THE

Tacos

of

TEXAS

THE

Tacos

of

TEXAS

★

Mando Rayo
& Jarod Neece

UNIVERSITY OF TEXAS PRESS ⛆ AUSTIN

"Shark-BLT Tacos" from *Nuevo Tex-Mex* by David Garrido and Robb Walsh.
Copyright © 1998 by David Garrido and Robb Walsh. Used with permission
from Chronicle Books, San Francisco.

Requests for permission to reproduce material from this work should be
sent to:
    Permissions
    University of Texas Press
    P.O. Box 7819
    Austin, TX 78713-7819
    http://utpress.utexas.edu/index.php/rp-form

♾ The paper used in this book meets the minimum requirements of
ANSI/NISO Z39.48-1992 (R1997) (Permanence of Paper).

Book designed by Derek George

LIBRARY OF CONGRESS CATALOGING-IN-PUBLICATION DATA

Names: Rayo, Mando, author. | Neece, Jarod, author.
Title: The tacos of Texas / Mando Rayo and Jarod Neece.
Description: First edition. | Austin : University of Texas Press, 2016. |
    Includes bibliographical references and index.
Identifiers: LCCN 2016002920
    ISBN 978-1-4773-1043-4 (pbk. : alk. paper)
    ISBN 978-1-4773-1190-5 (library e-book)
    ISBN 978-1-4773-1191-2 (non-library e-book)
Subjects: LCSH: Tacos—Texas—History. | Mexican American cooking. |
    Texas—Social life and customs—Anecdotes.
Classification: LCC TX836.R395 2016 | DDC 641.84—dc23
LC record available at http://lccn.loc.gov/2016002920

doi:10.7560/310434

The Tacos of Texas is dedicated to my little familia, Ixchel Granda de Rayo, Quetzal Trinidad Rayo, and Diego Armando Tenoch Rayo. Gracias for your love and patience, for letting me eat so many tacos, and for believing in me. Los quiero un monton!

—MR

Dedicated to my favorite ladies, Andrea Yz, Tessa Neece, and Francesca Neece.

—JN

CONTENTS

THE
Tacos
of
TEXAS

Rooted in tradición Mexicana and infused with Texas food culture, tacos can be eaten all across the Lone Star State. And in Texas, there are plenty of tacos for everyone, from puffy tacos in San Antonio to trompo tacos in Dallas, breakfast tacos in Austin, carnitas tacos in El Paso, fish tacos in Corpus Christi, and barbacoa in the Rio Grande Valley.

Covering the traditional to the modern, this story is about Texans' love for tacos. We've been behind the scenes with the trailers, stands, trucks, taqueros, home cooks, families, and even some ranchos. We tell the stories, share the traditions, and identify the iconic tacos from all over the state.

As a kid in El Paso, a.k.a. El Chuco, I grew up with fresh flour tortillas. But I also enjoyed corn tortillas with my caldos, discadas, and carnitas. The tortilla choice depends on what you're having. I usually like my pork—carnitas, al pastor, chicharrones with corn, and breakfast tacos—with flour. I also go flour with red meats like chile colorado, machacado, or carne deshebrada.

That reminds me of the time when we were kids, cue song, "allá en el rancho grande, allá donde viviaaa!" On special occasions, Tío Santiago would invite la familia y la chusma to his rancho para matar un marrano. Yeah, the family and the riffraff would get together to slaughter a pig—it's a family tradition. I remember the moment of the squeal, the cutting up of la panza, the cleaning out of las tripas, and the strong smell of "rancho." I mostly watched except when I would sneak in to stir the pork rinds in their own fat in a giant cazo three times my size. (For the record, my tío would not allow anyone to touch or stir the chicharrones.) I would bite into a few of those chicharrones that still had some hair, but the crunchiness and fattiness wrapped up in a corn tortilla . . . yeah, that's rancho perfection.

MEXICAN TO TEX-MEX TO NEW AMERICANO

I remember working at an "undisclosed" restaurant in Austin and they had a plate with one corn tortilla smothered with queso, accompanied by rice and beans. I was like, you call that a Mexican plate? Of course, I was wrong. You call that Tex-Mex! But then, this was the lowest of Tex-Mex places. Coming from a border town, I was used to real Mexican food (enchiladas in rich red sauce, gorditas, burritos, flautas, and chile, lots of it) and when I had my first plate of Tex-Mex, I really thought it was a watered-down version of Mexican food. As I ate my way through Austin and San Antonio and other parts of Texas, I began to appreciate and understand the sabores—the flavors—and the roots of Tex-Mex, from the queso to crispy beef tacos to the best thing this side of the Pecos, breakfast tacos. The main difference between Mexican and Tex-Mex is that one is rich in earth tones and sauces and the other is rich in queso. (See Robb Walsh's *The Tex-Mex Cookbook* for more on this subject.) The two cuisines are intertwined and both deserve a place on our tables.

Texas is not just cowboys and barbecue. Texas is tacos, Tejanos, Mexicans, immigrants, y más, all way before Texas was Texas. With the influx of different peoples and their cultures, all adding their own sabores to their taco-making ways, what you get is what I call the "New Americano," where culture meets tacos.

Founded in tradition and fused con creativity, the New Americano captures the evolution of the taco. Take a fresh tortilla, cilantro, onions, salsa, and match those up with Korean bbq, fried oysters, or portabella mushrooms and you're going to get pretty tasty tacos coming from muchos mundos. Cooks and chefs are experimenting with tacos in whole new ways, and some are going back to the basics like the Farm to Table movement, where you can get locally sourced carnes, huevos, and vegetables—y paz y zaz, you got a muy orgánico taco! It really is exciting to try new tacos and you'll get a taste of these en el book. *The Tacos of Texas* shows just how much these foods have influenced what Texas is today.

To make it simpler, here's a quick way to look at the categories de los tacos:

Tacos of Texas

TRADITIONAL

★

Authentically
Mexicano

TACOS AL PASTOR

LaMacro
(Houston)

Urban Taco
(Dallas)

TRIPITAS

Chef David Rodriguez
(Houston)

TAQUERIA STYLE

El Ultimo Taco (Brownsville)

Traditional—Mexican all the way, including taqueria style, alambres, al pastor, barbacoa, bistec, callejeros, and trompo.

Tacos of Texas

TEX-MEX

Part Mexican,
Part American,
100% Tejano

CRISPY TACOS
El Corazon Vintage Tex-Mex (Dallas)

BEEF FAJITAS
Farolito Restaurant
(Abilene)

BREAKFAST TACOS
Hi-Ho Restaurant (Corpus Christi)

Tex-Mex—part Mexican, part American, 100 percent Tejano.
Breakfast tacos, puffy tacos, crispy tacos, fajitas—top it all off with
queso, of course—and don't forget the mariachis and piratas.

NEW AMERICANO

★

Founded in Tradition, Fused with Creativity

CORNMEAL FRIED OYSTER TACOS

Velvet Taco (Dallas)

BEEF BULGOGI

Tacoholics (El Paso)

CHILE EN NOGADA

Tacodeli (Austin)

New Americano—founded in tradition, mixed with creativity. Fusion- and chef-inspired concoctions like Caribbean, Korean bbq, New Orleans shrimp po boy, pork belly, sushi, todo gluten-free, orgánico, and vegetarian tacos.

TACO REGIONS

While doing our very important research, we discovered and rediscovered different parts of Texas, all in the name of tacos. From West Texas to the Gulf Coast, if people were making tacos, we were there to eat them. No tacos were left untouched. And, yes, Texas does have a ton of taco options, and as we drove thousands of miles for *The Tacos of Texas*, we found that each region has different flavors and styles. Here's a sampling . . .

West Texas—carnitas tacos, taqueria-style (or "street") tacos, and asados made with rich tones of red and green chiles influenced by Mexico and New Mexico.

South Texas—giant breakfast tacos, or "mariachis" as they call them in Laredo. Taqueria-style and barbacoa tacos in the Rio Grande Valley. (Barbacoa is a weekend ritual down there.) And, of course, San Antonio is the king of the puffy taco, barbacoa, and Big Red and a solid breakfast taco town as well.

Central Texas—Austin loves their breakfast tacos and Tex-Mex variety. Nothing goes better with tacos than some Velveeta-y melt-y queso. Fusion also defines the Austin scene, and they are expanding the way that people are eating tacos, one taco trailer at a time.

North Texas—Dallas-Fort Worth is the home of Tex-Mex institutions. Gas station tacos, chef-inspired tacos, and newcomers from Monterrey, among others (trompo and al pastor), bring in a big mix to the North Texas scene.

Gulf Coast—Corpus Christi has great breakfast tacos, but the

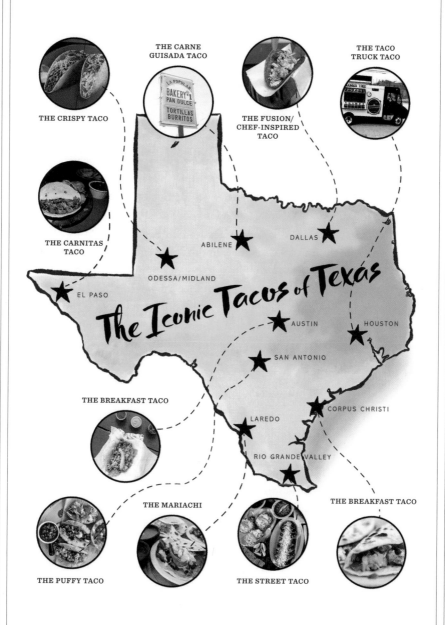

THE CARNE GUISADA TACO

THE CRISPY TACO

THE TACO TRUCK TACO

THE FUSION/ CHEF-INSPIRED TACO

THE CARNITAS TACO

The Iconic Tacos of Texas

EL PASO

ODESSA/MIDLAND

ABILENE

DALLAS

AUSTIN

HOUSTON

SAN ANTONIO

CORPUS CHRISTI

LAREDO

RIO GRANDE VALLEY

THE BREAKFAST TACO

THE BREAKFAST TACO

THE MARIACHI

THE PUFFY TACO

THE STREET TACO

fish tacos are amazing, too. Houston packs a big variety, from al pastor to bistec, with their taco truck scene.

THE TEXAS TACO COUNCIL: PEOPLE, PLACES, AND THE TACO JOURNEY

Ever been through Small Town, Texas, and wandered into a local Mexican restaurant and found the most incredible tacos? Have you been to Port Isabel and seen their ginormous tortillas and eaten their ginormous tacos? How about Juárez-style taquerias in El Paso or that crispy beef taco in Dallas? In this taco journey, we're exploring the ones you know—and the ones yet to be discovered. But *The Tacos of Texas* is not only a story of comida folded in a tortilla, but also of the people behind the tacos, from the taqueros to home cooks, chefs, and people who just love to eat tacos.

But you don't have to take our word for it. While we have some pretty extensive taco knowledge, we know that there are other taco diehards in the great state of Tejas. We're proud to say that the secret society of taco lovers (that's us) has formed the first official Texas Taco Council. The purpose of the Council is to provide local flavor, research, and credibility, and these aficionados represent their cities and regions, providing insights into a particular taco scene as only a local can. The Council represents Texas in true form, with community leaders, creative types, chefs, and foodies. They'll cook up some of their best tacos and give us their go-to taquerias in Texas.

INAUGURAL TEXAS TACO COUNCIL MEMBERS

Austin
Jose Miguel Anwar Velasquez
Timothy Braun and
Dusty Danger

Rio Grande Valley (Brownsville/McAllen)
Melinda Rodriguez
Hector Guerra
Letty Fernandez

Laredo
Sammy "The House" Ramirez

Corpus Christi
Gerald Flores
Joe Hilliard

Dallas-Fort Worth
José Ralat
Robert Strickland

El Paso
"Super" Mario Kato
Sara Macias
Seth Wilson

Houston
Iveth Reyes
Jay Roscoe

Midland-Odessa
Dennis Harris
Carlos Hernandez

San Antonio
Edmund Tijerina
Eddie Vega

Abilene
Blake Kammerdiener

Just like the breaking of bread (well, in this case, tortillas), the eating of tacos is about more than just eating. It's about understanding culture and history, about community, about sharing

★ Texas Taco Council ★

JOSE VELASQUEZ
AUSTIN

TIMOTHY BRAUN
AUSTIN

BLAKE KAMMERDIENER
ABILENE

MELINDA RODRIGUEZ
BROWNSVILLE

LETTY FERNANDEZ
BROWNSVILLE

HECTOR GUERRA
McALLEN

SAMMY "THE HOUSE" RAMIREZ
LAREDO

GERALD FLORES
CORPUS CHRISTI

JOE HILLIARD
CORPUS CHRISTI

JOSÉ RALAT
DALLAS-FORT WORTH

ROBERT STRICKLAND
DALLAS-FORT WORTH

"SUPER" MARIO KATO
EL PASO

SARA MACIAS
EL PASO

SETH WILSON
EL PASO

IVETH REYES
HOUSTON

JAY ROSCOE
HOUSTON

DENNIS HARRIS
MIDLAND-ODESSA

CARLOS HERNANDEZ
MIDLAND-ODESSA

EDMUND TIJERINA
SAN ANTONIO

EDDIE VEGA
SAN ANTONIO

experiences and recipes, and about appreciating where food and people come from. We'll explore places that truly represent the state food of Texas. (Yes, that's the taco. Petition starts now!) Beyond the Texas Taco Council, we'll hear from such personalities as Dr. Ricardo Romo, president, University of Texas at San Antonio; Rosie Castro, community organizer and mother of Secretary of Housing and Urban Development Julián Castro and Congressman Joaquin Castro; James Beard award-winning Chef Chris Shepherd (Underbelly); author Daniel Vaughn (*The Prophets of Smoked Meat*); beef curator Armando Vera (Vera's Backyard Bar-B-Que); Austin Police Chief Art Acevedo, and several city mayors, among others. We'll reveal the hidden gems and explore the world-famous spots. In all, we drove more than seven thousand miles in the great state of Texas, interviewed more than one hundred and forty people, and documented these taco stories in writing, film, and photos. We ate more than five hundred tacos and grew about three taco sizes.

Ladies and gentlemen, cowboys and vaqueros, these are the Tacos of Texas!

THE "MAKING OF": THE TACO JOURNALISTS

Mando Rayo

I was pretty much born with a tortilla in my hand. As far as I can recall, I've been eating tacos since forever. I remember just hanging around the kitchen at home while my mom, my tías, and my abuelita would cook up the most amazing food this side of the Pecos. (Yes, I am from El Paso, Texas. I'm a West Texas boy, not gonna deny it.) We would wake up to the smell of fresh, powdery flour tortillas. Just add butter and rajas de jalapeño con cebollitas. Now that'll get you going in the mornin'.

Growing up, I was more of an observer and a taster in the kitchen; yeah, I would taste a lot of the food. I was lucky coming from a Mexican family—there were plenty of people cooking up a storm. To be honest, I didn't really get into cooking and food until later in life. I stuck to the basics: chiles, beans, tacos, enchiladas, tortillas, and the 2-for-99-cents mystery meat tacos with that square American cheese on it. But I've evolved. Now I'm in my Golden Age of Cooking Super-Terrific Tacos stage. I love to cook all kinds of tacos, salsas, carnes, and even veggie-friendly dishes for my wife, Ixchel, and gluten-free kids, Quetzal and Diego. They always want Daddy to cook, so who am I to say no?

So way before I struggled with writing books about food, my friend Sammy Armstrong asked me to give him my top cinco tacos for a blog. So I did, and man, did it get people hungry! Then my

amigo El Jarod told me about this blog (TacoJournalism) that he started with Justin Bankston. He told me to come write with them because the blog was just a couple of white boys talking about tacos. Of course, I accepted and pretty much gave them the street cred they desperately needed. That was around 2007. Being the community guy that I am, I suggested that we host taco meet-ups and taco tours. We hit it big with the local media, and then one day, the *New York Times* called and we showed them the way of the taco. Our first book, *Austin Breakfast Tacos: The Story of the Most Important Taco of the Day* was a best seller (just ask my mom).

Today some people call me the Taco Whisperer. I've also been called the Taco King, and I've heard people say, "damn, that guy eats a lot of tacos!" That last one is la verdad. All in all, I'm no chef, I'm no historian, and I'm not a rapper either. I'm just a guy who loves tacos.

Jarod Neece

I was born in Beaumont, Texas, in the late 70s. My earliest memories are of my mother, Kathy Perry, dipping fresh flour tortillas, rolled up like tubes, into a hot bowl of queso at the Monterey House. The owner would hide candies underneath the pile of warm tortilla chips for kids—it was a five-year-old's version of heaven. I was hooked for life.

After my parents split up, I ended up in Louisiana. One of my first jobs in high school was at Tampico—part karaoke bar, part Tex-Mex restaurant—in Lafayette. I learned how a fifty-dollar bag of beans is where you are making the real money. I learned how to heat up a tortilla on a flat top and use my "not-so-Mexican" hands for real. I learned to take care of the dishwashers and cooks because they were the ones really in charge.

But slinging margaritas and deep-fried burritos was just a starting point, and it wasn't until I ended up at the University of Texas in Austin that my true taco knowledge started forming. I think every UT student in the late 90s survived primarily on breakfast tacos from Taco Shack and margaritas from Trudy's. It was the next step in a process, but those were not my finest hours.

After college, I met my wife, Andrea Yz, who opened up my world, introducing me to a magical new land called "South Austin." We ate lunch at Polvo's and dinner at La Mexicana. We ate plates of enchiladas while listening to the Gourds play at Jovita's. We ordered 3:00 a.m. tacos at La Mexicana while she used Spanish to confront the cat-callers who thought she was just some white girl. She stuck with me during my brief vegetarian phase and tolerated me ordering avocado tacos at Taqueria Arandas. And this was all just on South First Street. We now share our meals with our two taco-loving daughters, Tessa and Francesca, and they are more adventurous than either of us!

My next phase of taco growth began when I found a coworker as excited about tacos as I am. Justin Bankston and I ate tacos a lot. Like, everyday. We were on a mission and so birthed "Cornbitter Deluxe," JB's taco pseudonym, and TacoJournalism.com. Taco Journalism, our attempt at providing a one-stop shop for all things Tacos and Austin, won a "Best Of Austin" award. Our love for tacos had found a home. People liked reading about tacos and then eating those tacos. It was a super-easy formula for success.

Another great thing my wife has done is to introduce me to wonderful and exciting people. When she introduced me to Mando Rayo, I knew this man was on another level. I met Mando in his kitchen in the Miriam Mansion. The Mansion, Mando's old party house in East Austin, was legendary. Halloween, Miriam

Mansion! Poker Night, Miriam Mansion! Just party because, Miriam Mansion!

It was a hot summer night and there were tons of people at the Mansion. People sitting on chairs, smoking in the backyard, standing on the stairs—it was a proper party. We made our way into the kitchen where a sweaty dude was making huge piles of chiles rellenos from the New Mexico chile harvest. His handshake was a mixture of sweat and grease and Tecate and I knew this dude meant business. We became fast friends.

Years later, I was reading an online article about the top tacos in Austin and I noticed that the guy they were asking was Mando. I called him immediately and recruited him for the Taco Journalism Team. We have eaten many tacos together, written many words about those tacos, and, as they say, the rest is taco history.

THE
Holy
TRINITY

LAS TORTILLAS, LOS FILLINGS, Y LAS SALSAS

nd on Sunday morning, God made tacos. And those tacos are made up of something we call the "Holy Trinity": tortillas, fillings, and salsas. So yes, the taco is divine. What better way to start your morning or end your night but with fresh tortillas, some barbacoa, carnitas, eggs, chorizo, beans, carne guisada, fajitas, pollo asado, you name it, topped off with green or red salsa or some pico de gallo? Am I right?

LAS TORTILLAS

The story of the taco begins with the tortilla. Don't be fooled by the marketing campaigns trying to sell you a taco bowl without a friggin' tortilla! Whether it's corn or flour, all you gotta do is fill it, salsa it, fold it, and eat it. While that may sound easy enough to do, it is an art and a skill that not everyone can master—unless, that is, you've been taught by an abuelita, a mama, a tía, and sometimes a tío. Even the best chefs can't cut into that masa like an abuelita can, con mucho amor, cariño, sweat, guilt, tears, culture, and tradition that were passed down to her from the previous generation. And I've experienced the love and art of making tortillas firsthand: there's nothing like waking up to fresh tortillas con mantequilla and that warm feeling that you get when you take your first bite and know that this was made con mucho amor.

Whether you like corn or flour, just remember that you have to eat the tortilla "hot off the press," a comal, or an open fire. If it comes out cold, you must send it back. The best tortillas are made with corn or flour masa, lard (yes, manteca—it's making a comeback), salt, and water. Okay, you can also make tortillas with olive or vegetable oil to replace the lard, or you can buy organic lard off what was once a happy pig. Here's a starter lesson to make your life simpler and, in case you don't have an abuelita with Mexican roots, a how-to for tortilla making from my best amiga Patricia Sánchez. Actually, it's from her mom in San Antonio. She would make the best tortillas when I would visit. Muy ricas!

FLOUR TORTILLAS

ANTONIA G. SÁNCHEZ

I learned how to make flour tortillas at the age of nine. My tía taught me on a small ejido in Chihuahua, and I remember making my first dozen on a comal on a wood-burning stove. Nearly sixty years later, I'm still making homemade flour tortillas for my kids and grandkids.

I moved to El Paso, Texas, in 1979. Back then there weren't any stores that sold packaged tortillas. We used to make tortillas every Saturday for the week's meals, and it was cheaper than buying sliced bread. That was in the 80s. When my daughter was away in college, she would ask for homemade tortillas so I would mail them to her, and I think it was a delicious reminder of home. Now that we live in San Antonio, we enjoy making them together.

Makes about 25 average-sized tortillas

- 4 cups flour
- 1½ teaspoons salt
- 1 tablespoon baking powder
- ⅓ cup lard or vegetable shortening
- 1⅛ cups warm water

Note:

Please do not use spoons, whisks, hand mixers, or stand mixers with this recipe. Your hands and fingers are the best mixers!

Gently combine all dry ingredients in a large bowl. Add lard/vegetable shortening and gently mix with the dry mixture. Squeeze through fingers to combine well. Slowly add warm water, about ¼ cup at a time. Gently, and constantly, mix with hands to begin forming the dough. Use up each ¼ cup of water before adding any additional water. Do not oversqueeze dough as it can toughen. Once the water is added, knead the dough into one giant bola (ball). Leave the dough in the bowl, and let it rest for 20 minutes at room temperature; cover with a plate or a dish towel.

Once dough has rested, roll into small egg-sized balls. (These are called "testales.") To form a tortilla, place a testal on a flat surface, press down with four fingers to flatten it, then roll it with a rolling pin. (You may need to sprinkle flour onto the rolling pin or surface to keep the dough from sticking.) Pick up and gently turn the testal counter-clockwise about one inch and roll again; this ensures that it rolls out into a well-formed circle.

Now cook the raw tortillas, one by one, on a pre-heated comal at medium heat. Flip the tortilla once you can tell that it is cooked and it slides around on the comal. At this point, you will need to place something slightly heavy onto the tortilla to ensure that the heat is evenly distributed. Mrs. Sánchez uses a circular piece of wood with a handle; other folks cover the tortilla with a dish towel and use their fingers to press firmly as their tortillas cook.

Repeat until all testales are rolled out and cooked. Serve warm and with butter. Or fill with beans or prepared meat. (The smallest leftover testal becomes the smallest tortilla, given to the smallest member of the household.)

LOS FILLINGS

Now what you put inside a taco is just as important as the type of tortilla you choose. These fillings are what give the taco its name, from a breakfast taco to un taco de . . . (fill in the blank). Some tacos are more traditionally Mexican than others (Tex-Mex), and some are taking the taco to a whole different level (New Americano). While we can't include all varieties, these are the classics and the ones most commonly eaten in Texas.

TRADITIONAL: AUTHENTICALLY MEXICAN

Bistec—thinly-cut steak cooked over a flat grill.

Carne asada—thick-cut steak—grilled over mesquite.

Barbacoa—slow-cooked beef head. Extra points if it's cooked in a pozo wrapped in maguey leaves.

Pollo asado—grilled chicken with spices. Get the family style with two big roasted onions and plenty of corn tortillas.

Tacos al pastor—sweet pork with dried chiles and achiote and topped with pineapple chunks. We prefer the tacos prepared "al trompo" (cut from the vertical roasting spit).

Tripitas—fried intestines. 'Nuff said.

Lengua—boiled beef tongue cooked with garlic, onions, and jalapeños.

Carnitas—pork butt or shoulder fried in lard (yes!) and garlic, oregano, and orange slices. Best if cooked en el rancho in a large cazo. Bite into a hot chunk and let the grease just drip down your chin.

Cabrito—young goat with a hint of rancho.

Cecina—cured and aged, really thin beef. Kind of like a softer version of beef jerky.

Cabeza—beef head meat. So tender yet so smart!

Chicharrón—fried pork rinds. Pig skin (lonja) cooked in its own fat—the only way to do it.

Deshebrada—marinated, slow-cooked shredded beef.

Campechana—mixto style with beef, pork, and chorizo.

Alambres—beef with bacon, peppers, onions, and Oaxaca cheese.

Discada—beef, bacon, sausage, chorizo, jalapeños, onions, and tomatoes cooked in a disc-shaped pan. Think Mexican wok.

Picadillo tacos—a muy mushy seasoned blend of ground beef, potatoes, and onions. Potatoes are optional (y'know, carbs).

Guisados—stewed meats with green or red chile. Home style, like mom used to make.

TEX-MEX: PART MEXICAN, PART AMERICAN, 100 PERCENT TEJANO!

Puffy tacos—ground beef or pulled chicken, lettuce, tomatoes, and shredded cheese in fried masa puffed to perfection.

Crispy tacos—ground beef or pulled chicken on a fried tortilla with lettuce, tomatoes, and shredded cheese. A Tex-Mex classic.

Brisket tacos—slow-cooked barbecue brisket topped with fresh pico de gallo or salsa. Cowboy meets vaquero!

Breakfast tacos—eggs, bacon, chorizo, beans, potatoes, migas, cheese, pico, and salsa. Eat 'em in the morning, for lunch, dinner, or late at night. Nothing beats a breakfast taco.

Fajitas—juicy, marinated skirt steak on flour tortillas with all the trimmings: sautéed onions and peppers, guacamole, and cheese.

Carne guisada—stewed meat a.k.a. beef chuck roast with gravy.

NEW AMERICANO: FOUNDED IN TRADITION, FUSED WITH CREATIVITY

Korean bbq tacos—bbq pulled pork, kimchi, cucumbers, cilantro, and jalapeños.

Bulgogi beef tacos—marinated beef, usually with sesame seeds and scallions.

Chile en nogada taco—an orgánico homage to the Mexican flag with a roasted green chile stuffed with Texas wagyu picadillo, topped with a walnut goat cheese cream sauce, pomegranate seeds, chopped cilantro.

Cornmeal-fried oyster taco—remoulade, Napa slaw, corn pico, chili butter, micro cilantro on a hibiscus corn tortilla.

LAS SALSAS

It's midnight, you're at a taco trailer with a taco in hand, and before you take a bite, you must select red or green, mild or spicy, cooked or fresh, smooth or thick and chunky? What do you choose? How will this decision affect the taco you're about to eat, or, even worse,

will the taco ladies look at you with approval or disappointment? If you chose salsa then you got it right for that night. The salsa is key to taking your taco to the taco greatness level. Seriously, I don't know anyone who eats a dry taco. Just sayin'. To get you started, here are the classics:

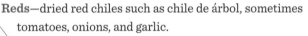

> **Reds**—dried red chiles such as chile de árbol, sometimes tomatoes, onions, and garlic.
> **Greens**—a mix of jalapeños, serranos, tomatillos, garlic, and onions.
> **Pico de gallo**—chopped jalapeños or serranos, tomatoes, onions, cilantro with lime.
> **Molcajete**—mashed aguacates and/or the traditional ingredients of green or red salsas.

It's not a salsa, but I love my chile de "amor" a mordida. Yes, that's taking bites of fresh jalapeño, serrano, piquin, or habanero with my tacos.

SALSA DE MOLCAJETE

CHEF DAVID RODRIGUEZ

Serves 4 to 6

- 4 to 5 ripe tomatoes
- 2 serrano peppers
- 1 to 2 garlic cloves
- ½ white onion
- Salt and pepper

Toast all the ingredients (except salt and pepper) in a nonstick skillet. Make sure to turn each to get an even char. After they are all nicely and evenly charred, pull the items from the heat and let cool for 10 to 15 minutes. Place the ingredients in the molcajete and break them down with the molcajete stone. Season the salsa with salt and pepper. Place the molcajete with the salsa in the middle of the table and enjoy.

SALSA QUEMADA

MARY RANGEL-GOMEZ

Serves 4 to 6

4 Roma tomatoes

2 jalapeños or serranos

1 medium onion

2 garlic cloves, chopped

⅓ cup water

2 tablespoons olive oil

¼ teaspoon cumin

Salt and pepper

¼ bunch cilantro, just
the leaves

Cook the tomatoes, jalapeños, and onion on the grill for about 10 minutes until the entire skin of each is charred and the vegetables are soft. Remove them from the fire and allow about 3 minutes to cool. Remove the skin from the tomatoes and cut each in half. Cut the ends of the jalapeños and cut each in half. Remove the outer layer of the onion and cut it into 4 pieces. Place tomatoes, jalapeños, onion, and garlic in the blender and add the ⅓ of cup of water. Press the chop button for about 10 seconds (or longer, depending on your preference). Add the 2 tablespoons of olive oil to a pan. Once the pan is hot, very carefully put the salsa in the pan and season with salt, pepper, and cumin. Reduce the heat and let it cook for about 10 minutes. Add the cilantro and let it cook for about 1 more minute. If you like your salsa very hot, then just add more jalapeños to the recipe. Enjoy your salsa quemada!

VERACRUZ ALL-NATURAL

SALSA DE CHILE DE ÁRBOL

VERACRUZ ALL NATURAL

Serves 4 to 6

5 Roma tomatoes
Handful of dried chile de árbol
3 teaspoons canola oil
2 garlic cloves
Salt

Boil the tomatoes for 20 to 30 minutes. Sauté the dried chile de árbol with the oil until the chiles turn a dark red. Blend the tomatoes and chiles with the 2 cloves of garlic and add salt. Consistency must be thick. Listo!

EL MUNDO DE MANDO'S
GREEN CREAMY SAUCE

Most taquerias offer a mix of reds and greens, but for me, it's the creamy green that does it. You'll see this salsa and think it contains avocado, but it does not! The secret ingredient is the oil. That's what makes it creamy. So here you are. Kids, please do try this at home.

Serves 4 to 6

5 jalapeños
2 cloves garlic
3 teaspoons canola oil (the secret!)
Salt

MY CUATRO-STEP PROCESS:

Step Uno: Grab a bunch of chiles—or just 5 for this recipe. You can take out the seeds and membranes if you prefer, but I don't. ¿Quién es más macho?

Step Dos: Boil 'em til it hurts. The chiles should be nice and soft before you take them out.

Step Tres: Put 'em in the blender and add the garlic, canola oil, and salt.

Step Cuatro: Pour it in your favorite bowl or add it to your tacos and go to town on it. You can also bottle it and try to sell it on the streets. I was thinking about doing this, but who has the time? I got tacos to eat!

Paz y zaz, there you go!

#TacoLife

OBSERVATIONS AND LESSONS

1. Mexicans tilt the head. Americans tilt the taco.
2. You roll a flauta, burrito, and enchilada; you fold a taco (except for taquitos of course).
3. Beans are The Mexican Mayonnaise.
4. Tortillas are a must. It's not a taco if you're eating it out of a bowl!
5. In order to get good tacos you must be proficient in restaurant Spanish. (Y'know, *Tres de asada, una cerveza más!*)
6. Don't ever, ever eat a dry taco. Salsa is your friend!
7. When you bring tacos, you make friends.
8. Tacos. Never. Die.

Rio Grande Valley

Hey, baby, que paso? I thought I was your only taco! #TacoLyrics. That was the theme as we headed to South Texas and the Rio Grande Valley. On the first leg of the Tacos of Texas Tour, we ate fifty-four tacos in the first twenty-four hours. Yeah, we were pretty excited. I think starting out in Brownsville and McAllen was the best way to begin the tour: these two cities are the home of giant flour tortillas and

breakfast tacos, barbacoa, and taqueria-style (or street) tacos. The RGV is all about big hearts, family, friends, palm trees, and tacos.

So where did we go once we were in the Valley? Well, being Taco Journalists, we went straight to the sources, la gente! For the inaugural Texas Taco Council, we enlisted taco aficionados. They represented their cities in the best taco way possible and were instrumental in helping us find the best places to eat tacos. The Taco Ambassadors for the Valley included Letty Fernandez, Melinda Rodriguez, and Hector Guerra. You'll learn more about them later. Now if we had awards for most connected Taco Ambassador, I would have to recognize Letty Fernandez. Being in communications and born and raised in Brownsville, she pretty much knows not only everybody in the Valley, but also, of course, the best taquerias there.

THE RIO GRANDE VALLEY ICONIC TACO: STREET TACOS

While you can get some great breakfast tacos with handmade tortillas, the street taco is king in the Rio Grande Valley. Besides south of the border, where else can you get so many taqueria-style tacos, a.k.a. street tacos, in Texas? I say nowhere. From bistec to al pastor, at a taqueria or a puesto, people all over the RGV are making and eating these iconic Mexican taquitos. Taqueria-style tacos are served on smaller-than-usual corn tortillas with small-ish portions of al pastor, bistec, tripitas, barbacoa, y más. That's the beauty of street tacos: you can eat three to six, mix and match, and you can eat them on the street or at your favorite taqueria. So next time you're in the RGV, all you have to do is put your hand up and order tres de bistec on double corn (always #doublecorn), add salsa, and then order three more!

TACO JOURNALISM'S TOP CINCO

With a focus on people and places, we wanted to taste the best tacos in each city and region. While we couldn't hit all the possibilities, we did get to some community gems and local favorites and they were muy rico! Here's our top five list for the Rio Grande Valley.

1. **El Ultimo Taco**—Matamoros-inspired taqueria serving up a whole assembly of street tacos—al pastor, mollejas, tripitas, and don't forget the frijoles especiales! This Brownsville place was so packed with families, they didn't need decorations on the wall.

2. **Vera's Backyard Bar-B-Que**—generations of ranch-style barbacoa making en pozo (in-ground pit). One of the only places in Texas that has been grandfathered to cook barbacoa heads in pozos.

3. **La Calle del Taco**—the Holy Grail for taco seekers. Garage-style tiendas line this taco mile on the outskirts of Pharr, Texas.

4. **Gourmet Central by Cel**—La International, Brownsville Chef Celia Galindo will take you beyond the border with customized dinners, from tacos de canasta to the salsas.

5. **El Rodeo Taco Express**—this McAllen restaurant started as a meat market and grew into an outdoor taqueria filled with músicos, families, and hella good tacos.

THE TACO MILE A.K.A. LA CALLE DEL TACO

You've heard of the Taco Mile, right? You go down to the Valley and somewhere in one of the smaller towns, you'll see taco stand after taco stand after taco stand. Yup, that's what our taco sources told us.

So we kept looking for the Taco Mile. We heard it was in Mission and right outside McAllen. We asked around, in Spanish, English, Spanglish, in whistles (yes, some of us Mexicans communicate by whistling to each other), but, alas, no Taco Mile to be found. But we did not despair. In fact, we were told by Rolando Curiel, the owner of El Ultimo Taco, about one place that sells way more tacos than they do and it's near a bunch of taquerias. So after a long day of multiple interviews between Brownsville and McAllen, we were off to find a place called Herradura's. It was now 11:00 p.m., and we were just south of McAllen on FM 2061/South

Jackson Road. It was dark, it was dingy, and it was the country. But then we came across a taco stand made out of aluminum carports. Then another one. And another one. To our left was Herradura's, which was a restaurant that looked like an old unfinished movie set. To our right was a dirt parking lot with neon signs and a row of taco stands. Ahhhh. We had found the Taco Mile!

As we came to learn, it was not called the Taco Mile but La Calle del Taco. No wonder no one knew what we were talking about. Anyway, La Calle del Taco is a row of taco stands made of aluminum carports, with seating for the whole family, including neon lighting, backed up next to a trailer. The amenities were limitless! Free charro beans while you wait, salsa bar with really hot chiles, conversations in español with the locals, and drive-in style service. You can park, order, and eat in your troca or sit under the carport with your friends and familia. Sure, there were some stray dogs and dust from the parking lot, but it was so worth it. You had your pick of bistec, alambres, carne asada, al pastor—all estilo Mexicano. We had some of the best tacos at El Chilango Vago, a Mexico City-style taco stand (or carport, in this case).

So if you're ever in the Valley, want to hit up some amazing tacos, and are feeling a little bit adventurous, look for La Calle del Taco.

Rolando and Ivan Curiel

EL ULTIMO TACO, BROWNSVILLE

Tell us your story.

Well, we started El Ultimo Taco back in 1999 and then from there people started coming more and more. We went about a decade with the same style, and then the past four years, we changed our concept to more modern, more high-quality food, and more freshness, so business started booming.

At first, it was just a business idea. The taqueria style that crossed over the Mexican border. We're originally from Brownsville, but our family comes from Matamoros, Mexico. We're really a family-owned business.

What's your go-to taco and why?

The traditional styles we make are bistec, tripas suave or crispy, mollejas (sweetbread tacos), al pastor, and barbacoa.

When customers come to El Ultimo Taco, they like to order the bistec and the frijoles especiales, and it comes with cilantro, cebolla, cheese, and a slice of avocado. Our beans have our own style, with bistec, cheese, and avocado. We do it a little bit differently than everyone else.

The taqueria-style taco is popular because the ingredients are really fresh, and it has a great flavor at a good price ($1.09 per taco). This style is what you see on the South Texas border.

Armando Vera

VERA'S BACKYARD BAR-B-QUE, BROWNSVILLE

Tell us your story.
It all started in the early 1950s with my father and his brother. Actually, they started in another location, and then my father went on his own in 1955. And then he did it for a long time. After that, I took over. And I guess I was born into it. I really had no choice; it's always been a family business. I got into it for family reasons when I was about twelve years old. I was born into it and we just had to do it. It had to be done. I thank God, he helped me a lot with that. He helps you when you need the help. And with him, I was able to do a lot of things. I look at my kids and they are ten and twelve years old and by that age, I was already doing this. No complaining, no hard feelings, no regrets.

What is your most popular taco and why? What makes it a standout or unique?
Barbacoa. It is something that originated in Mexico.

I guess we brought it over. It's beef head barbacoa. That's what makes the difference between barbacoa and American or Tex-Mex barbecue, the American brisket. The American/Texas barbecue is a different part of the calf. So mostly down here, there is not really a market for American barbecue. It's more of the barbacoa since we have more Hispanics in the area. Not that Hispanics don't eat brisket; they do eat American barbecue.

They will eat brisket one time and then eat barbacoa forty to fifty times before they eat brisket again. It's more of a tradition in the Hispanic culture.

We cook the beef head barbacoa in a pit on the ground, on an open fire and we cook it for eight to twelve hours before it's ready. The barbacoa we serve is the cachete, lengua, mixed, and the eyes. The mixed is composed of whatever is not from the beef head. We take out the eyes, the cheek, the lengua, the palate, the jeta (face), and whatever other meats are left from the cow. Over the years, we have added carnitas. And, of course, all the salsas are homemade. We make them here.

The ojos are a Mexican delicacy. It's something like caviar, I would say. That's one of the things that sells the most. We run out at about 7:00 or 8:00 in the morning. So the eyeballs are a hot deal.

Executive Chef
Celia Samano Galindo

GOURMET CENTRAL BY CEL, BROWNSVILLE

Tell us your story.

I was born in Brownsville, but when I was two, we moved to Mexico City. I inherited my love and passion for the kitchen and food from my grandmother, Celia Champion Samano. I established Gourmet Central by Cel in 2009 with the support of my "bread specialist," Chickie Samano, my mother. So you can see this is a true family effort.

What's your connection with tacos?

I lived in Mexico City as a child and the taco was part of my growing up and still is a part of me.

TACOS DE CANASTA

EXECUTIVE CHEF CELIA SAMANO GALINDO

Makes 12 tacos

Vegetable oil for frying
½-inch slice white onion
3 garlic cloves
12 corn tortillas
½ cup scallions, or cebollitas de cambray in Mexico, finely sliced
1 jalapeño, seeded and finely chopped
1 pound Roma tomatoes, chopped
½ teaspoon kosher or coarse sea salt
½ cup chopped cilantro or epazote
1 pound (about 2½ cups) requesón or farmer's cheese

Line a basket with large, thick layers of plastic wrap. The layers should be big enough to cover the interior of the basket and fold over the top. Place a couple of kitchen towels in the bottom of the basket on top of the plastic. Add butcher-style or parchment paper on top of the kitchen towels and on the sides of the basket.

Add enough oil to a large skillet to come ½-inch up the sides.

Heat the oil over medium heat. Once hot, add the onion slice and garlic cloves and let brown for at least 10 minutes.

Using tongs, pass the corn tortillas, one by one, through the hot oil containing the onion and garlic. That is, quickly fry each tortilla for 3 seconds per side and set each on a cooling rack, or a plate covered with paper towels, until all are done.

In another skillet, set over medium heat, pour 3 tablespoons of the onion- and garlic-seasoned oil. Once the skillet is hot, add the scallions or cebollitas and the jalapeño and cook for about 3 to 4 minutes until softened. Add the tomatoes and salt and cook, stirring occasionally, for about 8 to 10 minutes until completely cooked and mushy. Stir in the cilantro or epazote, cook for a couple more minutes, then remove skillet from heat. In a mixing bowl, combine the requesón with the tomato mixture and season with more salt, if needed.

Preheat a comal or skillet over medium heat.

Add a couple of tablespoons of the cheese and tomato mixture to a fried tortilla and fold into a half-moon shape. Repeat with the rest of the tortillas. (You may eat them at this point, but they won't be "basket," or "sweaty," tacos yet.) Place the filled tortillas on the hot comal or skillet.

Heat thoroughly for about one minute per side.

Arrange the heated tacos in layers in the basket as they come off the comal. Once you are done, add another layer of paper over the tacos, cover with another kitchen towel, and then the plastic, which should fold over it all from the interior lining of the basket. Let the tacos rest and sweat for at least 10 minutes and keep covered until ready to eat.

Serve with your choice of salsa, slices of avocado, or pickled jalapeños.

Mayor Tony Martinez

BROWNSVILLE

Tell us your story.

I am a Valley resident and a lifelong native, born on New Year's Eve in the mid 1940s. I attended schools in Harlingen up until the eighth grade and left for high school in San Antonio. I graduated from the University of Texas in 1967 and continued my studies to become a lawyer from St. Mary's School of Law in 1970. Along the way, I got married and became the proud father of four beautiful children, one of whom is now deceased. I moved to Brownsville in my pursuit of a career in trial law and spent the next forty years practicing law. Four years ago in 2010, I decided to run for mayor. I have been mayor of Brownsville for the last four-and-a-half years and was recently reelected, and I'm starting my second four-year term.

Throughout my life, one of my favorite hobbies, of course, is cooking. This makes the taco world a central part of my life in the Valley. I can tell you that tacos have certainly been an important part in our daily living. For me, it started with my blessed mother who would make us try and eat everything possible. This would include meats ranging from chicken to kidneys to barbacoa, including sesos. The ingredients, besides these meats, were lettuce, tomato, onion, cilantro, and white cheese.

What's your connection with tacos?

It's simply a staple of the household. The Mexican culture lends itself to the taco because it's easy to make and you can eat rice and beans as sides. And being on a limited budget, and having five other siblings, as well as mom and pop, we had to stretch the dollar.

Tacos are the "fast food" of our region and probably everywhere else in South Texas. Although tacos weren't considered a fast food because they were homemade, they have all the essential ingredients of good Mexican cooking, which includes onions, garlic, tomato, cumin, and oregano.

Hector Guerra

MARIACHI CONTINENTAL, McALLEN
TEXAS TACO COUNCIL

Tell us your story.

I was born in San Fernando, California, but as the saying goes, "I got to Texas as fast as I could!" During my summers, I lived in V. Guerrerro Durango, Mexico, learning guitar and music from my grandfather Victor Tejada. I've been in McAllen since I was twelve.

I was fortunate enough to be a founding member of Texas A&M Kingsville's mariachi program, the Mariachi Javelina, and I finally put my grandfather's teachings to good use by becoming the director of the mariachi program for the next four years. I moved back home to McAllen in 1980 and started the Mariachi Continental de Hector Guerra and to work in my family's restaurants making (what else?) tacos.

You're on the Texas Taco Council. Why are you a Taco Ambassador for your city/region?

I'm an Ambassador for my city because I've probably eaten tacos from every hole-in-the-wall to every beautifully appointed restaurant, backyard barbecue, and truck/taco stand in the whole Rio Grande Valley! Tacos should be simple—you can make a taco out of almost anything as long as it tastes good. My family taught me to enjoy life, music, laughter, and food to its fullest extent while remaining honest, hard-working, and decent people throughout your life. Viva el taco!

Give us the taco landscape for your city/region. Give us your top ten list and why they're the best.

1. **El Rodeo Taco Express**—It took exhaustive research (after many late-night gigs) to find the right combination of freshly prepared and delicious tacos in this "Mecca" of tacos! But there's no doubt we hit pay dirt with Rodeo's varieties, full

of flavor and freshness you can see as they prepare the best tacos in town right before your eyes. It's a mouthwatering jaw drop! The best of the best fajita (chicken or beef) tacos anywhere with fresh tortillas and salsas (red or green).

2. **Los Cazadores Restaurant**—talk about fresh! The fajitas are still sizzling when they come to you with fresh-made tortillas and salsa. Also try the brisket tacos.

3. **El Pato Mexican Food**—a Rio Grande Valley staple for more than thirty years. Fresh "patos," as the tacos are known, come in dozens of varieties, but my personal favorite is the beef, bean, cheese, and avocado pato—mmmm good!

4. **Mrs. G's**—the founder of El Pato, Mrs. G's family kept those original recipes and ran with them. Try the chorizo, potato, and refried beans—simply too good to pass up!

5. **Taqueria El Zarape**—all the tacos are delicious, but the tacos norteños with trompo are the bomb! Cilantro, grilled onions, and lime to taste and enjoy.

6. **Taco Rico**—the original taco pirata. Shredded beef with white cheese and avocado on a giant flour tortilla, toasted on the outside with charro beans on the side.

7. **Taqueria La Mexicana**—the tacos de tripas are exceptional.

8. **Morado's Restaurant**—cabrito and al pastor tacos on a fresh handmade flour tortilla. OMG!

9. **Leo's Drive In**—convenience store tacos, but unbelievably fresh and good. Try their Taco Tuesdays Specials, including the pork carnitas with salsa verde.

10. **Laredo Taco Company (inside Stripes)**—I never thought I would have picked a convenience store for good food, including the biggest tacos since Cueva's Restaurant closed

down a few years back. They have a wide variety of tacos, but definitely try the Crazy Taco—potato, egg, cheese, refried beans with two slices of bacon.

Letty Fernandez

UNIVERSITY OF TEXAS RIO GRANDE VALLEY TEXAS TACO COUNCIL

Tell us your story.
I was born and raised in Brownsville, Texas. I am a former television journalist, having spent nearly seventeen years covering the border. My current position is director of Presidential Media Relations for the University of Texas Rio Grande Valley. I am passionate about helping students succeed in college, anything UT,

the Texas Longhorns, and historic preservation. I love food and am always ready to try something new.

What's your connection with tacos?

I grew up on tacos. I have been eating tacos since I was a kid. My mother and grandmother made the best tacos. They had one of those old meat grinders and we would all take turns grinding the meat. It made the meat taste so good. Tacos are comfort food at its best, and when I eat tacos, it reminds me of home.

Give us the taco landscape for your city/region. Give us your top ten list and why they're the best.

1. **Taqueria Gonzalez**—small red tacos with shredded beef. So tasty, served with fresh, warm salsa. You've got to have at least a dozen. These tacos are like the ones they sell across the river. In fact, Taqueria Gonzalez used to be in Matamoros and many people from Brownsville would go across to eat these tacos.

2. **The Vermillion**—fajita, fish, shrimp. All are good and they come with a cup of charro beans. The "V" is an institution in Brownsville and they treat you like family. Everything on the menu is comfort food.

3. **Treviño's**—all kinds of tacos, chicken, barbacoa. My favorite is the lengua with flour or corn, both are good. The service is great.

4. **Café Amiga**—the fajita tacos with cilantro, white cheese, onions, and cilantro—so good. Great service, another place that treats customers like a family.

5. **Mota's Tacos**—you can do takeout or sit at the outside tables. With shredded beef, these tacos are so good.

6. **Taco Palenque**—fajitas are the best here. They fill their tacos with lots of meat, so order just one and then order extra tortillas to share or not to share.

7. **El Ultimo Taco**—fajita, bistec, molleja, al pastor, or tripa . . . all are good. Make sure you order the frijoles especiales—they have everything in them.

8. **Vera's Backyard Bar-B-Que**—order the barbacoa tacos. You can eat them there and get your onions, avocado, cilantro, and even a cup of coffee. Perfect for breakfast.

9. **Brownsville Coffee Shop**—chicken tacos are so good here. The owner, Jovita Chase, treats you like family. This place is an institution.

10. **International Coffee Shop**—if you order tacos, make sure you get the homemade corn tortillas, and I mean *homemade*. They are real and so good.

Manuel Medrano, PhD

UNIVERSITY OF TEXAS RIO GRANDE VALLEY

Tell us your story.

I was born and grew up on a small farm in Brownsville and now reside in Laguna Vista. I received my bachelor's and master's degrees at Texas A&I in Kingsville and my doctorate at the University of Houston. I have taught US and Mexican American history for more than forty years at Texas Southmost College and the University of Texas at Brownsville. I have authored or co-authored six books, including three poetry books, and more than a dozen journal articles, most about Valley people and their culture. Additionally, I have produced and directed twenty-seven documentaries about individuals and events in South Texas, including UT professor and scholar Américo Paredes, World War II Medal of Honor

recipient José M. López, and Chicana artist and author Carmen Lomas Garza. I am still inspired by my wife, Chavela, and three sons, Estevan, Daniel, and Noe.

What's your connection with tacos?

I have eaten tacos from the time I began eating solid food. My grandmothers, my mother, and several of my tías all prepared delicious tacos. My Tía Fela prepared some of the most unique, using albóndigas de kurbina (red drum) for filling. Throughout my travels in the United States, Mexico, and Central America, I have eaten a variety of tacos with regional ingredients. People in South Texas have a strong connection with tacos. I think they are the best in Texas because Tejano history includes them in a rich culinary and cultural tradition.

José M. Barroso

MANUEL'S RESTAURANT, PORT ISABEL

Tell us your story.

Manuel's was started back in 1983 on South Padre Island. My mother cooked and I served the first couple of years in business. Getting to know my customers throughout all these years has led to great friendships, people I consider family. After sixteen years, we moved our location to Port Isabel, which has led to great success. People from all over the country stop in to try us out, sometimes forming a line

outside to wait for a table. My boys, Frank and Jay, are a big part of this business. They both keep everything afloat when I'm not present. My grandson, Isaac, is also following in his dad's footsteps, helping us out on the weekends.

What is your most popular taco and why? What makes it a standout or unique?

Most popular taco would have to be the breakfast con todo. Why? Because everyone loves bacon! It consists of potato, egg, beans, cheese, and bacon. This heavily packed taco is about twelve inches long and can feed two, but you don't have to share.

Melinda Rodriguez

CEO, BROWNSVILLE CHAMBER OF COMMERCE
TEXAS TACO COUNCIL

Tell us your story.

I'm a native of the Rio Grande Valley, which is very likely the geography by which the taco migrated from the mines of Mexico into what was then northern Mexico, now known as San Antonio. I'm the oldest of three and the only girl. I am a foodie and no longer afraid to say it. I remember getting my first cookbook when I was in second grade. I loved it. I started with baking, but by the third grade, I was cooking dinner for my family, including making homemade taco shells. Pre-formed taco shells weren't sold in grocery stores. They were made from scratch. I love to eat, but I love to cook more. When I was a child, fast food was not what it is today, so I learned to cook "real food" from my mother and maternal grandmother. Today, I'm a business executive, raising a family, caring for my parents, and back home in the Valley. Over the years, I've adapted the recipes that my mother and grandmother taught me and made them simple, healthier, and quicker to make.

What's your connection with tacos?

My palate for tacos ranges from simple picadillo tacos to carnita tacos with all the fixin's. I love them all! As a child, I remember loving to eat homemade, crispy corned beef hash tacos and bean and cheese tacos. Of course, for years, my taco carrier of choice was the flour tortilla, but after taking a healthier approach to life, losing more than eighty pounds, and realizing that I have a high gluten sensitivity, my new taco carrier is the corn tortilla or lettuce. Yep! While I could choose to lament eating fewer flour tortillas, I'm learning to adapt my favorite taco fillings into lettuce and gluten-free tortillas. While the taco vessel might change, the essence of the taco remains.

You're on the Texas Taco Council. Why are you a Taco Ambassador for your city/region?

I'm a Taco Ambassador because I feel that I represent a taco generation that was on the cusp of an era when fast food was non-existent. We ate fresh taco ingredients, made with hand-crushed and -minced spices that filled a home with sweet and tangy aromas. Generations after me grew up with taquerias and fast-food establishments like Taco Cabaña and Taco Bell. In my day, coffee shops were the only places that sold tacos. Otherwise, you ate tacos at home. My parents' generation was conditioned to hide their fondness of tacos—a main food staple in any Hispanic home. Tacos were considered street food and therefore not a sign of good social status. They were ridiculed and embarrassed for publicly eating tacos. My generation was the first to herald the social status of tacos that would pave the way for foodies and taco aficionados like Aaron Sanchez and Mando Rayo.

Why do you think people love tacos in your region and in Texas?

People love tacos because they are a part of our ancestry and tradition. Tacos are a mainstay in Hispanic homes across the world. They are a breakfast, lunch, and dinner meal. We share laughs, worries, and wonderful family milestones over tacos, coffee, and other spirited libations. You can eat them sitting or standing, which makes them a great food to eat in just about any social setting. The taco has been adapted to meet diverse palates, but one thing remains . . . it is an intimate food eaten with your hands, and the person eating a taco knows it will make his/her mouth water.

Give us the taco landscape for Brownsville. Give us your top ten list and why they're the best.

1. **The Vermillion**—fish, shrimp, ceviche tacos. They are done to perfection.
2. **The Toddle Inn**—carne guisada tacos. The beef is perfectly braised, and the stew is perfect.
3. **Café Amiga**—picadillo tacos. The picadillo is spiced just right and the salsa is the perfect complement.
4. **Brownsville Coffee Shop #2**—bean, cheese, and bacon taco. Sometimes I like to revert back to elementary school palate choices. Simple and delicious always works.
5. **Bigo's**—tacos de fajitas. The fajita is tender, but juicy. The tortillas are consistently good and well done.
6. **Taco Palenque**—taco Matamoros. They consistently deliver this taco to perfection, and they "oil" the tortilla. The guacamole is great and the Cotija cheese finishes it just right!
7. **Treviño's**—any taco. This place is old school and everything is right with that. The flour tortillas are some of the best in the area. I always get the chorizo and egg taco on a flour tortilla.
8. **El Torito**—huevo con chorizo taco. The tortillas are perfect. Someone's grandmother is in the kitchen making them.
9. **Mota's Tacos**—simple, tasty. They serve one-of-a-kind carnitas and pollo asado tacos.
10. **Laredo Taco Company (a.k.a. Stripes)**—bean, cheese, and bacon. It's my go-to for a taco on the go.

YUCATAN-STYLE CARNITA TACOS WITH ACHIOTE (COCHINITA PIBIL TACOS)

MELINDA RODRIGUEZ

Makes 8 tacos

4 ounces achiote paste

1 cup fresh lime juice

1 cup fresh orange juice

1⅓ cups white vinegar

3 tablespoons dried oregano, preferably Mexican

4 pounds boneless pork shoulder, cut into 2-inch pieces

2 banana leaves, each 28 inches long

2 cups boiling water

1 medium red onion, thinly sliced

2 teaspoons kosher salt

4 cloves garlic, thinly sliced

3–4 habanero peppers (optional), de-seeded, thinly sliced, and roasted

1 bay leaf

Corn tortillas, warmed

Cilantro, roughly chopped

Combine achiote paste, lime and orange juices, ⅓ cup vinegar, and oregano in a blender. Season with the salt and purée until smooth. Strain marinade through a fine-mesh sieve into a bowl. Add pork and toss to combine.

Line the bottom of a 6-quart dutch oven with banana leaves, letting the excess hang over the side of the pot. Add pork and its marinade, fold leaves over pork, and place lid on pot. Bring to a boil. Reduce heat to medium low; cook until pork is tender, about

2½ hours. (Sometimes I also add carrots, celery, and onions to the pork to give it a sweetness.)

Meanwhile, stir water and onion in a bowl; let sit 3 minutes and drain. Stir in remaining vinegar, 2 teaspoons salt, garlic, habaneros, and bay leaf; cover and let sit at room temperature for at least 1 hour before serving.

Unwrap and transfer pork to a cutting board; shred into bite-size pieces and transfer to a bowl. Stir in 1 cup cooking liquid from the pot. Divide pork among tortillas; top with pickled onion mixture, cilantro, grilled onions, and Cotija cheese. Serve with lime wedges, sliced radishes, and salsa of your choice. (I prefer tomatillo salsa with these tacos.)

Romeo Cantu

FOOD BANK OF THE RIO GRANDE VALLEY, PHARR

Tell us your story.

I was born and raised in the Rio Grande Valley. For more than twenty years, I've worked in television as a news anchor, weathercaster, and reporter and have won several local and national awards, including two Emmy nominations. I'm currently the chief development officer for the Food Bank RGV and serve on the board of directors for the Boys and Girls Club of McAllen and I'm also the founder of the McAllen Tamale Fest.

What's your connection with tacos?

I grew up eating tacos at a very young age. My earliest memory of eating a taco was when I was about ten years old and it was just plain ground beef on a crispy corn tortilla with shredded cheese (the free government cheese, of course). One of my favorite tacos is the beef fajita taco made from Angus beef, with chipotle sauce, cheese, and on a flour tortilla. The chipotle sauce really complements the beef and brings out its delicious flavors.

Give us your top five taco list and why they're the best.

1. **Costa Messa**—the best fajita taco with chipotle sauce.
2. **Republic of the Rio Grande**—best dessert taco, made with fresh cream and strawberries.
3. **Armando's Taco Hut**—it's no longer around, but it served the best big fajita tacos back in the old high school days in Pharr, Texas.
4. **Taco Bell**—their chicken cantina tacos are good, especially when I'm in a hurry.
5. **Dairy Queen**—still the best crispy tacos around: just plain, simple, and good.

Dora Ramos and America Bonilla

ISABEL'S CAFÉ, PORT ISABEL

Tell us your story.
Isabel's Café started with my mom, Isabel Gonzalez. My mom used to work for other restaurants and, to be honest, she wasn't treated very well. In 1973, she decided to open up her own place, and we've been here since. Back then, my sister America and I used to come help after school and stay till 10:00 p.m. We used

to wash dishes, clean tables, and do our homework. Recently, our mom passed away. It was hard, but we want to carry her legacy forward. She loved everyone and would feed everyone, too. It didn't matter if you didn't have money, she would feed you. My mom had a big heart.

What is your most popular taco and why? What makes it a standout or unique?

Our breakfast tacos and tortillas. When my mom first opened the café with my grandmother, they started making the tortillas fresh and big. They started big and became very popular, being homemade and fresh, and it reminded everyone of eating at home. Just eating the food today, it reminds me of my mom. We make it just like she did with a lot of love.

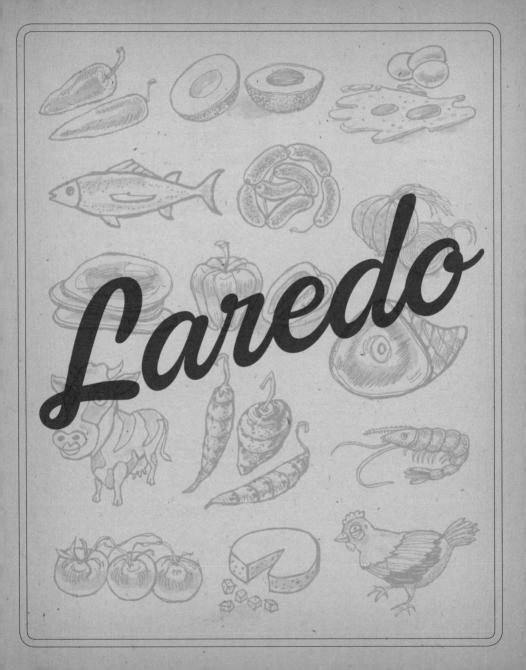

Laredo

In Laredo, there are mariachis en la noche—the kind who sing and give you one hell of a grito! And in the morning, there are the mariachis that you eat—breakfast tacos. That's the way to wake up in Laredo: con mariachis in freshly made flour tortillas. Also, if you ask anyone from Laredo about tacos, you're going to get one major response and that is Taco Palenque. The famous piratas—fajitas, beans, and cheese—of this famed quick-serve spot will have you wanting más.

Being a border town, Laredo is a mix of the old and the new and the creative. Driving around, you can see old barrios and people crossing the border, and you also see new shops opening up. From artists to musicians to chefs, Laredoans are making things happen.

THE LAREDO ICONIC TACO: MARIACHIS A.K.A. BREAKFAST TACOS

When you wake up in Laredo, you wake up with mariachis, anything from eggs and bacon to carne guisada to chilaquiles to huevos con chorizo and mostly cacheteados—that is, spread with a thin layer of beans on each taco. How they came to be called mariachis is folklore, one story passing to the next over tacos. Some say it comes from mariachis playing at 5:00 a.m. in Nuevo Laredo while you eat your early morning tacos; others say eating muy spicy salsa makes you do a big grito. We like the name and sabor, so we'll just leave it at that.

TACO JOURNALISM'S TOP CINCO

1. **Taco Palenque**—world famous for the pirata, fajitas, beans, and cheese wrapped in a tortilla.
2. **Paulita's Restaurant**—super breakfast tacos, including El Bombero.
3. **Lira's Restaurant**—the sweetest barbacoa I ever tasted.
4. **Chano's Patio**—Chano Aldrete, the Taco Mystic, comes out with the Sexy Mexy brisket taco.
5. **Los Reyes del Taco de Caballo**—estilo Nuevo León, this taqueria does not disappoint.

THE LAREDO ROUNDTABLE

When in Laredo, it's best if you speak in Laredo-isms, the unofficial language of that city. It's a mix of borderspeak, Spanglish, and terms that only locals know. And we experienced that firsthand during our plática at Chano's Patio, where our Laredo Taco Ambassador, Sammy "The House" Ramirez, gathered us for a conversation about tacos, Laredo-isms, and border culture. El mayor of Laredo Pete Saenz and company all shared that feeling of growing up in a border town. Below are some highlights from our plática . . .

MAYOR PETE SAENZ

First of all, we call ourselves Laredoenses. I was born and raised here. A lot of things are happening. Now as far as food is concerned, I personally enjoy the home-cooked tacos that we make, like barbacoa—of course, barbecue as well, but I've got to say that just a tortilla de maiz with potato salad makes it for me. You combine the Hispanic, Mexicano, and, with the potato salad, a little country.

CHANO ALDRETE

As people living in a bicultural city, we're united by our Rio Grande, sharing the food and culture as one family. Our strong family roots keep us a kind, loving, generous people who love to eat, drink, dance, and party hard. Salud!

CHEF GABRIELA PANTOJA

In Laredo, if you want a breakfast taco, it is called a "mariachi." I don't care if you work at city hall or whether you work in the oil fields, you're going to want that breakfast taco, that mariachi. Especially if you are going to be late. If you bring tacos—in Laredo or El Paso or all over Texas—then you are never late. Then you are forgiven.

CHANO: THE TACO MYSTIC

As I walked up to Chano to meet him for the first time, I saw his beautiful aura all around him. It was that or maybe it was the brisket he was smoking at his shop. Anyway, I knew we were going to connect de volada! Instant amigos.

Donaciano "Chano" Aldrete runs Chano's Patio in Laredo, is a food artist and chef, and from this point forward, he will be known as the Taco Mystic. With this power comes responsibility and good taco quotes like "tacos make strangers into friends," "a day without tacos is like a day without sunshine," and "spreading love, one taco at a time." He actually had me at brisket tacos.

Juan Francisco Ochoa (Don Pancho)

FOUNDER, TACO PALENQUE

Tell us your story.

I come from a family that had little experience in the food business, but had a great love for cooking. In 1974, I decided to work on creating a restaurant that would offer traditional Mexican food. As I started the planning process, I was introduced to pollo asada, and it completely changed my thought process. In my hometown, with my mom's pollo asada recipe, we came up with our exclusive flavor formula, and in 1975, we opened the very first El Pollo Loco in Guasave, Sinaloa, Mexico.

The next big step was bringing El Pollo Loco to the United States, and in 1980, we opened the first location in Los Angeles. This was bittersweet as it marked us as the first Mexican restaurant chain to ever cross the border.

There were a lot of people who told me that it was a crazy idea to come and compete against major national brands with a similar product, but the flavor and the quality came to play their part. In 1983, we sold the El Pollo Loco rights in the US, and I returned to live in Monterrey, Nuevo León, Mexico.

The desire to offer the public a great restaurant with traditional Mexican cuisine was still very much alive. In July of 1987, I did just that with Taco Palenque in Laredo, Texas. A memorable moment I recall was when the architect gave me the keys for our first location on San Bernardo. I said, "What are those for? I'm never going to close this one. It'll be open 24/7 the whole year." Today, twenty-eight years later, I've kept my word. In Taco Palenque, we serve real Mexican flavors, with recipes brought from throughout Mexico. Some of these great recipes were created by my wife Flerida and our sons. Our unique flavor has gained in popularity, allowing us to reach a total of nineteen locations across Texas, in cities like McAllen, Brownsville, San Antonio, Houston, and New Braunfels.

What is your most popular taco and why? What makes it a standout or unique?

Definitely the pirata taco. It has been on our menu for twenty-eight years, almost since the beginning of Taco Palenque. What makes it unique is its flavor, which comes from the use of the best quality ingredients in the market and our delicious recipe. The pirata has become a staple in South Texas. In fact, we've heard many stories of people coming back home after being away for some time and heading straight to a Taco Palenque to get their pirata fix, even before visiting family! It is so popular, we've added a breakfast version of the pirata to our menu. You can always take your pirata to another level by adding any of the salsas and fresh ingredients from our salsa bar such as our guacamole salsa, salsa tatemada, traditional salsa roja, pickled red onions, cilantro, and much more.

Donaciano "Chano" Aldrete

CHANO'S PATIO

Tell us your story.

I'm a chef and food artist. I've been part of the culinary world for more than twenty years. I guess you can say that I'm the creative genius behind all that is Chano's Patio. My passion for the kitchen and the grill stem from my early years as a child at the ranch. I'm carrying what I learned at the ranch into my career, and I continue to evolve each and every day. My respect, passion, and love flows into the essence of every meal I create, with love being the greatest of the three. My wish is to share the love I have for food with everyone who comes in, through every meal I prepare, todo hecho con mucho amor!

What is your most popular taco and why? What makes it a standout or unique?

My most popular taco is the El Mexy. This taco starts with a fire-grilled tortilla smeared with creamy avocado and *stuffed* with pecan-smoked brisket, topped with roasted poblanos and red onions. It's served with a side of our house-made El Sol salsa and just enough of our delicious barbecue sauce. It's the most popular because it's the sexiest of all.

Why do you think people love tacos so much?

Tacos break all social barriers and transcend cultural preferences. The foundation of the taco, the tortilla, has become the melting pot of all foods used to fill these flour delights and their endless combinations and possibilities of different and unique sexy taco options.

EL MEXY TACO

DONACIANO "CHANO" ALDRETE

I love my abuela's tortillas. María Montemayor Treviño Chapa Del Fuego is gone now, but her legacy lives on. It's important to keep your family's recipes that give you comfort and make you feel good.

FLOUR TORTILLAS
Makes 18 tortillas

4 cups all-purpose flour

¼ teaspoon salt

¼ teaspoon baking powder

1 cup vegetable shortening/lard

1 cup warm water (depending on humidity and altitude)

Mix and sift the flour, salt, and baking powder until blended and then work in lard until the mixture is incorporated and crumbly. Gradually add the warm water and continue mixing until the dough is smooth and not sticky.

Knead dough, cover with a towel, and let rest at room temperature at least 30 minutes or up to 1 hour.

After letting dough rest and rise, make 18 2-ounce dough balls. On a lightly floured board, roll each ball into a 6½-inch circle (más o menos).

Heat a dry griddle or 12-inch skillet (Teflon or cast iron) over medium high heat. Cook the tortillas one at a time, until puffy and golden brown, 45 seconds to 1 minute per side. Set aside to cool slightly. Bring the tortillas to the table wrapped in abuelita's dish-towel for warmth and nostalgia. Practice makes perfect.

EL MEXY BRISKET
Serves approximately 12 to 16 hungry taco lovers

We cook our brisket like a low rider: low and slow. We use pecan firewood from an orchard on the edge of the Rio Grande. I gather and chop the wood to fire log sizes for a stable and continuous burn.

1 10- to 12-pound trimmed brisket	2 cups coarse black pepper
	2 cups kosher salt

Mix the salt and pepper together and rub freely, and with love, on brisket. Shake off excess before putting the meat, fat side toward the fire, in the smoker. Smoke 12–14 hours at 225–250 degrees until tender.

Once cooked, the meat should rest for 30 minutes before cut-ting. (Start making more tortillas for your leftover brisket.)

EL MEXY CONDIMENTS
Serves about 16 tacos

4-6 large poblanos (size matters), julienned	3 medium to large avocados (set aside to use later)
2 medium red onions, sliced	

Preheat oven to 400 degrees. Toss peppers and onion slices in a bowl with oil of choice (we use cooled, rendered bacon fat). Coat well then place the peppers and onions on a flat sheet pan and

roast in the oven for 12–15 minutes until charred. Remove from oven, set aside, and keep warm.

SOL SALSA
Serves 3 Mexicans or 50 gringos (a "Chanoism")

3 tablespoons oil
5 to 7 chiles de árbol
4 garlic cloves
1 large red onion, quartered

2 large ripe tomatoes,
    cut in half
½ bunch cilantro

Place oil, chiles, and garlic in a sauté pan and toast on medium high heat. Cook chiles and garlic until they are smoking, charred, and a little black.

Coat onion pieces and tomato halves with a little oil and place in oven at 400 degrees for 20 minutes until tender and cooked.

Place all ingredients in blender and blend till smooth. Add cilantro and a pinch of kosher or sea salt and blend again.

Now you're ready to construct your El Mexy taco.

Fold a hot tortilla in half. Smear 3 thin slices of avocado on one side. Add 6 ounces of brisket, a pinch of the poblano and onion mix, and serve with a side of Sol Salsa and your favorite barbecue sauce. Celebrate with a Mexican Coke, a shot of tequila, or a Dos Equis. Salud!

Mayor Pete Saenz

Tell us your story.

I am a man from humble beginnings. I was born and raised in Laredo, Texas, in a ranching family. From the time I was six years old, I worked at the ranch, feeding pigs, cleaning pens, and helping my father sell anything he could for a profit. We owned and operated a dairy, and I remember my mother preparing breakfast tacos for all the employees every morning. The tacos consisted of flour tortillas filled with eggs and chorizo, potatoes, bacon, or ham. These tacos that everyone loved are now referred to as "mariachis" in Laredo.

I also remember going to elementary school, and my mother packing tacos for lunch. I was totally embarrassed to let anyone see my tacos because the other students were eating sandwiches. Those experiences are weaved into the fabric of my being. During those times, I learned a work ethic, respect for others, and to not

be embarrassed about my background, my culture, and my love for eating tacos—whether tacos were in style or not.

I carried those life lessons with me when I went to college and through law school and throughout my law practice for more than thirty years.

I have been married for more than forty years and God has blessed me with three children and five grandchildren, who now share that same love of tacos.

I love my community! It has provided me with many blessings, including a home, family, lifelong friends, faith, and the opportunity to build a successful business. As mayor, I will continue to move Laredo forward by starting each day with a delicious mariachi taco.

What's your connection with tacos?

Tacos are a part of my history. When I was growing up at the ranch, we had tacos for dinner after a hard day's work. When I was a boy, my family would go to Nuevo Laredo and eat tacos together. Once I had my own family, we celebrated special occasions—birthday parties, graduations, Easter—with carne asadas and tacos. Our tacos consisted of refried beans, tripas, sausage, guacamole, and we even created our own taco that was a little bit Mexican and a little bit American. My wife loves potato salad so she started preparing potato salad tacos and they are now a family favorite and can be eaten with either tortillas de maiz (corn) or tortillas de harina (flour).

Samuel Ramirez (Sammy "The House")

TEXAS TACO COUNCIL

Tell us your story.

Everybody pretty much knows me as Sammy "The House." I have been on the radio for the past twenty-three years. I have two kids and am married to their amazing mom. I love tacos, music, and life. Being on the radio, I've met great people, both regular everyday people and celebrities. Turns out, all these people love tacos! I love my kids and my wife, and I'm chubby, Catholic, sexy, and awesome.

What's your connection with tacos?

I was born Ramirez on the Tex-Mex border. It doesn't get more connected than that. Also, every time you look at me you know "he just had a taco."

Give us the taco landscape for your city/region. Give us your top ten list and why they're the best.

Landscape? It's Laredo. You can smell the tacos from fifty miles outside the city limits.

1. **El Mexy from Chano's Patio (I named this one)**—brisket and onions with special toppings like guacamole with a combination of barbecue sauce and homemade salsa.
2. **The pirata from Taco Palenque**—the perfect fajita with the right amount of beans and cheese.
3. **Bacon and egg with beans and cheese (custom order) from Laredo Taco Company**—it's perfect.
4. **Pollo te quiero from Chano's (I named this one, too)**—everything Chano makes is "hecho con amor."
5. **Tres carnes (en lechuga) from Taco Villa**—you have to try it in lettuce instead of a tortilla. It will change your life.
6. **Barbacoa from Lira's Restaurant**—best barbacoa in the state.
7. **Chicharrón from Laredo Taco Company**—quick, fast, and dirty.
8. **Adobado pork from El Taco Tote**—you can't get this flavor anywhere else.
9. **Shrimp from El Taco Tote**—I'm Catholic and this makes my Lent go by easier.
10. **Tacos de caballo from Tacos de Caballo**—inexplicable.

Elsa Rodriguez Arguindegui

LA INDIA PACKING COMPANY
AND THE TASTING ROOM CAFÉ

Tell us your story.

La India Packing Co. was founded in 1924 by our grandparents, Antonio and Antonia Rodriguez. The business was founded as a general store. Antonio used to take orders for medicinal herbs from the soldiers during the Mexican Revolution and went to an "Indian woman" from Lampazos, Mexico, who would prescribe herbs according to the described ailment. Antonio was blind since he was a younger man, but had the foresight to create his chorizo and menudo blends with medicinal herbs as natural acid neutralizers. Our spice blends are not only good but are also good for you. For ninety-one years, we have worked with many of the same

suppliers who maintain the highest level of quality that is expected from our products year after year. We use our grandparents' recipes created many years ago. Our mother, Guadalupe Rodriguez, bought the business in 1990, which is also when I became general manager. Today a few of the original employees who were teens when I was growing up continue to help keep the traditions while transitioning to the world of technology.

In 2000, we opened up the Tasting Room Café on site. It has become one of our city's regular tourist attractions. We are known for our historically significant spice company; the colorful, artistic, and relaxing atmosphere; and the flavors of our homemade meals using our specialty blends. We are now part of Frontera Fusion, a pilot project intended to preserve our Hispanic heritage. It is important to educate people on how to use herbs and not lose our culture's traditions.

What is your most popular taco and why? What makes it a standout or unique?

La India Specialty taco, which includes a rich selection of herbs and spices, blended in our mesquite-grilled chicken and fajitas. Another popular taco is our very own Shroomizo taco, which is a tasty vegetarian option for chorizo lovers.

Chef Gabriela Pantoja

GP RESTAURANT & CULINARY CONSULTING AND ACADEMY

Tell us your story.

I was born and raised in Nuevo Laredo, Tamaulipas, Mexico, and later immigrated to the United States in search of better opportunities. I was raised with the importance of traditional values, religion, higher education, and practicing sports as a way of life. My passion was always in the food industry, so I moved to Austin to pursue my dream at the Texas Culinary Academy/Le Cordon Bleu. I have worked in restaurants since the age of sixteen, from retail, chain, and local to five-star hotels, from catering and food distributor to owning my own restaurant and culinary consulting and academy.

What's your connection with tacos?

My connection with tacos has been since I can remember. As a native Mexican, I grew up with tacos, from a simple tortilla con chile to gourmet tacos. It's has been part of my diet, and I keep visiting Mexico in search of new variations and creating my own recipes. Every time I travel to different countries, I must take my corn flour to make my own tortillas and, of course, my chiles to make salsa. So, no, I cannot live without tacos!

Give us your top taco spots and why.

My kitchen—you can't find tacos just the way you want them but at home. Fresh ingredients, everything homemade, and produce from the garden.

Villa Antigua—fresh ingredients. There is love in every taco that comes out of the kitchen, from mariachis to fajita tacos to Oaxacan tlayudas.

Tensai Sushi—another type of taco. Jicama tacos with seafood mix is another variation of taquitos. Amazing combinations and experimentation.

Don Panino—an Italian restaurant that serves tacos! Yes, Italian tacos with the infusion of Mexican ingredients.

Gisela Sanchez

PAULITA'S RESTAURANT

Tell us your story.

I was born in Mexico but have always lived in Laredo. Paulita's has been around since the 1960s. All of our food is homemade and we stay true to the Mexican culture of food. There are a lot of taquerias, and because we are closer to the border, our food stays authentic. The farther up you go in Texas, the food loses its authenticity and becomes more Tejano.

What is your most popular taco and why? What makes it a standout or unique?

One of our most popular tacos is the bombero. It stands out

because of the homemade tortillas. It comes with beans, three fried eggs, and two slices of bacon. It is very simple but very good.

Why do you think people love tacos so much?

People love tacos because of the homemade tortilla. On this side of the frontera, the handmade tortillas aren't made as much anymore. People tend to buy them already made. We offer them homemade and fresh, so it feels like they are coming from the kitchen of your own home.

Rebeca and Luis Guzman

Tell us your story.

We met in Guanajuato Mexico at the age of nineteen. Thirty-seven years later, here we are. In 1983, Luis miraculously made it to Laredo, Texas. He was lucky enough to receive amnesty from Ronald Reagan and soon after that, we joined him in the US. Luis now owns a successful landscaping business, and I take care of our home. We feel blessed to have six children and twelve grandchildren.

What's your connection with tacos?

Well, we're Mexican. We can both cook tacos, tortas, carne asada, and all the best Mexican food.

PUERCO EN SALSA ROJA

REBECA GUZMAN

Makes 25 tacos

SALSA ROJA

20 chile cascabel pods	3 cups water
2 garlic cloves	Salt

Remove stems, devein, and remove seeds from the chiles. Soak chile pods in the water until soft, then mix the chiles, garlic, and salt in a blender. Remove mixture from blender and strain into a large bowl. Set aside until pork is ready.

8 pounds pork butt	1 cup manteca/lard
1 cup water	1 tablespoon salt

Chop the pork into 1-inch squares. Add pork and 1 cup of water to pan. Cover and cook on medium heat until the water evaporates. (If the cubes begin to fall apart, empty out the water before evaporation.)

After water evaporates, add the manteca (or lard) and cook until golden brown. Remove excess grease. Remove from heat. Allow the pork to cool, then shred the meat.

In a large pan, combine shredded pork and salsa roja. Cook over low to medium heat. Let simmer 15 minutes.

Warm corn tortillas on a comal or griddle. Add the puerco en salsa roja to tortillas and you're ready to eat your tacos!

David Lira

LIRA'S RESTAURANT

Tell us your story.

I've been in Laredo for five years now. We started originally in Nuevo Laredo in 1986 and opened in Laredo in 2010. Our specialty is barbacoa and menudo. We've been in the barbacoa business for thirty years now. People line up to get their barbacoa on Sundays and it makes me proud to serve our clients—it makes me happy.

What is your most popular taco and why? What makes it a standout or unique?

It's definitely our barbacoa tacos. We serve it by the pound and you can make as many tacos as you want. We sell it every day, but our lines are out the door on Saturdays and Sundays, usually before and after church. We put a special touch on our barbacoa to make it sweet and with lots of love and hard work.

Gilberto Rocha Rochelli

ARTIST

Tell us your story.

I am an artist and, needless to say, not a starving one, thanks to our abundance of tacos.

What's your connection with tacos?

Tacos have been a part of my culture since the day I was born. I was actually born out of a taco. I love tacos. Even tacos love tacos sometimes.

My favorite tacos are "tacos the papa" and you can find them in Nuevo Laredo, Mexico. They are tiny and they consist of a corn tortilla deep fried with mashed potatoes and cabbage inside. You eat them at the side of the street and the surrounding sounds and street life are what give them a magical flavor.

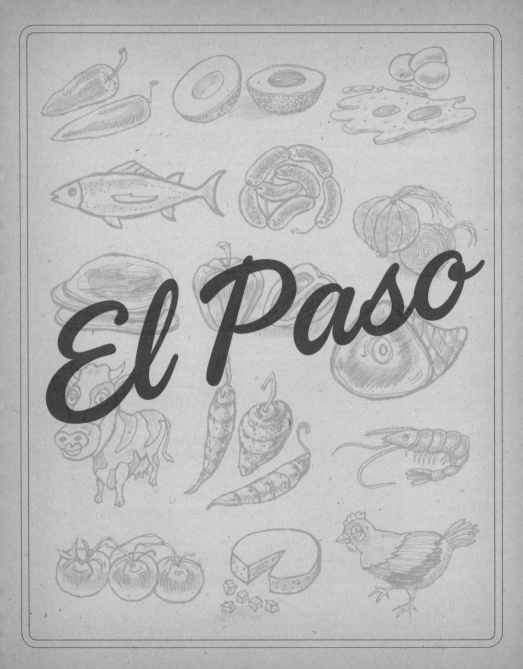

El Paso

El Paso, Texas, home of Mando Rayo, this Taco Journalist! The land where people talk in song, where the minorities are the majority, and where the Pachucos came from. El Paso is home to the L&J Cafe, the star atop the Franklin Mountains, El Segundo Barrio, Ysleta, and it's the place where I grew up. Going back to El Paso for the *Tacos of Texas* was a great homecoming. I've been away for twenty years with sporadic visits, but this taco tour helped me reconnect with my roots and learn about what's been happening in Chucotown.

When I started this project, I asked about the tacos in El Paso and I would get the same response: "We eat burritos here." But after digging deeper, visiting people's homes, and finding the food scene, I noticed that the tacos just kept popping up! From the newest and trendiest to the Juárez-style taquerias and the iconic restaurants, tacos are everywhere in El Paso.

Being away and only going back once a year, I knew I needed to reach out to my El Paso community. So I contacted my amigos, ex-pats, cousins and other family members, neighbors, y paisanos, and I combed el internet. El Paso Taco Ambassadors unite! Yes, I made a call to the Texas Taco Council to help me find the best of the best. Official Taco Ambassadors "Super" Mario Kato, Sara Macias, and Seth Wilson responded to my call. From the West Side to way east, Horizon, and Clint, we ate some of the best tacos the El Paso area has to offer.

THE EL PASO ICONIC TACO: CARNITAS

Traditionally, carnitas are made during the winter months, but now you don't have to wait all year to get your carnitas fix. If you're lucky, you have a tío who can fry them up in a cazo. If you're not so lucky, you can go directly to your local carniceria and then cook them up yourself. Or buy them ready-made. As a border town, El Paso is influenced by the food, people, and culture of Mexico. Carnitas originated in Michoacán, but El Paso has made them their own—in the farmlands, taquerias, fiestas, and restaurants. While also known for other styles and foods—like Juárez-style taquerias and enchiladas with muenster cheese (yes!)—El Pasoans sure know their carnitas.

TACO JOURNALISM'S TOP CINCO

1. **L&J Cafe**—an El Paso institution doing it up crispy.
2. **Tacoholics**—taking tacos to the next level with their Korean bbq tacos.
3. **Tacos El Charly**—Juárez-style taqueria con todo, tacos, papa asada and grilled cebollitas and jalapeños.
4. **Carnitas Queretaro**—solid, juicy carnitas!
5. **El Taco Tote**—Meat lovers unite! Grilling is what they do and carne is what you'll have.

I do have to mention my nostalgia for the rolled taco shop, Chico's Tacos. Late nights in El Paso, I used to order not a single but a triple order of rolled taquitos drowned in tomato sauce topped off with shredded yellow cheese and green spicy salsa. Like so many El Pasoans, I grew up with Chico's and I think that's the connection El Pasoans have with it. My taco palate has grown up, too, and, in the words of my loving children, I must say about Chico's: "it's not my favorite." That's all I have to say about that.

OF MEN, DISCADAS, AND CARNITAS

Being Mexican means a hell of a lot of machismo. Pero I'm a modern Mexican, so I left that behind me years ago . . . sort of. One of the traditions I hold dear to my corazón is cooking with family. I was influenced in the kitchen by mi mama, tías, primas, and sisters, as well as my brothers, tíos, y primos. Now I'm the cook at home. Daddy always cooks when he's at home for Quetzal y Dieguito. (I gotta say that my wife Ixchel is an excellent baker, too.)

Anyway, part of my experience was around the kitchen with the matriarchs, but another part was outside con los hombres. Cooking outdoors—doing up a carne asada (grilling) or a discada or even an annual matanza del marrano, slaughtering a pig, for carnitas and chicharrones—still falls in the hombre category. It's part of the Mexican culture where men cook together, share stories, drink (lots), and bond over an open fire, cazo, or grill.

One of the ways we do this is with a discada and using a disco, a pan developed somewhere between the farmlands of Mexico and Texas. Large tractor tills are welded together to form a concave pan used for outdoor cooking. El disco is more than a pan; it's a way for Mexican men (mostly) to share the experience of cooking and bringing families together with food and culture. The discada is the process of cooking up the red meats, pork, sausages, weenies, bacon, chorizo, jalapeños, and cebollitas as the corn tortillas warm up on the edges of the pan and we converse about life, politics, food, family, beers, tequila, y más. All while giving each other a hard time, laughing, and, yes, sometimes hugging and crying, depending on the amount of alcohol consumed. I love a good discada. Somebody should write a book about that.

The disco is so special in my family that one year my older brother Javier received a custom-made one from my Tío Santiago and, man, that Christmas I was pretty jealous and disappointed. But I got over it because the next year, I got El Disco 2000; it was larger, better, and with welded horseshoe handles. Win!

Lucky for us, we set up a couple of discadas while in West Texas. Below, you'll read about discadas with Jessie Peña y familia in El Paso and then later with the Flores family in the Midland-Odessa chapter.

Allá en el rancho grande, allá donde viviaaa!

Not really. My tío and tía and cousins lived there and we just loved to visit them. I remember the killings—pigs, chickens, cabras—and, you know, that was la vida en el rancho. La matanza del marrano was typically done in the winter months, and the whole family came together to help out, making carnitas and chicharrones and tacos, flautas, chile rellenos, chile con queso, tortillas, and lots of chiles and salsas. I got to relive that on the Tacos of Texas Tour.

While we didn't slaughter a pig, we did cook up one hundred and sixty pounds of carnitas and chicharrones, led by my father figure, Tío Santiago, the hardest-working and shortest Mexican in West Texas. (Well, they do call him "Chaparro," his nickname for shorty.) Old school, hard-working, loving in his own way, and one hell of a ballbuster, mi Tío Santiago is all heart. Even if he still makes me nervous for the first hour when we get together and he gives me life lessons like "you're not a man unless you own your own home and your fence line is in a straight line" or a simple "don't be lazy, cabrón." And then there's the one he says about nuestra gente (our people) or about you when you make a mistake in his presence: "por eso no avanzan los Mexicanos." Loosely translated, it means "that's why Mexicans do not progress." So for this project, I had to endure being twelve years old again—and it was worth it. After six hours of preparation, cutting pork skin and meat and cooking it in a muy hot cazo, we made some pretty amazing carnitas and chicharrones. You'll see how it's done in the Familia Garcia section of this chapter.

Jessie Peña

TACOHOLICS

Tell us your story.

I am the proud father of two, a husband, and an entrepreneur. A culinary dropout, with the vision to give people some of my best interpretations of what good tacos should taste like.

I am a born-and-raised El Pasoan. I have five brothers, two sisters, and proud parents who still won't hesitate to tell me when I'm screwing up. Growing up, we appreciated food a bit more because we raised much of what we ate. We raised cattle, hogs, chickens, to name a few. The appreciation for food started early. Some of the fondest memories growing up always seemed to revolve around food. We had fritangas—I'd call them feasts. They included lots of cerveza, fresh tortillas, two or three great salsas, various types of proteins, and a lotta love. No matter what the problems in the world are, a family-style meal is always a warm welcome.

After a few years in school, I jumped into the food business. Bought a food truck and started slinging tacos. The whole idea of Tacoholics started as a dream and is now a reality, vibrant and healthy.

Tacoholics started from a food truck in 2010 and we are humbled by all the support that we have received over the last few years. Our first brick-and-mortar place opened in early 2016. Our concept is ever evolving, but the flavors and hustle are still there! Our food is still true to the street food vibe: elotes, charro beans, tacos, flautas ahogadas, chicharrones, huaraches, and more. We've become more involved with the community over the last few years through volunteering and donations.

What is your most popular taco and why? What makes it a standout or unique?

Our Korean bbq taco is the most popular because it bridges the gap between old and new, hip and cultural. I've heard that taco referred to as "KMEX"—Korean Mexican, essentially. A fusion of cultures, where the concept of a taco meets bulgogi; hints of pear, sweet yet still tasting the essence of the tortilla, topped with an Asian slaw and a vinaigrette, and let's not forget the sesame seeds. Oh, and yeah, cilantro, onions, limes, and salsa. It works, oddly enough.

Why do you think people love tacos so much?

A good taco makes most people happy, and who doesn't want to be happy? Ok, well that's part of it. It's simple meets beauty, humble yet loud. They're easily held, you can get 'em rolled, soft, hard, fried, flat, stuffed, wet or dry, with veggies, meat, or seafood. For breakfast or dinner. They're tacos!

DISCADA

JESSIE PEÑA

Makes about 100 tacos

½ cup lard or canola oil
1 pound bacon
2 pounds Mexican-style
   chorizo, beef, or pork
5 pounds chopped pork
   cushion
5 pounds chopped beef,
   boneless chuck
One package of all-beef
   franks, sliced

2 Roma tomatoes, grated
1 Mexican beer
6 jalapeños
6 Fresno peppers
   (red peppers, shaped
   like jalapeños, but hotter
   and fatter)
1 bunch chopped cilantro
Salt and pepper

Serve with:

Tortillas
Chopped onions
Chopped cilantro
Lime wedges

Salsa
Pickled red onions, optional
Avocado slices, optional

It starts with the disco. Add the lard or oil. Let it smoke just a bit, then add the bacon. While cooking all the proteins, you may want to have the flame at a medium to high temperature.

After the bacon renders some of the fat, push the bacon toward the top or remove and save for integration later.

Add the chorizo and cook for approximately 3 to 4 minutes, being careful not to overcook. After the bacon and chorizo have let out all that magical grease, place the chorizo toward the top of the disco or remove and save for integration later.

Next add the pork cushion, cooking approximately five minutes. Remove it and save for integration later.

Add the beef and cook for five minutes. At this point, you are ready to integrate all the cooked items along with the sliced franks.

While everything starts to cook together, add the tomato zest and Mexican beer.

Most of the time, this is where you would add the peppers, tomatoes, and onions. We didn't add onions in this mix because we have them as a condiment. What we *did* add were the peppers, but whole, not sliced or chopped. This allows the discada to have some flavor and depth, but doesn't make it too spicy for those who just don't like a lot of heat.

The boil. This part is extremely important because everything just comes together. Lower the flame a bit to a medium heat. This slow boil may take seven to ten minutes while the juices start to evaporate a bit. Some people like their discada really juicy; others prefer it dry. I say that if you use good quality ingredients, the discada shouldn't be too wet or dry, but just right. I've eaten discada that has a lot of fat or is a bit too oily because of the ingredients used. Sticking to good lean proteins will eliminate that.

Add the aromatics; we use cilantro for the discada. Also add salt and pepper. Warm up some tortillas and start plating. Pop a cerveza or two, and enjoy, my friends! This whole process from start to finish should take about forty-five minutes or so.

Rosa Guerrero

Tell us your story.

I'm a native El Pasoan and the first in many things. First in my family of seven to graduate from college; first living Latina artist and educator to have an elementary school named in my honor, the Rosa Guerrero Elementary School, which opened in 1992; first Latina to be named Distinguished Alumnas at UTEP in 1997; and first to have founded the folkloricos in El Paso. My International Ballet Folklorico was the first US folklorico to dance at the

Kennedy Center in 1991 and at the Central Intelligence Agency in 1992. My folkloricos are intergenerational, as I also started the first senior citizens folklorico. I was the first El Pasoan to win a Golden Cine Award for my film, *Tapestry*, made in 1974. At eighty, I still do motivational talks on Mexican/Latino cultures and international cultures, using music and dance.

I believe corn is the basic and most important food in Mexican/American cultures. History, products, and byproducts were made from the corn and our own tacos were first made from corn, before the flour tortillas.

What is your connection with tacos?

My mother is part Indian, Chichimeca, and my grandmother was full Indian from Toluca, Mexico. This taco recipe is hundreds of years old. It was passed from family to family.

TACOS DE ENSALADA DE NOPALITOS/ TACOS WITH CACTUS PADS

ROSA GUERRERO

Makes 10 tacos

- 2 1-pound packages precut cactus leaves (nopales)
- 1 cup diced onions
- 3 large or 6 small avocados, diced
- 1 cup diced tomatoes
- 1 cup chopped cilantro
- 2 to 4 (or more if you like chiles) fresh jalapeño peppers, diced
- 1 cup diced cheese such as Monterey Jack
- 1 5-10-ounce package very small pork rinds with no fat
- 1 pound bacon, fried and crumbled
- 1 cup diced cooked ham
- 2 boiled and diced medium-sized potatoes
- Salt and pepper
- Fresh hot tortillas for your taquitos or tacotes

Rinse then boil the cactus leaves in a little water. Add onions and 1 teaspoon of bicarbonate powder so it will not get so slimy. Cook for ½ hour. Rinse again and let cool. Mix all ingredients in a large bowl.

If you are a vegetarian, omit ham, bacon, and pork rinds. This salad is nutritious and great for people with diabetes. Native Americans have eaten nopalitos for thousands of years.

Carlos Serrato

TACOS EL CHARLY

Tell us your story.

We started as a family business in Juárez, Mexico. It's where our father started selling tacos, and as young boys, we started our business by learning from him. We started a lonchera (truck) in 2006, only being open three days a week. As time went on, our business began to grow.

As young boys, we saw our father sell tacos, and he taught us and continued that tradition, and we continued to get more and more customers. Our brother still sells tacos in Juárez. So you can say, we are a family of taqueros.

What is your most popular taco and why? What makes it a standout or unique?

It is our taco al pastor with the meat that is prepared with adobo sauce with the estilo Juárez. My father passed down the cooking tradition. Unlike most taquerias that serve only tacos, we serve our tacos with plenty of sides, baked potatoes, grilled long green onions and jalapeños, radishes, and corn tortilla quesadillas.

Why do you think people love tacos so much?

People love tacos because they love the feeling they get when eating tacos. They feel as if they are in Mexico, eating real Mexican food.

Estela Casas

KVIA-ABC NEWS ANCHOR

Tell us your story.

I am a news anchor at KVIA, the ABC affiliate in El Paso, and have been in broadcast journalism for thirty-two years. I enjoy telling "people stories" and my proudest moments have been covering Pope John Paul II's visit to Chihuahua City in 1990 and stories featuring women and children battling cancer. Last year, the White House invited me to speak with President Obama about the Trans-Pacific Partnership, that added twelve countries to the NAFTA agreement between the US, Mexico, and Canada. In my free time, I enjoy cooking, traveling, dancing, and karaoke.

What's your connection with tacos?

I love to eat! You can turn any meal into a taco—just grab a tortilla and fill it.

I also enjoy arrachera tacos and tacos de deshebrada. They are easy to make. You have to remember that it's all in the salsa.

Why do you think people love tacos in your region and in Texas?

I believe people in the Borderland love tacos because you don't need a spoon. You just scoop up the meat, chicken, shrimp, mushrooms, kale with a corn tortilla and a tablespoon of home-made salsa morita and enjoy! People have a connection with food because in the Mexican American community, we celebrate with food and many times it's with tacos!

Give me your top five taco spots and why.

I like the shrimp tacos at Little Shack and the Korean beef tacos at Tacoholics. Any taco stand along Alameda Street has great tacos and, of course, my arrachera tacos.

Jose Pacifico Heras

EL TACO TOTE

Tell us your story.

Everything began in 1988, when my family and I moved to Ciudad Juárez, Mexico, and noticed something was missing in the local cuisine; it was the "Heras" touch. We felt the need for authentic Mexican tacos and salsas, the kind that we were used to having at home.

The first restaurant was small, with six or seven tables for customers and just four employees. It was a south-of-the-border traditional taqueria, but the quality of the food made the business prosper and become what it is now. We are without a doubt 100 percent Mexican style!

We are really proud to be an "all fresh" restaurant. Everything,

from our tortillas to our distinctive salsa bar, is made fresh every day, with no preservatives and with the best quality in produce, meats, and ingredients.

What is your most popular taco and why? What makes it a standout or unique?

I have to say all of our tacos are popular in some way and for specific niches, but the all-time favorite is the sirloin taco.

It is made from deliciously seasoned and grilled top butt, wrapped inside a corn or flour tortilla, which is made from scratch by the hands of our experienced and very talented "tortilleras."

This taco is the definition of quality, juiciness, and succulent flavor!

Why do you think people love tacos so much?

Because they're freaking delicious! People nowadays crave exciting, strong, and unique flavors, and that's exactly what a taco represents.

Also, when you talk about tacos, the possibilities are endless; we currently have twelve different kinds of tacos . . . and we still have new recipes in mind.

Tacos are 100 percent customizable, you can put anything you want inside a warm tortilla and create an amazing taco. So practically, there is always a taco recipe to satisfy every single person.

A taco is an easy dish to eat; you don't even need utensils or a fancy plate, just your bare hands and a big appetite.

And, of course, the taco will always be a Mexican tradition, and who doesn't love tradition?

"Super" Mario Kato

KLAQ-FM
TEXAS TACO COUNCIL

Tell us your story.

I was born in El Paso, Texas. My father was a mechanic by trade and my mother was a garment worker. I'm the oldest of four boys who lived in a two-bedroom house in central El Paso. We were taught at an early age to enjoy life, and for me, it's family, music, and food. They all blend together in one way or another.

I'm a proud father of four kids, two girls and two boys, and I've been married to my soul mate and travel partner, Patricia, for ten years.

I've worked for the same rock radio station for twenty-four years, touching every aspect of the business. I've met some great musicians and chefs. When a great band or group is playing, food and cookouts are always close by. That's why I'm known as the "KLAQ Foodie."

What's your connection with tacos?

A quick bite to eat is always on my list. I'm always on the run and tacos are a man's best friend while on the road—easy to grab, easy to eat.

You're on the Texas Taco Council. Why are you the Taco Ambassador for your city/region?

I was nominated by a few people in El Paso. Being on the radio, I've had the chance to explore some great food establishments, and I talk passionately about the food from our little big city. I'm the vato who likes good company, a good beer, and a great meal.

Give us the taco landscape for your city/region. Give us your top few list and why they're the best.

Tacos have always been around in El Paso. Now, with the food truck revolution that has recently popped up in El Paso, there's more variety, and more foodies and backyard chefs are exploring the world of the taco.

1. **Tacoholics**—Korean bbq taco. Amazing flavor.
2. **Rulis' International Kitchen**—chicken chicharrón tacos are one of kind.
3. **Tacos El Charly**—tacos al pastor are salty, sweet, and spicy.
4. **Tacos Ay Cocula**—tripitas are very clean, and the red salsa is excellent.
5. **Roli Taco Truck**—the barbacoa tacos are very tasty.
6. **Steve O's**—the carnitas tacos have a spice that will make you want more.
7. **Chico's Tacos**—flautas in a tomato-based sauce. It's an El Paso thing.

Zulem Arellano-Bordier

CARNITAS QUERETARO

Tell us your story.

Carnitas Queretaro is all about the people. Our mission is to create a restaurant environment that satisfies the tastes and expectations of our core customers. Our customers are like family—they have grown with us for all these years and we are always happy to serve them!

What is your most popular taco and why? What makes it a standout or unique?

The carnitas taco is our most popular taco. The way the carnitas is prepared is very unique. Our technique originally comes from Queretaro, Mexico, and is definitely what sets us apart in El Paso.

Familia Garcia

SANTIAGO GARCIA

Tell us your story.

I was born in my family's home on July 25, 1940, in a small town on the Mexican border named Porvenir, Chihuahua. My father owned a three-thousand-acre ranch and kept cattle for selling and providing beef for our family of eight. Once or twice a year, during the winter, my father and uncles would butcher a cow for the family. Every part of the cow was eaten. Dishes were made from the organs: liver and heart tacos, tripitas tacos, and morcilla tacos (a thickening of the blood until it looks like ground beef). The tripe was used to make menudo. I was not fond of all these dishes, but I remember the adults in my family enjoyed them. The head of the cow was used to make beef and tongue tacos. The meat was then cut into fourths. Some of the meat was ground in our family's molino to make ground beef and some of the meat was used to make shredded beef, enough to last a couple of days. I was raised eating ground beef tacos and shredded beef tacos. My mother prepared ground beef tacos with handmade corn tortillas topped with lettuce, cheese, and green chile salsa.

Back then, we didn't have refrigerators, so the rest of the meat was cut into strips and air

dried, and that was the only meat that was available for the rest of the year. Dishes were made with dried meat, including sopa de fideo with meat, chile verde con carne, and chile colorado con carne. We also made machaca. The dried meat was tenderized with a tenderizer on a metal base almost to crumbs and then fried with eggs. Poultry was available year round. I remember butchering chickens with my mother and making dishes for the day like chile verde and chile colorado with chicken, regular chicken tacos, pipian, and caldo de pollo.

I married Olga in 1971 and moved to Clint, Texas, where we both raised chickens, goats, cows, and pigs. I raised a pig every year for butchering to make chicharrones with the rind, carnitas, and asados. It was a winter tradition; our family and friends would get together. It became a festive tradition with our wooden stove, food, and music. Over the years, I've practiced to make the perfect chicharrones.

Olga Garcia

Tell us your story.
I was born in 1948 in El Paso, Texas. I'm one of eight siblings, a daughter of bracero parents in Arizona. When I was two, my parents moved to a small town in Chihuahua, Mexico, where I grew up on a farm. My four older brothers helped our father tend the crops, while the three daughters of the family helped clean the house and make the food. Growing up, I remember eating vegetables from the fields like squash, chile, tomatoes, onions, cucumbers, carrots, corn, peas, wheat, pinto beans, lentils, peanuts, and fruit,

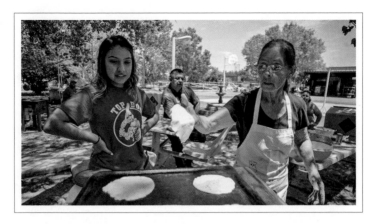

including watermelon, cantaloupe, and honeydew, and sugar cane and sweet potatoes. Every year these crops were grown, enough to last through winter, until the next fresh batch came the following year. We saved the dry goods, the beans, lentils, and corn in sacks. The wheat was sent to the mill to be ground and put into sacks as well. All the dry goods and flour were kept in a large adobe room, the family pantry, where up to one hundred sacks were stored. My mother preserved many of these foods. She canned chile and tomato jam. My two sisters and I helped make up to two hundred tortillas per day. The flour tortillas were then used to make bean, potato, and chile tacos or eggs, chile tomato and onion tacos for the family of ten and the family workers. When I was thirteen, I left our little town, Ejido Benito Juárez, to work in the United States. I married Santiago in 1971 and moved to a farm in Clint where we raised animals for our family. Although we had many chickens, goats, and cows, we only raised one pig each year. We fed it corn for six months and fattened it for the annual slaughter and that was the beginning of my famous asado.

CHICHARRONES

OLGA AND SANTIAGO GARCIA

Chicharrones are fried pork belly or skin. You can buy them at local meat markets.

Makes about 100 tacos

  60 pounds pork rind
  3 tablespoons salt
  ½ gallon water

Cut pork rind into 2 × 2-inch squares. Place in a cazo and turn on medium heat. At the beginning of the cooking process, mix salt and water in separate container and pour into cazo.

Turn pieces of pork rinds constantly with large wooden paddle for at least 2 hours until crisp and fluffy.

Take chicharrones out of the liquid lard left in the cazo. Place them into a cardboard box lined with paper towels and let cool.

ASADO DE CHILE COLORADO

OLGA AND SANTIAGO GARCIA

3 pounds dried New Mexico red chiles

1 head garlic, peeled

Place chile in pot, cover fully with water. Bring to full boil for ¾ of an hour or until chile is soft.

Let cool. Blend in blender with peeled garlic. Sieve into a large pot. Refrigerate until needed.

CARNITAS

OLGA AND SANTIAGO GARCIA

60 pounds pork shoulder or butt	10 bay leaves
3 tablespoons salt	3 to 4 teaspoons salt (or to taste)
flour to cover	3 tablespoons oregano
½ cup manteca (lard or oil)	10 cloves garlic
4 pounds chile colorado	½ cup flour

Cut pork into 2 × 2-inch squares. Place manteca and pork in cazo on medium heat. Turn pieces of pork constantly with large wooden paddle for approximately 2 hours or until golden brown. Pork will fry in its own fat until crisp on the outside and moist on the inside. You may pour off excess fat as the pork cooks to prevent the carnitas from becoming too greasy. Remove carnitas from cazo, place them in a large bowl, and set aside.

Once carnitas are done, select the larger pieces and return them to the cazo to cook on medium heat. Add flour and mix, then add the chile colorado, bay leaves, salt, oregano, and garlic. Slowly bring to a boil on medium heat for 10 minutes. Simmer for another 10 to 15 minutes on low until the asado is done.

Now you are ready for tacos de chicharrones, carnitas, and asado de puerco. In a corn tortilla, add the chicharrones or carnitas with your favorite salsa or just put the asado de puerco on your tortilla and you're set for a Sunday afternoon.

Chef Raul Gonzalez III

RULIS' INTERNATIONAL KITCHEN

Tell us your story.

I was born in Chihuahua, Chihuahua, Mexico, in 1971, but lived in Quito, Ecuador, until the first grade. My grandmother lived in Parral, Chihuahua, and my family moved back there briefly until we moved to El Paso.

Parral was very special for me because one, I loved my grandmother very much, and two, my great uncle Cesar ("Checha" we called him) owned a taco shop right on one of the main streets in town. It was at Uncle Checha's place that my love affair with the taco began. Tacos de bistec and sangria señorial is the first food/drink pairing that I remember. I was probably four or five years old. I also remember always having tortillas at the table for every meal. I would make everything on my plate into a taco. Spaghetti tacos, egg tacos, tacos de fideo, fish tacos, picadillo tacos, tacos de albóndigas, you name it!

My palate developed early, and by the time I was fifteen, I was experimenting in the kitchen. I inherited my taste buds from my father and my cooking skills from my mother. Through good times and bad, delicious food and eating together as a family has always been our tradition. Our home, when I was growing up, always smelled heavenly, but summer time was the best. My dad would grill arrachera every weekend, and my aunts, uncles, and cousins would come over to swim and eat tacos. Grilled onions, baked potatoes, and charro beans were always on the menu, too.

In 2004, I funded a restaurant for my mom's sister (a prolific cooking instructor) and my cousin in Torreón, Coahuila, Mexico. It was a great experience in building a restaurant, and it was the step that drew me closer to opening my own. By 2008, I was ready to leave the corporate world and that's when Rulis' International Kitchen was born. We opened to the public in 2008, and I've never looked back. Now my entire family (mom, dad, sister, son, and three nieces) work with me. And we all love tacos!

What is your most popular taco and why? What makes it a standout or unique?

The most popular taco is the shrimp taco. I sauté the shrimp with bacon and top it with a mango avocado salsa. This taco became popular because of the salsa and the bacon. The salsa gives the taco a cool tropical feel, and bacon makes everything taste better.

Why do you think people love tacos so much?

Tacos are the ultimate comfort food. Tacos transcend social class and bring people together. You eat them with your hands, and you can stuff them with just about anything. Tacos are versatile and delicious and now take on more flavors than ever.

PORK BELLY TACOS

CHEF RAUL GONZALEZ III

Makes 24 tacos

TERIYAKI SAUCE

10 serranos

½ cup oil

2 cups soy sauce

2 cups sugar

Fry serranos in the oil until the skin blisters and peels off easily. Remove the skin and set the peppers aside. Blend soy sauce and sugar with the serranos toreados. Once blended, bring the mixture to a boil in a small pot, reduce heat, and simmer until it thickens, about 10 to 15 minutes.

SLAW

2 Granny Smith apples

¼ cup cilantro, chopped

½ Persian lime, juiced

Kosher salt

Julienne apples and mix with cilantro and lime juice. Season with kosher salt.

PORK BELLY

1 pound pork belly with a
    half-inch dice

Tortillas

Sesame seeds

Sauté the pork belly and glaze it with the teriyaki sauce. Put pork in the tortilla and top with the apple slaw. Add sesame seeds for extra flair.

SIRLOIN TOREADO TACOS

CHEF RAUL GONZALEZ III

Makes 12 street tacos

TOREADO SALSA

10 serrano peppers

½ cup oil

1 white onion, diced

2 cloves of garlic, minced

⅓ cup of soy sauce

1 pound sirloin, shaved

GARNISH

1 cup red onion, diced

¼ cup chopped cilantro

2 avocados, sliced

Heat the oil in a pan, add the serranos. Cook until the peppers blister and the skin comes off easily. Remove the serranos, then peel, chop, and set aside. Heat the pan to medium and add a tablespoon of oil, the white onions, and the garlic. Cook until the onion is translucent (about 10 minutes), then add the chopped serranos and the soy sauce. Cook down for another 10 minutes. Set aside.

Cook the sirloin in a pan with a tablespoon of oil over medium high heat. Add the salsa and mix with the beef.

Build your tacos and garnish with the red onion, cilantro, and avocado slices.

Sara Macias

TEXAS TACO COUNCIL

Tell us your story.

I was born and raised here in El Paso. I'm a fashion designer, crafter, baker, mother, wife, and foodie. I've been married to the same man for eight glorious years, and we have two sons.

I've been pursuing my dream of designing clothes. One year, I submitted my portfolio to Project Runway, and while I was on an internship on the set of a movie, they called me to say they really liked my portfolio. But they said they couldn't send it to the casting director because I was missing something, so I sent my missing documents and that was the last I heard from them. That phone call was the ultimate thrill in my journey. (No, seriously, they actually called me.) A couple years after that, I did the El Paso Fashion Week, and I continue to craft and sew.

What's your connection with tacos?

I can remember being very young, and my grandma would make these ghetto tacos from leftovers that consisted of lettuce, tomatoes, cheese, and day-old mashed potatoes. I thought they were the best things, and it was comforting. Tacos are a great comfort food. You can have them any way you want, at any time you want. If I'm out late at night, and everyone is starving, who is there to save us from hunger? The food truck on the corner that makes amazing quick little tacos. If a taco does not comfort you, it's not a good taco.

You're on the Texas Taco Council. Why are you the Taco Ambassador for your city/region?

I am one of the Ambassadors because I know good food when I see it, and I'm not afraid to chow down and let you know my opinion. I would never let someone eat terrible tacos; that's my duty as an Ambassador.

Why do you think people love tacos in your region and in Texas?

It's part of the Tex-Mex culture. You can change it up and make it new and exciting or traditional. And once you have the meat cooked just right, they are easy to assemble. It's an easy food to make and eat.

Give us the taco landscape for your city/region. Give us your top ten list and why they're the best.

Here are my favorite places in the Sun City to grab a good taco.

1. Tacos El Charly—the gem of Horizon City. The flavor, moistness, and quality are always consistent. They make a small variety of tacos, but each one is as flavorful as the next. When a taco place can make tripitas good, you've struck gold.

2. Gabriel's Restaurant—my first job ever was as a hostess

here. I tried almost the whole menu, and they have the best tacos de alambre. I have yet to find a place that can beat it.

3. **L&J Cafe**—great tacos with freshly made shells and the meat is terrific. Having a well-prepared clamato to go with the tacos is the best.
4. **Kiki's Mexican Restaurant**—famous for their machaca. But everything else on the menu is amazing, tacos included.
5. **Tacoholics**—great tacos getting national attention. They are delicious, customizable, and a culinary fusion.
6. **Delicious Mexican Eatery**—another famous El Paso spot. They make all kinds of tasty Mexican food, and the tacos are no exception.
7. **Forti's Mexican Elder Restaurant**—a very nice restaurant for dinner. Tacos are delicious.
8. **Los Bandidos de Carlos & Mickey's**—everything on the menu is out of this world, including the tacos and enchiladas.
9. **Lucy's Diner**—really good food. Expect great quality and tasty tacos.
10. **Good Luck Cafe**—a great late-night eatery with good tacos. If you're craving simple diner food, this is your place.

Leo Duran Jr.

L&J CAFE

Tell us your story.

The L&J Cafe was founded by my grandfather Antonio Flores, my maternal grandparents, back in 1927, and this area of town, Central El Paso, was the outskirts of town. Historically, we've been next door to the old landmark Concordia Cemetery, which was here long before we were back in 1850. We are blessed to have such a legacy for almost eighty-eight years of just providing good, authentic Mexican food, which is unique to the area because of the infusion that we have in El Paso due to the proximity of Ciudad Juárez, Chihuahua, and New Mexico, but, all in all, it is very unique to this one particular region in El Paso.

What is your most popular taco and why? What makes it a standout or unique?

Our steak tacos are the most popular. We started with the main steak plate and burritos, then we made it into tacos. I think it's part of the culture around the border that makes our steak tacos so popular. It's that influence with the border.

Mike Guerrero

THE FOX JUKEBOX
THE FOX 92.3 FM

Tell us your story.

I'm born and raised in El Paso. I'm a proud resident of El Paso's Lower Valley. I've been in the radio business twenty-eight years.

Currently, I'm the host of *The Fox Jukebox*, a Sunday afternoon request and dedication oldies radio show. I love music, movies, and hanging out with friends and family. I like to travel when I get the chance, and I love El Paso's diversity and culture.

What's your connection with tacos?

I've been eating tacos my whole life. I love deshebrada, buche, tripitas, and more. I'm amazed with the current food truck craze because it has introduced all types of tacos—such as Korean, tropical, and Hawaiian—to El Paso in a very creative way.

What's your go-to taco and why?

For years, the El Paso tradition has been the rolled tacos at Chico's Tacos. They have always been a late-night eatery; it's an El Paso thing. Over the years, a lot of new and good restaurants from Ciudad Juárez have been opening up in El Paso, and it's brought in a good mix. One of my favorite places is Don Cuco, for sure.

Give me your top five taco spots and why.

1. **Chico's Tacos**—the tomato juice and melted cheese are like no other.
2. **Tacos Don Cuco**—it's like you walked across the border and got some great tacos!
3. **Tacoholics**—great, innovative flavors.
4. **Tacos Chinampa**—fresh ingredients and great salsas.
5. **Toro Bronco**—another Mexico-based restaurant that has a very delicious variety.

Victoria and Richard Piñeda

Tell us your story.

I'm a communications professor at UTEP, and Victoria is an associate vice chancellor for development at Texas Tech University Health Science Center, El Paso. We are El Paso natives who returned several years ago to try and make a difference in a community we love. Fate brought us together about two-and-a-half years ago, and after a year dating, we got married. We love food and trying new cuisines and styles, but we always return to the comfort of Tex-Mex and Mexican food; gorditas, enchiladas, and, of course, tacos!

What's your connection with tacos?

Being foodies, we think the best thing ever is seeing something simple like a taco transformed into something worthy of a gourmet restaurant.

Richard: I have a Proustian relationship with ground beef tacos; one bite of meat and potato with a dash of cumin and I remember all of the delicious tacos my grandmother used to make me. They were always crisp and a little oily, definitely a little lumpy but delicious. She was a master when it came to whipping up those tacos, and that smell is always going to be home for me.

Victoria: I associate tacos with place and space. The puffy taco, rarely found in El Paso, was a staple when I lived in Austin and worked in San Antonio. Made right, it is a pillow of loveliness with yummy meat. I don't like a lot on my puffy tacos, just meat and cheese and, maybe if I'm feeling provocative, a splash of salsa.

What's your go-to taco and why?

Richard: For me, it's a tie: ground beef and potato tacos or egg and cheese tacos with bacon. I will go out of my way for a breakfast taco, especially late at night. It's the mark of versatility in my mind when a taquero can throw on eggs in the middle of the post-bar rush to make breakfast tacos.

Victoria: The puffy taco all the way. And just like with migas, I can't figure out why people don't make them in El Paso.

Why do you think people love tacos in your region and in Texas?

Some of it is ease and some of it is comfort. They're portable and cheap and you can get them anywhere. When you see someone eating a taco in a Dairy Queen, you know you are in Texas!

Give me your top five taco spots and why.

1. **L&J Cafe**—family owned, consistent, and unique. The crispy beef tacos have a great flavor—staple in El Paso.

2. **El Taco Tote**—as traditional as it gets but quick and easy. Their variety of salsas and meat choices are flavorful and extensive. My go-to is the sirloin taco.
3. **Rincon de Cortez**—a multifaceted greasy spoon that makes a phenomenal carne molida taco paired with a spicy salsa made fresh daily.
4. **Ode Brewery**—El Paso's new brew pub with a gourmet twist. Shrimp tacos are the name of the game at Norbert Portillo's joint. Citrus and spice all in one.
5. **Tacoholics**—a great variety of tacos that are only outdone by a variety of salsas. From a truck to a snack bar to a brick-and-mortar restaurant, these guys make great pork tacos and orange sauce. These are classic little tacos big on flavor.

Seth Wilson

TEXAS TACO COUNCIL

Tell us your story.

I grew up in the Lower Valley, on the family farm in an area called La Isla (the Rio Grande was pretty much right in the front yard). I went to college and grad school in New Mexico and have recently returned to El Paso, where my family has lived and farmed for more than one hundred years. I'm a husband, a writer, a voracious reader, and, much as I hate the term, you'd probably say I was a foodie. I love West Texas and being from El Paso County because this is still a wild, untamed place, full of hard-headed, generous, hilarious people.

What's your connection with tacos?

Living on the border, everyone eats Mexican food, everyone cooks Mexican food. My grandmother made enchiladas and tacos. My folks made burritos. Gordita sale fundraisers were always anticipated. It's such a deeply ingrained part of the culture, regardless of your ethnicity. I like tacos specifically because they're so versatile and so comforting.

You're on the Texas Taco Council. Why are you the Taco Ambassador for your city/region?

Probably because I'm so vocal about food on Twitter. Also because I'm rediscovering the taco scene in El Paso, what's changed and what's stayed the same.

What's your go-to taco and why?

As much as I love al pastor or fifth-quarter meats like tripitas or buche, I'll take carne asada every time, to start. If a place can't nail a good, simple carne asada taco then I have serious reservations about the rest of the menu. I'm a big believer in basics.

Why do you think people love tacos in your region and in Texas?

I think because we're right next to Juárez, and Juárez is a huge gateway for people coming into the US. We're always getting the newest recipes and styles from Mexico, as well as specialties from other regions of Mexico. The food is always changing; everywhere you look, there's always something new to try next to the old standbys we all grew up eating. It's the whole range from really established places like L&J Cafe to street-style tacos from trucks to more adventurous, modern takes on tacos.

Give us the taco landscape for your city/region. Give us your favorites list and why they're the best.

1. **Tacos El Charly in Horizon**—just simple, expertly prepared tacos callejeros with excellent sides and salsas.

2. **Chico's Tacos**—even with locals, they're an acquired taste. Philly has cheesesteaks, Chicago has pizza, New York has everything, but Chico's Tacos are our thing. I go there when I need my fix.

3. **Taco trucks in San Elizario**—this is Texas, we love stuff that comes off trucks. You're buying tacos off a truck in the shade of an old mission, while dudes are riding their horses around. It's like a movie. Take a bite, close your eyes, and for a moment, you're in the best of all possible Texases.

4. **Plain old tacos dorados at any cafe**—all the little neighborhood places south of I-10 or the cafes in the small towns of the Lower Valley. Just sitting down and drinking a huge glass of iced tea and eating the taco plate with beans and rice. Watching everyone joke with the waitresses and argue about football. It's a definitive West Texas experience.

5. **L&J Cafe**—last couple of times I went, people were smuggling the table salsa out of the restaurant in Tupperware. It's not the most current menu, or the most representative of what El Paso cuisine is like right now, but it's a local landmark and the food there has stood the test of time.

6. **El Taco Tote**—for a place with an eye toward being a big national chain, they do stuff right. Freshly made tortillas (the corn tortillas are like silk!), freshly grilled meats, great trimmings. The kitchen is a thing of wonder to watch. It's not exactly fast food, but they do have a drive-through. Plus, they started out as one taco stand in Juárez. There's something great about that success story.

Is Austin the breakfast taco capital of the world? If you ask an Austinite, you'll get a resounding hell, yeah! If you ask anyone outside of Austin, you'll get a loud hell, nah! Austin does love its breakfast tacos. You can probably get breakfast tacos any time of day or night in more than five hundred places, and not just at Tex-Mex restaurants, but also at Mexican joints, barbecue pits, diners, drive-throughs, supermarkets and meat markets, donut shops,

bars, coffee shops, and tons of food trailers around town. And you know Austin does love Austin, and we'll tell the world about the latest and greatest food creation or trendiest trend that is trending in this town. New Yorkers and Portlandinos, in particular, seem to heed the call and come to eat up this town, one breakfast taco at a time.

Austin is a creative town, whether it's in tech, food, or music, and it's going through a lot of growing pains. But that's what makes Austin so special: it's a great place to create, from the old chili and tamale stands to the explosion of taco and food trailers that have helped make it a mecca in the US culinary scene.

That's the great thing about Austin—there's something for everyone. If you want traditional Mexican tacos, just go to Mi Tradición or hit up a trailer on East Riverside. If you want the real deal Tex-Mex, just go to Matt's El Rancho or Joe's Bakery. Or, if you want that quintessential Austin-style taco that is 100 percent local and orgánico, then hit up Tacodeli. The one thing I will fault Austin for is that they do need help in the fresh tortilla category. They definitely need to step it up in the masa department.

Of course, who better to represent the tacos than our Taco Ambassadors: East Austin advocate Jose Velasquez and writer Timothy Braun and his doggy, Dusty Danger. Backed by the taco intern team, Tanya Ramirez, Ciri Haugh, John Peña, and Jordan Schwartz, and the original Taco Journalists, El Jarod and El Mundo de Mando (yeah, that's me) and with our local personalities and places, we have Austin covered!

THE AUSTIN ICONIC TACO: MIGAS BREAKFAST TACO

We already know that breakfast tacos in Austin usually mean flour tortillas. Add fried corn tortilla chips, huevos, pico, cheese, and you got yourself a migas taco. You can find migas at just about any taco or breakfast joint in Austin. Even traditional Mexican places have adapted migas to fit their style of cooking. The funny thing is that I grew up eating migas in El Paso but didn't know it. We just called it "huevos con tortillas." The trick with good migas is to keep the tortilla chips crispy when you cook them with the eggs. Nobody likes soggy tortilla chips, right? Traditionally, migas are made from the remains of tortillas, usually in pieces and cooked with eggs to make sure no pieces go to waste but are enjoyed in a warm breakfast taco—the most important taco of the day!

TACO JOURNALISM'S TOP CINCO

1. **Veracruz All Natural**—best and freshest migas in Texas.
2. **Tacodeli**—the quintessential Austin-style taco shop. Todo orgánico, todo good!
3. **Joe's Bakery & Coffee Shop**—where every Mexican knows your name. And that battered bacon!
4. **Valentina's Tex Mex BBQ**—the most amazing brisket taco in the Lone Star State.
5. **Mi Tradición**—the tacos al pastor enchilados will take you back to Mexico.

EL FLACO ROJO

I never met a gringo who didn't love tacos! That goes for my amigo and official *Tacos of Texas* filmmaker, Dennis Burnett a.k.a. El Flaco Rojo. Yes, he is skinny, and there's a reddish hue in his beard. Also, we needed a nickname for him when we introduced him to all the taqueros in Texas.

Dennis has the work ethic of a Mexicano, the skills of a master filmmaker, the ganas (desire and ambition) of a Taco Journalist, and an appetite to match that enthusiasm. As our one-man film team, Dennis jumped on the opportunity to eat more than five hundred tacos with us and venture across Texas. Not only is he a master of his domain, Dennis also took on this project con puro corazón, from 4:00 a.m. to midnight (at times), and with limited restaurant Spanish skills, venturing onto country roads in the Valley, eating out of cazos in ranchos, learning the differences between chicharrones and tripitas, using our truck as his cama at times, and realizing his dream of understanding the essence of the tortilla. For that, I thank El Flaco Rojo. Mil gracias, Dennis!

Miguel Vidal

VALENTINA'S TEX MEX BBQ

Tell us your story.

I grew up on the south side of San Antonio and we ate home-cooked meals every day out of necessity. I didn't know what was fine dining. I didn't know what was the best barbecue around. I grew up eating my family's food, my parents' food, Isidoro and Dolores Vidal. Whenever we had extra money, my dad would buy steaks or brisket. And he would barbecue most of the time. He would make chicken, a lot of ribs, and, of course, fajitas. It was cheap. But my mom would always serve homemade tortillas, rice, beans, fresh salsa, and avocado.

I started working at my first restaurant when I was thirteen. I started off as a dishwasher and then I started doing prep and ended up doing everything in the back of the house. When I moved to Austin, I worked for my cousin at Ranch 616 and did everything from the bottom up, from busboy, waiter, prep, kitchen, catering, and events. Eventually, I became the general manager and ran the restaurant for eight years.

The idea behind the trailer came from trying to replicate my dad's barbecue. In Austin, I couldn't really find a taco that had the same style and flavor of San Antonio. I would go down to San Antonio and eat my mom's food and come back and be like, man, I wish there was a place like that here. And I always had that idea of trying to open up a taco shop or something that represented what I got in San Antonio here in Austin. So I started working toward that for a good five or six years. I started using sketch and art books that I would draw in and write recipes in. I would create my ideas to practice and put those into play. I had books that were filled with half recipes, half ideas, and just random drawings.

So, what really prompted me to do it was that I fell in love with food, and I felt like Austin was missing something that was a part of Texas and Tex-Mex culture. And that is the combination of barbecue that was true to Texas but also has Mexican influences like barbacoa, roasting whole heads of cows or pigs and everything, you know, encompassing the two together. Bringing the fire-roasted veggies and salsas and homemade tortillas, beans and rice, and all the good peppers and stuff that you get out of Tex-Mex, but then the clean, simplified effect you get from having a really nice quality of smoked meat. And I think every Mexican American family has uncles and grandfathers that barbecue badass and grandmothers, aunts, and uncles that make the potato salad, rice and beans, and tortillas, and it's really something that is overlooked because it's done in the backyard. And it's something that's done for the familia, right? It's not in the mainstream. No one is putting that stuff out there as a restaurant and providing it for people. And I really felt like that's what I wanted to do. That's where the idea came from.

What is your most popular taco and why? What makes it a standout or unique?

Our brisket taco is the best seller. That was something we concentrated on by trying the top barbecue places in town and seeing who is doing what and kind of staying true to the way my dad cooked.

It's very simple, very traditional to Texas. We use a very light rub and the recipe is mostly salt and pepper. But it's really about a consistent fire. We cook it between 225 and 250 degrees, but it's time and temperature and patience that we use to create a good brisket.

We make our tortillas by hand, and the salsas are made fresh everyday. Our guacamole is very simple. It's just smashed avocado with a little bit of lime and salt. So we put those combinations together to stay true to Texas barbecue with a Mexican influence.

We didn't want to create barbecue tacos covered with cole

slaw and barbecue sauce—not to say that we don't do some of that stuff here, but the brisket taco is very clean. It's the meat, a little avocado, and the salsa. The flavors work together in harmony, so you can taste the smoke and the flavor of the meat, rather than anything overpowering it. When you do a brisket taco that has so many fillings and toppings, you lose the true essence and the flavors of what the protein is supposed to taste like. And it's not rocket science or anything new that I've come up with. It's just the way my family does it and the way we like to serve it.

Regina Estrada
JOE'S BAKERY & COFFEE SHOP

Tell us your story.
I was born and raised in Austin. I have lived here for thirty-four years. My parents were born and raised in Austin and so were my grandparents on both sides, so I'm a true native Austinite. When I was growing up, Joe's Bakery was my grandparents' house. I spent more time here at the restaurant doing family events around birthdays and holidays, and after school I spent time at my grandparents' restaurant. When I graduated, I came back to the restaurant and I've worked here ever since. I've had the opportunity to work with my mom, my aunt, and my grandmother, and it's both challenging and rewarding. My mom, Rose Ann Maciel, is one of my best friends and I get to see my grandmother, Pauline Avila, regularly, which is very special to me.

Joe's got started with my great-grandmother, Sophia, and her husband, Florentino, who was a baker. They had a small bakery outside of their home and would sell bread around the neighbor-hood. My grandparents married after the Korean War and opened the bakery soon after. It was his passion and the work ethic that made them successful. There were a lot of bad times and struggles. No one likes to talk about the bad times, but they had to keep going. My mother, Rose Ann, was really the saving grace because during the tough times, she was able to bring us to where we needed to be. And that's how my mother and I started working together. We work really well together. Even though it says "Joe's Bakery" on the sign and it's been five years since my grandfather passed, it is a team effort with my mom, my grandmother, my aunt, and myself. We always say that once it stops being fun, we'll think of other options. We all really enjoy what we do.

We stick with what we know and really focus on consistency. Our recipes have been mostly the same for the last forty years.

That's why Joe's has become such a staple in Austin. People remember when they were here in college, and when they come back, it's still the same. So we are staying true to who we are.

Some people call Joe's Bakery authentic Mexican food. I find that flattering, but it's not true. We serve Tex-Mex food. For some people, it's not that big of a deal, but I want people to know who we really are. We are authentic Tex-Mex. That's one thing I experienced growing up with my grandfather. He was a very proud American who fought for his country in Korea, and we are proud of our heritage. The restaurant has become a sense of identity for me and it's something to be proud of.

What is your most popular taco and why? What makes it a standout or unique?

Our most popular taco is our carne guisada taco. Ours is unique in that it is made of pork. Carne guisada is a staple on our menu and it's served all day from 6:30 a.m. to 3:00 p.m. It can be a taco, part of a breakfast plate served with beans, eggs, and potatoes, or on a lunch plate served with beans, rice, and salad.

Reyna and Maritza Vazquez

VERACRUZ ALL NATURAL

Tell us your story.

We were born and raised in Veracruz, Mexico. Our mother owned a small restaurant and we helped her in the kitchen. In 1999, we moved to Austin, and we worked as waitresses for almost eight years. We started our business back in 2008 with a small 12 × 8

truck. We sold snow cones, fruit cups, smoothies, and juices. We started out very small, barely making ends meet. We lived paycheck to paycheck. There were times when we had to decide between using the money we made to buy product for our truck or paying rent. Times were really hard, and we had no one but each other. Our mother supported us the best she could. For three years, we lived without a salary, working in the morning at a restaurant to provide for the food truck. As time went by, people started to ask us for more kinds of food, including tacos. Our plan from the beginning was always to sell tacos, tortas, and other Mexican food, but we didn't have the resources to make that possible. We were working with what we had at the moment.

Finally, after three years, we decided to make it happen. The truck was too small to fit a grill. We settled for a griddle, but it was too small for the amount of food we would have to make. At this point, we decided to invest in a bigger truck. With the help of our mom, we were able to purchase a 16 × 8 truck. From that moment on, the goals and dreams we had in the beginning have come true. Even now it's hard to work in such a small place, and we think that will always be our biggest challenge. We love what we do and there's no greater satisfaction than seeing our customers happy with the food we make. It makes all those years of struggle worth it.

What is your most popular taco and why? What makes it a standout or unique?

Our most popular taco has to be the migas taco. Austinites are known for being breakfast taco fanatics, and our migas taco is the perfect mixture of ingredients for a breakfast taco. Migas means leftovers in Spanish, and what makes this taco so unique is the crispy tortilla chips that the taco contains. The chips are blended with the perfect portions of egg, cilantro, onion, and tomato with just a little bit of salt and pepper. We put all these ingredients into our homemade tortillas.

MIGAS TACO

REYNA AND MARITZA VAZQUEZ

Makes 1 taco

½ cup tortilla chips
1 tablespoon oil
¼ cup tomato, diced
¼ cup onion, diced
¼ cup cilantro, chopped

2 eggs
Salt and pepper
1 corn or flour tortilla
¼ cup Monterey Jack cheese
1 slice avocado

Set the pan on medium heat. Break the tortilla chips and add a little oil to the pan. Add the tomato, onion, and cilantro to the chips. Beat the eggs, add to the chips and vegetables, mix together, and add a bit of salt and pepper. Cook until the eggs are fully cooked, but make sure the tortilla chips are not soggy. Place the mixture on your choice of warm tortilla, add cheese and a slice of avocado, and enjoy!

Art Acevedo

CHIEF, AUSTIN POLICE DEPARTMENT

What's your connection with tacos?

Having been born in Cuba and raised just outside of Los Angeles, I was introduced to tacos early in life and have a lifelong appreciation for them. As a member of the California Highway Patrol, I began my career on patrol in East Los Angeles and soon discovered the joy of carne asada and al pastor tacos at King Taco, one of the most famous taquerias in Los Angeles County.

What's your go-to taco and why?

I love carne asada tacos with avocado and salsa verde, onions, and cilantro. Avocado is a perfect add-on to any taco and a healthy choice. The lean beef provides the protein and energy I need to get me through my long workdays and gives me great comfort during the challenges we face. Yes, tacos are comfort food.

Why do you think people love tacos in your region and in Texas?

It is simple. Austin is home to some of the best taquerias in Texas and the nation. We have so many places to choose from, and the truth of the matter is that they range from food trucks to brick-and-mortar establishments.

Give me your top five taco spots and why.

I love many taquerias here in Austin and here are some of my favorites in no particular order:

Maria's Taco Xpress

Tacodeli

Torchy's Tacos

El Taquito

Del Taco—reminds me of the place where I grew up, and I love to eat their French fries.

Connie Rodriguez
LA COCINA DE CONSUELO

Tell us your story.

I am originally from Zacatecas, Mexico, and I've been in business for nine years. I started by making enchiladas for my daughters as they were attending college. People were enjoying my food so much, but I was told that I couldn't cook out of my own kitchen. It was at that time that I found this place of business and I have been here ever since.

What is your most popular taco and why? What makes it a standout or unique?

We have all types of tacos, but what makes our tacos stand out are that our tortillas are made of corn and are hand-made. Our crispy beef tacos have become popular. We fry and shape them by hand and add our own seasoning. The tacos that come in flour tortillas are also very popular probably because people in this part of the United States like their flour tortillas.

We take a healthy route with our crispy tacos by frying them in canola oil, and we make our own taco shells. We fill the shells with 80/20 angus beef. We cook the meat with chile colorado, ajo fresco, tomatoes, and some comino. We don't have any special recipes but just use the basic ingredients that are found in the house.

DJ Stout and Lana McGilvray

Tell us your story.

DJ Stout: I'm fifth- or sixth-generation Texan raised on Tex-Mex with a deep love of all things tortilla, meat, and salsa. I'm the former art director at *Texas Monthly* (thirteen years), a partner at Pentagram Design, and I recently published *Variations on a Rectangle: Thirty Years of Graphic Design from* Texas Monthly *to Pentagram* via the University of Texas Press.

Lana McGilvray: I'm a Yankee and was first introduced to tacos (now a passion) by Maria Corbalan, founder and proprietor of Maria's Taco Xpress. I'm the principal at Blast Public Relations.

What's your connection with tacos?

DJ: I've lived in Austin for thirty years and used to go religiously to

Las Manitas, down on Congress Avenue. I think I have the record: I went to Las Manitas or tried to go there every single day. My record was that I went there for ten days in a row. But when they closed it down for that hotel, I kind of panicked. I remember they did a whole segment on the closing of Las Manitas on NPR, and I just happened to be over there when they were filming on how people were going to miss Las Manitas, and I think they filmed me saying I was going to lay down in front of the bulldozers as long as the sisters fed me tacos.

Lana: I've been going to Maria's Taco Xpress religiously, too, for more than twenty years, and my time at Maria's is a time before DJ and after DJ. Most of my friends I made here in Austin I made at Maria's—starting with Maria, who is like a big sister to me. I became friends with the staff and the musicians who came here. And I would ride my bike. I live in South Austin and would come here almost every single day. A taco was my meal, and it's been that way for a long time.

What's your go-to taco and why?

Lana: Now our go-to taco at Maria's Taco Xpress is the migas taco because, as anyone will tell you, it's delicious and always "a lil bit crispy." Maria's taco sauces are several and spicy, a big plus in the taco accessory category.

DJ: But as far as Maria's goes, it was just a bitty trailer or like a small little shack. And a lot of people started going there because the tacos were so great. But also it had this funky vibe. It felt like Austin. It felt laid back and the decorations are kind of like it is here, kind of eclectic, just had this Austin feeling from the very beginning. We love coming here on Sundays when they have the Hippie Church and that's when you really see Austin, you know?

Lana: Maria's hasn't changed over the years. If you walk up to the counter, you still see Fernando working there. Or Oscar working at the counter. Oscar has two kids, and he's been working here since, I think, he was a teenager. And the same folks are slinging the tacos—and making the migas tacos and pollo asado. It's wonderful.

We come here a lot on Friday nights when Leeann Atherton is singing, and it's kind of like a round robin of songs. And it's one of the only times you'll see a sixty-five-year-old man dancing with your four-year-old and then that four-year-old grabs the tip jar and runs around the restaurant like a little rascal. You know, they are just collecting money, and there's not that many places you can go to have that kind of environment. And not just Austin—in modern culture. It's a really, really special place for us.

Why do you think people love tacos in your region and in Texas?

DJ: Who doesn't love tacos? Tacos are far more than just something to subside hunger or appetite. Tacos are peace, love, zen.

I think Austin is a hopeful place, that you can do anything you want. I always said that if you wanted to make it in Austin, just make a good taco. Open up a little trailer and make a good taco because people here are crazy about tacos. And they know if it's not a good taco. And because of that, they are kind of picky about it. But there are a lot of success stories like Maria's because people said, I know how to make a taco. And they did it, and it grew from there. At my office, usually because they are running late, they will call in and say, I'm running late but I'm going to go by and pick up a bunch of tacos. So then it makes everyone at the office very happy. In New York, the food is bagels and whatever. I think Austin is as snooty about their tacos as New Yorkers are about their bagels. Yeah, I think they are.

Lana: I think tacos transcend food though. I think tacos in Austin are a currency for friendship and freedom. We all have fantastic taco stories. Whether you're at Maria's Taco Xpress, or you went to Las Manitas and you're sitting near James McMurtry and you're watching what kind of taco he ate. You say, "We're bringing twenty tacos in the office this morning," and people get really excited and they start to talk about where their favorite taco joints are. You don't get that in New York. People don't bring twenty hot dogs into the office.

DJ: I just want to say that the taco to me is like the perfect food because it comes in a holder. You don't need a fork necessarily. It comes in a little container, a little holder that you can eat. But also it's better than a bagel or a sweet roll or something like that because it has a little bit of punch to it. You know? It's got peppers, it's hot. There's something about the combination of it that gets you going in the morning.

Jesus Guevara

MI TRADICIÓN PANADERIA

Tell us your story.

We are originally from Puebla, Mexico. We are a small family, my wife Imelda and our two boys. We have been in Austin for nine years now. I opened up my business when we moved here. We have a bakery and a taqueria. We started with a bakery—I am a born baker! I was raised baking in my home. In Mexico, my parents have a small bakery. So that's how I got my start.

I came to the US when I was sixteen—to Washington State. I came as a laborer, picking apples. It was a hard job. I was thinking about going back to Mexico and I spoke to my uncle in Houston. I told him the farm work was very difficult and I didn't like it much. When I went to Houston, I found some work, I started baking, and I liked it a lot. I kept working in bake shops here in the US. I really enjoy it.

Did you know that there is such a thing as Olympic bread competitions? They call it the "Bread Olympics." They are held in France. I once worked with a champion breadmaker from the Olympic team. He would tell me I needed to join the team; he insisted I had talent and unique style in baking. But because I didn't speak English very well it held me back.

But eventually I got the opportunity to get my business started in Austin. It was a lot of work to start up our business. My wife and I started off just with the bakery. And because of my experience, I knew that in the summer sales drop off. So I told my wife that in the summer we needed to continue sales. So we started selling tortas in the summer. And then we added the tacos al pastor because all our clients from Mexico wanted to know where were the tacos al pastor? The taco al pastor is simple, but I had a cook from Mexico come and show me the secret to making them.

But once we started to sell more off the menu, we needed to expand to have a place for people to sit. The space next to us was available and we rented it and now we have a place for people to sit. But also, we have a large window for everyone to see the food being prepared—our customers really like watching how everything is made.

So we have worked really hard to be a successful business. And a lot of people assume that Anglos own this business or someone with a lot of money owns this business. Many people can't imagine that a Mexican family owns such a successful business, and I'm here to tell you that Mexican families work hard, we put effort and excellence into what we do, and we can do everything that others do really well.

What's your go-to taco and why? Why is this the most popular and what makes it unique?

One of the most popular tacos is the taco al pastor. It's made up of a rich combination of ingredients that consist of a small corn tortilla with marinated pork, cilantro, onion, pineapple, and our own special sauce made in-house.

Deana Saukam

PARTNER, EAST SIDE KING/QUI

Tell us your story.

I was born and raised in Houston, Texas, and have been an Austinite since 2000. I'm a partner at both East Side King and Qui, and I have a lust for tacos, travel, fashion, and my Pomeranian, Buckingham, and my cats, Goose and Bear. I've built my own following on Instagram as @faimfatale, which highlights my travels around the globe, feasting on everything from Thai-spiced grasshoppers to Parisian éclairs, fresh-caught fish from Tsukiji in Tokyo, and egg curry in the Maldives.

What's your connection with tacos?

I love tacos. My go-to taco is al pastor because it is so delicious and has never failed me.

Why do you think people love tacos in your region and in Texas?

I think people love tacos in Austin because we have the best tacos in the world and they are available 24/7. Breakfast tacos are an Austin staple—and who doesn't want to start the day with a taco for breakfast? Tacos are easy to eat, fast, and inexpensive. Culturally, they are the perfect food for Austin's laid-back, delicious vibe.

Give me your top five taco spots and why.

1. **Las Trancas**—perfect filling-to-tortilla ratio, full of flavor and crispy lengua.
2. **Veracruz All Natural**—my favorites are the migas and La Reyna.
3. **Valentina's Tex Mex BBQ**—delicious barbecue in tacos? Who could want anything more?
4. **El Primo**—super tasty, delicious Austin staple.
5. **Anywhere in Mexico City**—seriously.

Nikki Ibarra

HABANERO MEXICAN CAFE

Tell us your story.

I am the daughter of Arturo Ibarra, the owner of Habanero. I have worked in the restaurant off and on for about seventeen years. Mostly off, with the exception of these last six years. I have watched my dad turn a small, hopeful restaurant into a busy, go-to spot for many Austinites. I hope to carry on this name and reputation for years to come.

Habanero started with Dos Hermanos. My grandpa and uncle were successfully running four restaurants throughout Austin. If you lived in Austin in the late 70s and 80s, you know the name. My dad was working in the Dos Hermanos Cesar Chavez location for years. He decided it was time for a change, so we packed up and moved to Ontario, Oregon. He had a small but rapidly growing tortilla factory that distributed preservative-free tortillas to eastern Oregon and western Idaho grocery stores. During our ten years of living in Ontario, the Dos Hermanos decided to retire and sell the restaurants. Arturo was offered the small Oltorf Street location and gladly accepted. One stipulation was that he had to change the name. It was Arturo's very own restaurant, opened with the help of the amazing food legacy of Dos Hermanos.

Habanero opened in August of 1998. Starting from scratch was not easy. Having a different name in the same building where Dos Hermanos once was so popular, Habanero didn't have people rushing in. Lucky for us, we were located in a very positive and welcoming neighborhood. People were skeptical at first, and it took

a few years to get the name out and show what we were made of, but eventually we were welcomed with open arms. We have been asked, "Why don't you open another location or stay open later?" We like the feeling of a mom-and-pop dive. There's not too many of us left in Austin, so we try to keep it simple but authentic. We want to stay true to our customers, the ones who have always been there for us. With the help of our amazing cooks and our servers, some of which have been with us from the start and are like family to us, we are able to stay and keep up with the ever-growing, beautiful new Austin.

What is your most popular taco and why? What makes it a standout or unique?

Our most popular taco is probably our beef fajitas. Having a recipe that can date back more than thirty years sure helps make it a customer favorite. We don't just cook skirt steak and call it fajitas. We trim the skirt, we marinate it, marinate it a little more, then throw it on the mesquite wood grill and wait for the magic to happen. For our brave patrons, they get fajita ranchera. It's the same fajitas just with grilled tomatoes, onions, and jalapeños. This is the best order; it's spicy and flavorful!

Why do you think people love tacos so much?

I'm happy that people are realizing tacos are the best. I mean how could you not? With tacos, it's simple. Put ingredients in a tortilla, and it's a meal! I think that people are always on the go and tacos are made for that. You can get a fajita taco with pico, and a grilled veggie taco, and you have your lunch. You can sit in your car, eat it in ten minutes, and be ready to go. There are so many varieties and even definitions on what tacos are. The possibilities are endless.

Jonathan "Chaka" Mahone and Ghislaine "Qi Dada" Jean

RIDERS AGAINST THE STORM

Tell us your story.

We moved to Austin in 2010. A lot of people know us for the way we curate programs for our community. We love to merge and shift cultures. Food is definitely a way to accomplish that awesome task. Our community helped us win "Band of the Year" in the Austin Music Awards two years in a row. We were the first hip-hop band to have achieved such an honor here in the capital city. We owe it to the amalgamation of friends and fans open to culture and new ideas.

What's your connection with tacos?

Qi Dada: My background is Caribbean. We don't really eat tacos, but when I came here, I had a longing for the traditional flavors of my Caribbean background, while at the same time experiencing tacos in Texas. This ultimately led me to come up with the Caribbean breakfast taco. And my go-to taco is simple: eggs and guac! I usually say, "Go get your life!" before I eat it.

Give me your top taco spots and why.

Veracruz All Natural—their story and flavor are unmatched! Most authentic flavors in town and still kind of a hidden gem.

Tyson's Tacos—incredible prices and right in our neighborhood. I am pretty sure you can get a free taco by playing a ukelele and singing.

Torchy's Tacos—portions meet flavor meets the mainstream, just in the right way.

Roberto Espinosa

TACODELI

Tell us your story.

I am a lover of good meals, which, for me, are usually simple preparations with quality ingredients. This is why I love the tortilla; it is a canvas for well-tended-to fillings. To me, the taco is very personal. I grew up eating tacos in Mexico City, which started my addiction to them, and now it is part of my daily existence that I get to share with family, friends, and our taco-loving customers.

We have some very dedicated customers. Some eat at our restaurants with frequency and sometimes even on a daily basis. It's funny when you run into them on consecutive days; for some reason, some of them feel embarrassed to be seen so frequently and apologize. But, frankly, nothing could make me happier. I like to put them at ease by telling them that I have been eating our food on a near-daily basis—twice and sometimes three times a day—for the past sixteen years! I will never get tired of eating tacos, especially ours.

What is your most popular taco and why? What makes it a standout or unique?

Hands down, the cowboy taco. It was named by *Texas Monthly* as one of the "63 Tacos You Must Eat Before You Die." It is a "cowboy"-seasoned beef tender with a garnish of caramelized onions, roasted red bell and poblano peppers, guacamole, and queso fresco. It is beautiful to look at and delicious.

CHILES EN NOGADA

TACODELI

Makes 6 tacos

PICADILLO

1 pound ground beef

½ cup chopped onion

2 teaspoons salt

½ cup chopped tomatoes

¼ cup chopped jalapeños, deseeded

2 tablespoons chopped garlic

1 teaspoon chili powder

1 teaspoon black pepper

1 teaspoon honey

Brown meat with onion and salt.

Once meat is browned and just cooked through, add tomatoes, jalapeños, garlic, chili powder, and black pepper. Cook for 5 to 10 minutes more until vegetables begin to soften.

Stir in honey. Season to taste.

SALSA DE NUEZ DE CASTILLA (EN NOGADA/IN WALNUT SAUCE)

½ cup walnuts

½ cup blanched, peeled
    almonds

½ cup milk

½ cup half-and-half

1 teaspoon sugar

1 teaspoon chopped garlic

1 teaspoon sherry

¼ cup goat cheese

1 tablespoon sour cream

1 teaspoon salt

Heat walnuts, almonds, milk, half-and-half, sugar, and garlic over medium high heat to the point of boiling.

Place in blender and blend on high for one minute.

Add the sherry, goat cheese, sour cream, and salt and blend for one additional minute. Texture should be smooth. Season to taste.

Plating *(use one pepper per taco)*

Roast, peel, and deseed poblano or Anaheim peppers, slit one side of the pepper, and fill with the picadillo. Garnish with the salsa de nuez, pomegranate seeds, and chopped cilantro. The red, green, and white of the dish are representative of the Mexican flag.

Jay B. Sauceda

TEXAS HUMOR

Tell us your story.

I'm from southeast of Houston. It's a little town called La Porte. I grew up in a Tejano-lovin' household with three siblings and two parents from South Texas. I moved to Austin to attend the University of Texas and despite focusing on political science in school, I found myself in advertising afterward and have spent the last roughly ten years working in the field as a photographer. In that time, I've shot for *Texas Monthly*, Dick's Sporting Goods, Pentagram, and the *New York Times*.

Recently, my wife Priscilla and I have worked on building an e-commerce and fulfillment logistics company in South Austin, which has grown tremendously since we started it.

Outside of work, I'm a pretty big Texas history buff and a private pilot. I spend a fair amount of time photographing the state, especially from the air. I love traveling all over, but there's so much to see and do in Texas, I just feel like my time is best spent traversing the Republic of Texas.

What's your connection with tacos?

My family is Tejano and our roots, especially on my mom's side, extend to the pre–Texas Revolution era. We grew up eating a lot of tacos and cheap street food-style plates when we'd visit family in South Texas. My father in particular loved eating barbacoa, so it was something we had around pretty much every weekend. I guess we're just genetically predisposed to liking tacos.

Why do you think people love tacos in your region and in Texas?

It's the food of the people. They're not pretentious, they're easy to customize, and even a cheap taco can be really good. It's the great equalizer in my opinion.

Give me your top five taco spots and why.

1. **Pueblo Viejo**—solid street taco. It's got my favorite al pastor.
2. **El Tacorrido**—for pretty much the same reason, but because of their steak taco.
3. **Casa Garcia**—the breakfast tacos are always amazing. They have the best tortillas in town.
4. **Piedras Negras**—one of my top taco spots, but it seems to have disappeared.
5. **My wife's crispy tacos**—some of my favorites. But our kitchen isn't open to the public, so I'm not sure if that counts.

Jessica Galindo Winters and Adam Winters

MELLIZOZ TACOS

Tell us your story.

We opened Mellizoz on a cold winter's day in December 2008. The business was then operated by my dad and brother, Tony and John Galindo. My brother John is a chef and created our signature tacos, and some recipes were taken from old family recipes as well. John was a chef at a few restaurants around Austin and decided to venture on his own, opening a food trailer. He already had a following, so it didn't take long for Austinites to recognize the quality food coming from the 42-foot stationary trailer parked on South 1st Street. A few years down the road, my husband Adam Winters and I moved to Austin to help out. Today, we run the trailer along with a great group of loyal and talented cooks and staff members.

During South by Southwest, we usually get quite a few foreign guests who've never tried a taco in their life! It's kind of funny

when they ask you, "What is a taco and how do you eat it?" I never thought I'd have to explain what a tortilla is. Then, the best part is when they come back to the order window to personally tell us, "That is *the* best food I've had since I've been in Austin!"

What is your most popular taco and why? What makes it a standout or unique?

We have a few tacos that go head-to-head on popularity. Our fried avocado has been known to make many people believers of a taco that is "sin carne." We batter with tempura, fry to order, then top with baby arugula, Roma tomatoes, Cotija cheese, and a tasty chipotle sherry vinaigrette. Our other popular taco is the Padre—ancho chile pork, braised for three-and-a-half hours, topped with sauteed pineapple, avocado, and salsa fresca.

Then, there's the Old School, which might be the best taco on the planet. House-fried taco shell, lean ground beef, fresh spinach, tomatoes, and cheddar. Crunchy goodness and beef seasoned to perfection with fresh veggies. Fresh and made to order is what makes all these tacos stand out.

Why do you think people love tacos so much?

People love tacos because there is absolutely no limit on what you can fill a tortilla with. Sometimes I like a plain ol' bean and cheese taco, but then I'll go for a chef-inspired taco like seared salmon with slaw, roasted corn relish, and chipotle aioli.

Grandmother Galindo used to tell us stories of how, back when she was in elementary school here in Austin, "taking a foil-wrapped taco out of a paper lunch sack was something we had to hide for fear of being made fun of by (non-Mexican) classmates." *What?* Now, everyone eats tacos for breakfast, lunch, brunch, linner, dinner, late-night snacks. And if you don't eat tacos daily, then you're missing out!

DEL MAR TACO

MELLIZOZ TACOS

With blackened tilapia, slaw, pickled red onion, and chipotle aioli.

Makes 4 tacos

4 tilapia fillets
Blackening seasoning
  (recipe below)
12 ounces finely shredded
  green cabbage

Slaw dressing (recipe below)
4 corn or flour tortillas
2 ounces pickled red onions
2 ounces chipotle aioli
  (recipe below)

In a shallow dish, coat both sides of each fillet with blackening seasoning and cook on medium to high heat until done—about 8 to 10 minutes.

Mix enough slaw dressing with cabbage until well coated, but not soggy.

Heat tortillas, then place one fillet in each tortilla. Top with cabbage, red onion, and chipotle aioli.

BLACKENING SEASONING

¾ cup paprika
¼ cup garlic powder
¼ cup onion powder
2 tablespoons white pepper
2 tablespoons dried oregano

½ tablespoon ground thyme
2 tablespoons ground cumin
2 tablespoons ground
  fennel seeds
1½ tablespoons kosher salt

Combine all ingredients in mixing bowl.

SLAW DRESSING

¼ cup red wine vinegar

¼ cup white or rice wine vinegar

¼ cup mayonnaise

¼ teasoon white pepper

Combine all ingredients in mixing bowl and whisk well.

CHIPOTLE AIOLI

1 cup mayonnaise

1 teaspoon garlic, minced

1 whole chipotle pepper (canned)

½ teaspoon white pepper

1 teaspoon kosher salt

Blend all ingredients well using a stick blender.

Orión García (DJ Orion)

DISCOS PELIGROSA

Tell us your story.

I am a half-generation son, a Puerto Rican and a Colombian, living in Austin, Tejas. I am a self-diagnosed workaholic and an avid proponent of the arts. Among these arts is music. Where it comes from. When it comes from. I like to share the music I find when I DJ, which I've been at for more than ten years now. I started a Latin party called "Peligrosa" in 2007 with some friends who shared a similar interest in music. This led to the formation of a record label, Discos Peligrosa, where I am at liberty to create projects using my many interests.

What's your connection with tacos?

I really started eating tacos when I was working my way through college. Caribbean and Colombian cuisine, what we mostly ate at home, used corn in a different way. Arepas, a corn cake, were our tacos growing up. And empanadas (Colombian). Flour empanadas, the kind my Puerto Rican mother makes, could be my tacos as well if we were going to make analogies.

These days I do make, eat, and procure tacos pretty regularly. Sometimes if you do it right, you don't even need a napkin.

Give me your top five taco spots and why.

1. **La Fruta Feliz**—they have lamb and goat and breakfast all the time. Very key for me.

2. **Piedras Negras (RIP)**—carne guisada and bomb greasy carnitas. They aren't around any longer.

3. **La Michoacana Meat Market**—chill vibes on East 7th Street. And you can shop for some extra meats while you're there.

4. **El Taquito**—the especial with six tacos (small tortillas). I love how they have a nice array of condiments, including roasted jalapeños, salsas, and veggies.

5. **Taco More**—I like these guys' tacos all right, but I really like their menudo, my favorite so far in Austin.

Eddie Campos (DJ Chorizo Funk)

Tell us your story.

I'm an Austin-based DJ, sound mixer, music curator, record collector, promoter, and party starter. I began DJ'ing in Austin in 2007 and haven't looked back. I'm a 2013 winner of the *Austin Chronicle* Critic's Pick "Best of Austin" award, and you can catch me most weekends here in Austin playing music with any of the numerous groups that I am a part of: Peligrosa, Body Rock ATX, and the Austin Boogie Crew. I have a huge range regarding music, but have a special love for cumbias and funk from the past, present, and future. El disco es cultura!

What's your connection with tacos?

I'm a Chicano with Mexican roots, so tacos have always been near. Living in El Paso as a kid means that burritos were more common growing up; there were a couple of summers that all I would eat for breakfast and lunch were frijoles con queso . . . by choice! Tacos with a cold Topo Chico . . . it doesn't get better than that in the summer!

Give me your top five taco spots and why.

1. **Rosita's Al Pastor**—off Riverside in front of the American Bingo. Perfect late-night spot!

2. **Veracruz All Natural**—I love their al pastor. High quality and quickly becoming an Austin institution.

3. **Mi Tradición Panaderia**—nothing like eating some amazing tacos and having a panaderia in the same building.

4. **Tamale House**—the original location on 51st Street. It was my go-to breakfast taco spot for years before they closed. It was an Austin institution, always packed, hot, and stuffy.

5. **Torchy's Tacos**—not traditional Mexican or Tex-Mex. But I love their tacos for what they are . . . an ATX twist on one of my favorite foods.

Gloria Reyna

MATT'S EL RANCHO

Tell us your story.

I was born and raised in Austin. I'm the oldest of three girls, Cecilia Muela, Kathy Kreitz, and my brother, Matt Martinez Jr. who passed away. My parents, Matt and Jenny Martinez, started the restaurant in 1952. When we were growing up, my mother and father spent a lot of time at the restaurant. Our birthday parties were there. We were fortunate to have my grandmother who would take care of us. She was a great cook, she had a garden, and she would prepare wonderful food. We were learning about the business by just watching them work. They loved what they did, and they loved doing things together, so it was a great atmosphere for us as children.

We're one of the oldest family restaurants in Austin and continue to grow. We always make sure we have quality food and ingredients. We make everything from scratch and have our own tortilla factory in the restaurant. My brother Matt was so wonderful, making sure that everyone felt comfortable in our restaurant. So it's not only the food and flavors but it's also the hospitality. In the beginning, my mom could only sit forty people in our restaurant and now we can sit more than five hundred. It's a beautiful business that just grew. My mother and father paid a lot of attention to detail. Both in the food and the way the restaurant looks. I think it's the combination of everything. It's a true family restaurant, and I enjoy seeing the generations of families visit us every day.

What is your most popular taco and why? What makes it a standout or unique?

Asadero tacos. Matt's El Rancho asadero tacos use beef tenderloin, the most tender of all beef cuts. Grilled with asadero cheese, onions, and rajas in house-made, non-GMO corn tortillas.

HOMEMADE ASADERO TACOS

MATT'S EL RANCHO

Make sure the beef tenderloin is fresh and high quality.

Makes 8 tacos

1 pound beef tenderloin
1 medium white onion
2 medium poblano peppers
2 ounces canola oil
3 ounces soy sauce

Spices such as salt, garlic,
  and black pepper
6 ounces asadero cheese
8 corn tortillas

Cut beef tenderloin into ¼-inch cubes. Cut the onion and poblanos into small strips. Heat canola oil in a cast-iron pan over medium heat. When the oil is hot, add the beef tenderloin and cook half way, then add the onions and poblano pepper strips. Add soy sauce with spices just before you remove meat to serve. In another pan, cook the asadero cheese over medium heat on both sides until soft.

Serve with hot corn tortillas. Put 4 tortillas on each plate. Make a large taco using two tortillas for each taco, adding first the asadero cheese, then the meat with the onions and poblano peppers.

Jose Miguel Anwar Velasquez

HERMANOS DE EAST AUSTIN
TEXAS TACO COUNCIL

Tell us your story.

I'm a third-generation, born-and-raised East Austinite. I've worked in public relations and political strategy, but my true passion is being of service to others.

I come from a long lineage of public servants and have a deep-seated commitment to community service and local matters. In 2007, I founded and currently serve as executive director for Hermanos De East Austin, a local nonprofit that focuses on promoting and advancing the people and rich culture of East Austin.

Some people know me as the "Mayor of East Austin," so any time, day or night, you can find me in East Austin, taking a meeting at my office at Joe's Bakery, getting "starched up" at Estrada's Cleaners, enjoying my favorite craft beer at Hops and Grain, or building coalition at the Hard Luck Lounge.

I'm a diehard Vicente Fernández fan. I even named my min-pin dog after El Idolo de Mexico, who carries the nickname "Chente."

My other interests include the Dallas Cowboys (I'm a self-proclaimed Romo-sexual); gangster rap, which I call the "new blues"; politics, the last true full-contact sport; my familia, a.k.a. my foundation; East Austin, a.k.a. my soul; and moving the Hispanic people forward, however difficult that can get. I would like to acknowledge that I'd be none of these things and a man in the wilderness without my amazing wife of three years, Dianna Sosa Velasquez.

What's your connection with tacos?

I've had a lifelong love affair with tacos. Growing up poor, you are required to become creative in order to feed yourself. The tortilla was my canvas with eggs, beans, and rice serving as my paintbrush.

You're on the Texas Taco Council. Why are you the Taco Ambassador for your city/region?

I'm on the Taco Council, representing my beautiful hometown of Austin, Texas, because, next to the vatos who wrote this book, I'm the guy you call when you want to know where to get the tastiest and least expensive tacos in town.

Why do you think people love tacos in your region and in Texas?

You can't cast a stone without hitting a taco spot in Austin. People in Central Texas *love* tacos! The reason being that they are quick to make, quick to take, and the ingredient possibilities are endless.

Give us the taco landscape for your city/region. Give us your top ten list and why they're the best.

1. **Joe's Bakery & Coffee Shop**—homemade tortillas and the best Tex-Mex in Austin.
2. **Cisco's Bakery**—chori-migas tacos, a one-of-a-kind, off-the-menu item.
3. **Donn's BBQ**—brisket and bean. Nobody does this taco like them.
4. **Porfirio's Tacos**—the carne guisada will kick your teeth out.
5. **Juan in a Million**—beans and nopales. Difficult to master, easy to mess up. They've got it down.
6. **Rosita's Al Pastor**—best al pastor in Austin. Hands down.

7. **La Michoacana Meat Market**—you can order *any* taco here and you'll be happy.
8. **Habanero Mexican Cafe**—the fajitas . . . mic drop.
9. **Tamale House East**—fish taco. Huge portion, fresh and fast.
10. **Tacodeli**—pollo en mole. Hard-to-find good mole in Austin.

Aurelio Torres

MI MADRE'S RESTAURANT

Tell us your story.

My wife and I started a tiny taco shop with only four tables. We were located in the bad part of town and struggled daily to make the rent. My children worked for us to help the small business flourish and, though we struggled, we have been in business for twenty-five years. Our neighborhood has changed tremendously for the better, and it has become a very popular place in Austin.

What is your most popular taco and why? What makes it a standout or unique?

Our number zero taco is the most popular. Bacon, eggs, potato, and cheese. It might seem simple, but we do it right and it always hits the spot. We are also known for having huge tacos.

CARNITAS TACO

MI MADRE'S

Makes 15 tacos

5 pounds pork shoulder	1 bunch cilantro, chopped
3 tablespoons salt	1 teaspoon pork fat or
1 avocado, sliced	vegetable oil

Cut the pork into 1-inch cubes and steam for 4 hours until pork is tender and pulls apart easily. Add salt and pull apart into smaller chunks. Heat oil or pork fat in a pan over medium heat and lightly fry the chunks. Add carnitas to tortillas and assemble the tacos (corn tortillas are preferred), adding the slices of avocado and the chopped cilantro.

Terrence and Christine Moline

Tell us your story.

We've been in fond admiration of the food and service culture since birth. We are incredibly passionate about building community by exchanging stories and cultures over memorable meals. As native New Orleanians, we enjoy infusing our go-to Creole and Cajun influences into dishes we've been introduced to since our relocation to Austin, as well as featuring standards in our weekly or seasonal meal plans.

We share the commonality of working in hospitality early in our adult lives. We worked at French Quarter institutions, including Arnaud's Restaurant and Dickie Brennan Steakhouse as a waiter (Terrence) and hostess (Christine). When we weren't working, we could be found a few times a week at a new fine dining or casual establishment. This allowed us to enjoy our city as much as tourists and to serve as ambassadors for anyone visiting the city for the first time.

We've been together since 2001 and now reside in Austin. Terrence is an independent illustrative designer and developer. He's an incredibly good cook who loves to entertain friends and family along with his wife. Christine is a communications and IT management consultant. When we aren't working or hanging out with friends, we enjoy walks around different neighborhoods in Austin, trying new restaurants, and traveling. Terrence is a martial arts enthusiast and Christine loves her Pilates and yoga.

What's your connection with tacos?
We didn't make a ton of tacos in New Orleans—if any at all. We started understanding the versatility of the tortilla when we moved to Austin. We were inundated with breakfast tacos, but we didn't really start making breakfast tacos until years later. Now it's a staple for breakfast and dinner.

SHRIMP PO BOY TACOS

TERRENCE MOLINE

Makes 4 tacos

2 fresh nopales	¾ cup vinegar, such as
(cactus pads)	apple cider vinegar
Whole cayenne pepper	½ cup sugar
2 cups water	

Remove prickly parts from cactus and cut into ¼-inch strips. Cut cayenne pepper into thin rings. Salt nopal strips and rub with cayenne pepper. Set aside for an hour.

Rinse nopales and place in jar or bowl. Bring to a boil the water, vinegar, and sugar. Pour boiling liquid over nopales with 10 cayenne pepper rings, cover, and place in refrigerator for two days.

SHRIMP FRY

24 shrimp with heads on	¼ cup baking powder
Salt	(enough to coat shrimp)
Pepper	1–2 cups buttermilk, enough
	to coat shrimp

CRUST FOR SHRIMP

1 cup Bob's Red Mill gluten-
free flour, or flour of your
choice (if using full gluten
flour, omit xanthan gum)

⅛ teaspoon xanthan gum

¼ cup cornmeal

¼ cup rolled oats

1 tablespoon cornstarch

¼ teaspoon onion powder

¼ teaspoon roasted garlic
powder

⅛ teaspoon cayenne pepper

¼ teaspoon salt

Combine all ingredients in a bowl.

Peel and devein shrimp. Reserve shrimp heads and all other discards for stock. Liberally salt and pepper shrimp on both sides. Dust shrimp with baking powder and shake off excess.

After dusting shrimp, coat by dipping in buttermilk. Next, dredge buttermilk-coated shrimp into the shrimp crust mixture. Cover shrimp and place in refrigerator until ready to fry.

CONCENTRATED SHRIMP STOCK

Shrimp heads, bodies, and
all shrimp discards

½ lemon, juiced

2 tablespoons salt

Celery stalk

½ red bell pepper

A few sprigs of lavender,
if you can find some

3 garlic cloves

4 cups water

5 cayenne pepper rings

1 teaspoon frozen butter

Place all ingredients in a pot with water, cover pot, and boil down to 1 cup of liquid. Strain and place remaining liquid in a clean pan. Cook down to a thick, dark paste, thick enough to heavily coat a spoon—about ¼ cup.

Once cooked down to a paste, take pan off stove and whisk in frozen butter. Set aside.

SHRIMP SAUCE

2 egg yolks

1 cup avocado oil, olive oil, or canola oil

3 cloves roasted garlic

1 teaspoon concentrated shrimp stock (because it's concentrated, you can store the rest in the refrigerator and use for other recipes)

¼ teaspoon of hot sauce

2 teaspoons creole mustard

1 teaspoon tomato paste

Dash Worcestershire sauce

6 chopped fried capers (salted capers fried, preferably in bacon fat)

½ tablespoon fresh dill

1 teaspoon chopped parsley

1 teaspoon green onion

¼ teaspoon sweet smoked paprika

Salt

Pinch of cayenne pepper

Add the egg yolks to a bowl and whip with wire whisk until slightly thick. Slowly drizzle in oil and continue to whisk. Eventually it will become a thick mayonnaise.

Mash roasted garlic with mortar and pestle with a little oil. Mix until smooth. Add roasted garlic and all other ingredients to mayonnaise.

Please wait until the end to taste sauce before adding pepper and salt. It may be to full flavor already.

PICKLED NOPALES SALSA

4 pickled nopal strips,
chopped into cubes

1 medium-sized tomato
(needs to be about the
size of a tennis ball)

½ tablespoon diced shallot

1 teaspoon chopped parsley

Juice of one small lime

Dash tequila

Salt, if needed

Remove seeds and chop tomato into cubes. Place all ingredients in bowl and add the lime juice and the dash of tequila. Mix together and set aside.

For taco assembly

8 tortillas

2–3 cups of oil (peanut, avocado, or olive)

1 head iceberg lettuce

On hot, dry skillet, slightly toast 8 tortillas on each side. Wrap in foil and set aside.

Put 2–3 cups oil—peanut, avocado, or olive—into a frying pan on medium to high heat until temperature reads 350 degrees. Wait until oil is shimmering but not smoking. Cook shrimp until golden brown then flip to brown other side, about 2 minutes.

Cut iceberg lettuce into strips and place on warm tortilla. Put shrimp sauce over lettuce. Place 3 shrimp over sauce. Spoon salsa over shrimp and serve.

Timothy Braun and Dusty Danger

TEXAS TACO COUNCIL

Tell us your story.

I'm a writer who lives in Austin with my writing partner, Dusty, a ten-year-old Australian shepherd. Basically just a guy and his dog, you know?

What's your connection with tacos?

We eat them almost every day. Almost.

You're on the Texas Taco Council. Why are you the Taco Ambassador for your city/region?

Because to me and Dusty, a taco is a noun, a verb, and an adjective all rolled into a tortilla. When you come to Austin, I take you inside the taco, we become one with tacos, and we aren't afraid to send a cease and desist letter to a gyro.

Give us the taco landscape for your city/region. Give us your top ten list and why they're the best.

In Austin, we like to think of ourselves as champions of fine food, but we like authentic tacos, classic recipes, and even creative third-wave-crazy-style tacos. For my list, I'm not just looking for a great taco, but also a place I can bring the ol' writing partner. Thus, most of these places are trucks or have a fine patio to boot.

1. **Tacodeli**—they have the freshest and highest-quality ingredients.
2. **A taco truck on E. Oltorf that pops up mysteriously next to a carwash.**
3. **Mi Madre's**—the classic Tex-Mex tacos are thick and mighty.
4. **Papalote Taco House**—the portions are huge and the prices are cheap.
5. **Tyson's Tacos**—their breakfast taco güera ("white girl") of potato, egg, and cheese might be the best in town.
6. **Tamale House East**—because of the atmosphere.
7. **Torchy's Tacos**—for me, Torchy's kicked it all off as part of the taco truck craze that now owns Austin.
8. **Mi Trailita**—the "tiny trailer" is a favorite among Eastsiders. The homemade corn and flour tortillas.
9. **Whole Foods**—I think their taco bar is one of the best-kept secrets in town.
10. **JW Marriot**—the downtown Austin hotel. Because these suckers know how to make a hearty taco.

POBLANO AND MUSHROOM TACOS

TIMOTHY BRAUN AND DUSTY DANGER

Makes 4 tacos

2 tablespoons vegetable oil, divided
1 fresh poblano chile, halved, seeded, thinly sliced into long strips
½ small red onion, sliced
3 ounces cremini (baby bella) mushrooms, thinly sliced, about 1¼ cups
1 teaspoon ground cumin

4 corn tortillas
4 thin slices Monterey Jack cheese
Chopped fresh cilantro
Crumbled feta or Cotija cheese
Assorted toppings, such as shredded lettuce, diced tomatoes, and hot sauce or salsa

Heat 1 tablespoon vegetable oil in large nonstick skillet over medium high heat. Add poblano chile, red onion, and mushrooms. Sauté mixture until brown, about 5 minutes. Mix in ground cumin. Season to taste with salt. Transfer mixture to medium bowl.

Heat remaining 1 tablespoon vegetable oil in same skillet over medium high heat. Add tortillas in single layer, draping up sides of skillet to fit. Divide mushroom mixture among tortillas, mounding on only one side. Place slice of Monterey Jack cheese atop filling in each tortilla. Fold plain tortilla halves over filling and press firmly. Cook until tortillas are brown, about 1 minute per side. Transfer tacos to plates. Open tacos; sprinkle with chopped cilantro, crumbled feta or Cotija cheese, and toppings.

Johnny Limon
COMMUNITY ADVOCATE

Tell us your story.

I come from a family of eleven children, three sisters and seven brothers. My passion is helping others. In 1980, I decided to give back to my community by volunteering with youth at Big Brothers Big Sisters for eight years. For the past twenty-three years, I have been delivering meals with Meals on Wheels. I have been appointed to serve on several boards and commissions of the City of Austin. I am an affordable housing advocate, serving on the board of HousingWorks Austin. I serve as president of our neighborhood association. For the past twenty-nine years, I have been choir director at St. Julia Catholic Church. The *most* important part of my life is caring for my 101-year-old mother, Eloisa Ojeda Limon.

What's your connection with tacos?

Growing up in a large Mexican American family, I remember my mom and sisters having to make two huge stacks of tortillas every day. With tortillas, you can put anything inside and make it a taco. When we were kids, tacos were our appetizers to hold us until it was time to sit down at the table to eat. The most popular taco appetizer was a quesadilla, cheese inside the tortilla and put on the hot comal. Bread was only used during holidays.

Why do you think people love tacos in your region and in Texas?

For those of us of Mexican descent, tacos are our culture, part of our life. The taste and texture of tortillas makes it possible for *anyone* to put *anything* inside it, without it coming apart. That makes it a great taco! I think that's why it's become such a popular food for anyone. We use tortillas as a spoon, too.

Give me your top taco spots and why.

Joe's Bakery & Coffee Shop—places that have good tacos start with homemade tortillas, like Joe's Bakery. Everything is great at Joe's including the carne guisada, refried beans, chorizo with eggs, and migas. Their tacos are always full and consistently good.

Juan in a Million—great tortillas. I love the chorizo and egg.

Los Huaraches—I love their tacos al pastor.

Tamale House East

CARMEN VALERA

Tell us your story.

One day Mom asked, so do you kids want to open up a restaurant? Two weeks later, we were open for business. With that simple question began the third generation's debut into the family business—although Juan, Jose, Robert, Colombina, and I literally grew up in all our family restaurants.

Beginning in the 1930s with our great-grandfather Antonio Villasaña, all the generations of our family have lived behind, above, next to, or in front of a tortilla factory or a restaurant.

Our Uncle Bobby (Robert Vasquez) opened up the iconic Tamale House #3 on Airport Boulevard and ended up in the pages of the *New York Times*, helping make the Austin breakfast taco famous around the world. This from a boy who grew up shamed for having tacos in his lunchbox.

Our mother Diane Valera, in the entrepreneurial spirit of her mother before her, opened up Mexico Tipico in the heart of East Austin in 1984. Now she is the heart and soul of our restaurant, Tamale House East. It is why we call it "Mom's Migas & Queso" because the recipes are mainly hers. Yes, we bring our talents to the table, and put our spin on classics as well, but we build on her legacy. She has taught us that food means family.

What better way to keep a family close-knit than to have a business that creates one of the most important components of our culture? What matters is the food. Is it authentic, is it real? Is it made with love and pride? Does it remind you of home?

Fresh homemade dishes that taste like your mother made it for you—because our mother made it using family recipes she learned from her mother who learned from her mother before her—are our specialty.

And, yes, we still make the same handmade tamales that you could buy from that tiny takeout restaurant on 1st and Congress in 1958.

What is your most popular taco and why? What makes it a standout or unique?

Well, for breakfast, our migas with queso taco is very popular because it a delicious twist on a classic with crispy pan-fried tortillas, mixed with eggs, and drenched in queso—and who doesn't love queso? It is Tex-Mex comfort food at its best.

But the taco we have decided to feature is our grilled fish taco. It is quickly becoming our most popular taco because it just tastes so good. And it tastes so good because it is made with love. Truly. It is a recipe created, as many of our dishes are, by our mother, who learned to cook from her mother Carmen Vasquez, who learned to cook from her mother, Carmen, who learned from her mother, Mama Maria. The secret to all of Diane's cooking is that she does almost everything by hand and takes the time to season, marinate, season some more, and slow cook delicious food. There are no shortcuts. It is innovative and fresh, served hot off the plancha and just a little bit spicy.

Michael Rypka

TORCHY'S TACOS

Tell us your story.

Torchy's Tacos was started by me in August of 2006 out of a food trailer in Austin on South 1st Street. I had a head full of ideas on how to take tacos to another level and elevate the common street taco and do something fun and different using authentic ingredients in an unusual way. With my twenty years of restaurant and chef experience, ranging from the World Bank to MTV, Disney animation, and many other fac-

ets of the industry, I've drawn on that experience to create new innovative and gourmet street tacos. Business was tough in the beginning with no customers in sight, so I had to drive my red Vespa and hand out free chips and salsa to get people interested in trying my food. After a write-up in the *Austin Chronicle* and after seven months of being open, the lines started to form and we haven't looked back since, becoming one of Austin's institutions for tacos. Nine years later, we have thirty-one stores all over Texas with more on the way. We've always kept the quality of our tacos top priority and make everything fresh in house every day, many times throughout the day. We've struggled many times like many other restaurants in the beginning, trying to operate and pay our bills and keep ahead. I was blessed many times with a friend or a family member who helped out to keep people paid, the lights on, and food coming in the back door. Now we can say we have a solid company with values in our food and the people who work for us and the people who visit us on a daily basis to serve them damn good tacos fresh and with a smile.

What is your most popular taco and why? What makes it a standout or unique?

Our most popular taco is our Trailer Park taco. It consists of a hand-battered chicken tender, roasted green chiles, lettuce, pico de gallo, shredded cheddar and Jack cheeses, served with creamy poblano ranch on a flour tortilla. I think what makes it stand out is everything is so fresh and the combination of ingredients hits all your senses. The chicken is marinated and the flour we use to batter the chicken is well seasoned, the sauce is made from scratch using roasted poblano peppers, and we have great quality green chiles we get from Hatch, New Mexico.

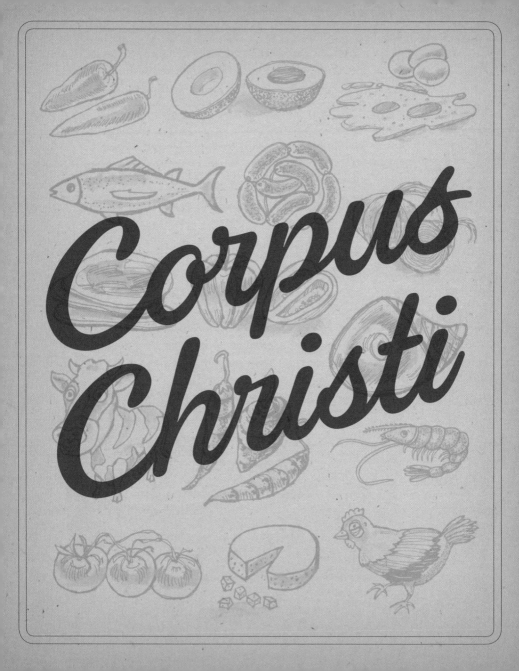

Corpus Christi

The big little city in the Coastal Bend, Corpus Christi is home of Selena—anything for Selena—the first Whataburger (taquitos, anyone?), beach life, big breakfast tacos, taquerias, and fish tacos. Corpus was definitely one of the friendliest places we visited on the Tacos of Texas Tour. Thanks to our Taco Ambassadors Gerald Flores and Joe Hilliard, the Taco Mafia and the #ChevyTacoTruck received a warm welcome.

It's like people knew we were coming—even Ben Resendez, the shrimp hustler, knew about *Tacos of Texas*!

We really didn't know what to expect, but the warm breezes of the coast, the neighborly attitudes, and the people willing to go out of their way to help us really made our experience extra special. We visited with local personalities, from a blogger to a singer to a fishmonger, to learn about taco life in Corpitos.

Now the tacos . . . well, let me just say that, during this trip, I had a taste of the biggest and baddest taco in Texas. That was the Almighty Chacho's Taco, which they said was three pounds, but it was more like cinco! That's the one that made me a taco meme. Taquerias were everywhere and the barbacoa was flowing. Being on the coast, we hit up one of our favorites, Coastal Sol Food Truck, for some mighty tasty fish and shrimp tacos. We finished the Corpus tour with a blessing from Monsignor Marcos Martinez.

Yeah, the tacos are good in Corpus Christi.

THE CORPUS CHRISTI ICONIC TACO: BREAKFAST TACOS

No one makes breakfast tacos like the ones in Corpitos. From the fresh tortillas to the warm hospitality of the taco makers themselves and the biggest breakfast taco we've ever tasted, breakfast tacos are loved by locals and Taco Journalists all over Texas. Whether you're an oil worker, a suit, or an abuelita, you know that Corpus has some of the freshest breakfast tacos.

So what makes them great? It's the fresh flour tortillas, just a tad bit thicker, rolled with lots of love and manteca. Chacho's Tacos not only had the tastiest tortilla but the biggest too, all made by hand. So take your pick, barbacoa or sausage or chorizo and eggs, but the crispy chicharrones con huevos a la Mexicana at Hi-Ho . . . I gotta say, hot damn, that's a good breakfast taco!

TACO JOURNALISM'S TOP CINCO

1. **Hi-Ho Restaurant**—warm hospitality and a tasty and crunchy chicharrón and eggs breakfast taco. Plus, it was one of Selena's favorite spots.

2. **Tacos El Tri**—the best taco trailers are usually in a parking lot next to a tire shop. Late-night spot for bistec and tacos al pastor and Mexican hot dogs.

3. **Coastal Sol Food Truck**—fresh-off-the-boat fish tacos.

4. **Southside Barbacoa**—sweet barbacoa, sweeter family.

5. **Chacho's Tacos**—the Almighty Chacho's Taco. That is all.

Just listen to our Taco Ambassador Gerald Flores:

Corpus Christi is known for its Hispanic and Mexican American heritage and with that, of course, comes tacos! Tacos are a huge part of some of our daily lives. Whether it's breakfast tacos on the way to work, during lunch or dinner or backyard barbecues with friends and family—tacos are everywhere here. In fact, I haven't ran into anyone who doesn't like tacos. I always say you're never late if you bring tacos.

Maria Gutierrez
CHACHO'S TACOS

Tell us your story.

Our story begins in Corpus Christi in 2001 when my husband Arnulfo "Chacho" Gutierrez and I, along with our two sons, Arnulfo Gutierrez Jr. and Michael D. Gutierrez, decided to pursue my dream of opening the best family-owned and -operated restaurant like no other in town. Immediately the response was outstanding, especially

when we revealed the Almighty Chacho's Taco challenge! With such a huge response from the community, lines became long and the restaurant full of customers. At one point, we had three locations. It was a struggle, but a struggle well spent. With all of our loyal customers, old and new, and, of course, by the grace of God, we have been able to keep the tradition going.

At this point in time, we only have one location. The difference between Chacho's Tacos and other restaurants is that we use some of Grandma's secret recipes, keeping the tradition of Tex-Mex home-style cooking. We invite you to come try us out and, if you're up for it, come try the Almighty Chacho's Taco Challenge!

What is your most popular taco and why? What makes it a standout or unique?

Our most popular taco is the Almighty Chacho's Taco! The combination of beans, potatoes, eggs, bacon, and the best carne guisada in town, topped with cheese, makes it a unique mouthful of goodness.

It's a fourteen-inch homemade tortilla that is stuffed with three-and-a-half pounds of food. It's also a challenge: if you can finish it in under ten minutes, it's free, and you also get our one-of-a-kind Chacho's Tacos T-shirt, letting everyone know that you accomplished the challenge!

Gerald Flores

TACOCREATIVE
TEXAS TACO COUNCIL

Tell us your story.

I am a creative, born and raised in beautiful Corpus Christi. I'm surrounded by a city of other creatives and, more importantly, taco lovers like myself. Tacos have always been a part of my life, whether it be for breakfast in the morning or dinner in the evening and especially for weekend cookouts.

My life as a graphic designer has brought me so many opportunities and so much fulfillment in life. I love tacos so much that I named my graphic design company TacoCreative. Naturally, it took some time for the public to really grasp the name, but before you knew it, everyone I knew was sharing everything and anything about tacos with me.

As if naming my company after tacos wasn't enough, I then went in search for some T-shirts that I could wear to show how much I loved tacos. To my surprise, there really weren't a whole lot of options out there, or at least one company that focused on the taco. Since I couldn't find a company I wanted to buy from, I decided to make one myself. That's how Taco Gear was born.

Taco Gear has allowed me to design some really fun and appealing apparel for taco lovers. From shirts to hats, mugs to tote bags, and more. I thoroughly enjoy designing fun stuff that people want to wear. Not just people—taco lovers! This company lets me express a new level of fun and creativity that I have always been itching to get out.

With my design career, living in a creative coastal community, being surrounded by great Hispanic culture, the support of my beautiful wife, family, and friends, I can honestly say I *love* everything about my life right now. It's perfect, and I can't wait to see what else is in store.

What's your connection with tacos?

As a Hispanic, I have always been around tacos. Tacos have always been a part of my mornings growing up, evenings at home, weekend cookouts, etc. There was always a family gathering and tacos were always there. Family and tradition are my connection to tacos.

You're on the Texas Taco Council. Why are you the Taco Ambassador for your city/region?

I love tacos so much that I named my company after them. I was also inspired to create an apparel line, Taco Gear, dedicated to tacos and taco lovers. It's because of this that I have been known by many to love everything and anything to do with tacos.

What's your go-to taco and why?

Chorizo egg and bacon. I *love* this taco. I just love chorizo because it has so much flavor. So you add that with egg *and* bacon? N'ombre, chut up! The flavor combination is just great.

Why do you think people love tacos in your region and in Texas?

Beside the fact that they are quick and easy to make, they are a staple of the Hispanic culture. Of course, not only Hispanics love them in this region and in the state of Texas. Tacos bring people together. "Let's get tacos"—it's a strong statement that people can definitely get behind. It's a specific mission to go out and get something awesome that we can enjoy together.

Give us the taco landscape for your city/region. Give us your top tacos list and why they're the best.

1. **Southside Barbacoa**—because of the barbacoa and my favorite taco, the chorizo, egg, and bacon.
2. **Nano's Taco Run**—the tortillas are great. They are quick and have a great drive-through.
3. **Molé**—their street tacos are delicious.
4. **Tacos El Tri Food Truck**—delicious tacos al pastor.
5. **Hi-Ho Restaurant**—chicharrón tacos are awesome.
6. **Coastal Sol Food Truck**—the best fish tacos!
7. **Señor Jaime's**—the fish tacos are delicious.
8. **Sonny's Barbacoa**—awesome brisket tacos.

Gary Schneider

COASTAL SOL FOOD TRUCK

Tell us your story.

I'm the owner of Coastal Sol Food Truck. It was a long time coming and a dream come true to have my own kitchen and to work with my son and the rest of my family. Coming up through the school of hard knocks in Corpus Christi and having great mentors that instilled a strong work ethic, I like to think it paid off. It was a lot of sacrifice, and many hours have been spent in the kitchen over the years. I would only like to say that I am proud of the quality of food that I serve off my food truck.

What is your most popular taco and why? What makes it a standout or unique?

That would be our grilled flounder taco with jalapeño slaw and pineapple salsa. I think that fresh, never frozen, has been key. Along with flavors from sauces made from scratch.

GRILLED FISH TACOS

COASTAL SOL FOOD TRUCK

Makes 2 tacos

3 ounces flounder
1 tablespoon butter
Creole seasoning
4 corn tortillas
Shredded green and red
cabbage

Jalapeño dressing (see
recipe below)
Chipotle crema (see recipe
below)
Pineapple salsa (see recipe
below)

Season fish with creole seasoning. Brush the fish with melted butter, then cook in hot skillet for a couple of minutes per side until done. Warm tortillas. Mix a little jalapeño dressing with cabbage to make a slaw. Then build your taco. Slaw . . . fish . . . crema . . . pineapple salsa.

JALAPEÑO DRESSING

1 tablespoon minced garlic
2 tablespoons chopped
pickled jalapeños
1 tablespoon Dijon mustard
½ teaspoon Worcestershire
sauce

½ teaspoon Tabasco
¼ teaspoon salt
½ tablespoon sugar
¼ cup apple cider vinegar
½ cup olive oil

In a food processor or blender, combine all but the last ingredient. Then gradually add the ½ cup olive oil while processor or blender is running.

PINEAPPLE SALSA

1 pineapple, diced small

½ cup minced red bell
   pepper

¼ cup diced red onion

1 jalapeño, diced

1 tablespoon brown sugar

2 tablespoons chopped
   cilantro

Juice from ½ lime

In a medium bowl, stir together the pineapple, red bell pepper, red onion, jalapeño, brown sugar. and chopped cilantro. Add lime to taste.

CHIPOTLE CREMA

1 cup sour cream

1 tablespoon chipotle in
   adobo sauce

Juice from ½ lime

Salt

Pepper

In a small bowl, stir together the sour cream, adobo sauce, and lime juice. Add salt and pepper to taste.

Clarissa Serna

SINGER/SONGWRITER

Tell us your story.

I was born and raised in Corpus Christi. I am a singer/songwriter who was featured on Season 6 of *The Voice* with Team Shakira. I'm currently working on my next album and setting up a tour along with it. In addition to music, I am a freelance makeup artist, painter, skincare consultant, and DJ for a local rock station.

What's your connection with tacos?

I was raised in a Hispanic family and tacos are at the top of my nutrition pyramid. I have always looked forward to my mother's cooking. I remember when I was in school, she would send me off with coffee and two tacos to go *every* morning. I'm obviously blessed. I've had to cut back on my taco addiction to balance my diet, but I will always have a special place in my heart for them.

What's your go-to taco and why?

Breakfast tacos. Chorizo and egg, bacon and egg, or barbacoa. They are all nostalgic of what my mom used to cook for me when I lived with her. No one beats mom tacos, but I've discovered a few competitors. For lunch, I love mini-tacos or chicken fajita with grilled bell peppers and onions. Somehow I convinced myself I'm eating healthy because it's chicken.

Give me your top five taco spots and why.

1. **Mom's house**—no one beats my mom's tacos, especially her infamous Spam tacos. Yeah, I said Spam.
2. **Taqueria El Potro**—family-owned and tastes like home cooking. I love their habanero salsa and they know me by name.
3. **Cancun Mexican Restaurant**—consistently good tacos. And their green sauce is to die for.
4. **Nano's Taco Run**—a family joint. Delicious special sauce. I have a lot of memories at Nano's because I ate there all the time in high school.
5. **Taqueria Acapulco**—it's close to home and they always take care of me.

Mary Rangel-Gomez and Eric Gomez

HOME COOKS

Tell us your story.

We have been married for seventeen years and formed a beautiful family that includes two daughters, Kate and Julia. Our family is extremely busy; however, for us, cooking is an event in which the entire family plays a role with the hope that our daughters do the same with their children and generations to come.

What's your connection with tacos?

Eric and I were raised in Matamoros, Mexico. My love for tacos has been part of my upbringing. I remember that no matter what time you got in the night before, you were expected to be seated at the table by breakfast time. Carnes asadas were a must during the weekends and barbacoa on Sundays and usually fajitas were the meat of choice. Helping out in the kitchen was quality family time: the girls were in the kitchen, helping Mom with all the sides, while Dad and his boys would stand next to the barbecue pit grilling. I was born in the United States but was raised in Mexico. My parents wanted to give me the opportunity to be raised in the Mexican culture.

Why do you think people love tacos in your region and in Texas?

We are Mexican descendants and proud to be. Tacos are a food that allows us to feel closer to our roots. When we prepare and eat tacos, we think of our abuelitas, mamas y tías; we think of our childhood. Tacos can bring memories of the simplest but happiest times.

LENGUA TACOS

MARY RANGEL-GOMEZ AND ERIC GOMEZ

Makes 40 tacos

1 lengua	Pepper
3 to 4 garlic cloves	1 onion
Salt	3 to 4 celery stalks

Rinse lengua thoroughly and dry with paper towels. Make small incisions in the lengua and insert the garlic cloves. Rub the lengua with salt and pepper. Slice the onion into 4 to 5 pieces.

Cut the celery stalks in half. Place onion and celery stalks in the slow cooker. Place the lengua on top of the onion and celery. Cover the slow cooker and cook on low for 10 to 12 hours.

When done, remove the skin from the lengua and discard along with the onion and celery. Place the lengua on a plate and finely shred while adding salt and pepper to taste. (For a leaner lengua, remove fat while shredding.)

Make tacos with corn tortillas, garnish with diced onions and cilantro, and top with salsa.

FAJITA TACOS

MARY RANGEL-GOMEZ AND ERIC GOMEZ

Makes 15 to 20 tacos

5 poblano peppers
1 full skirt steak
Generic garlic dry rub
Meltable cheese (asadero,
    mozzarella, etc.), enough
    to stuff poblano peppers
    (about ⅓ cup per pepper)

2 large yellow onions,
    cut in quarters
Salt
Pepper
1 lime, juiced
3 large avocados, sliced

Start fire in pit (preferably a pit with a smoke side and side fire box). While the flame is high, burn the poblano peppers on all sides. When done, place them on a plastic bag for a few minutes. Set aside.

Rinse skirt steak thoroughly and dry with paper towels. Place the steak on a cutting board and remove the membrane as much as possible, but leave the fat. Rub the steak with the dry rub.

When the fire is ready and the pit is hot, place a piece of aluminum foil on the smoke side of the pit and then place the skirt steak on top of the foil. The foil will keep the fat drippings from falling into the pit. Cook on slow fire for 2 to 3 hours while brushing the steak with the drippings every now and then.

Scrape the burned skin from the peppers. Make a side incision into the peppers and remove the seeds. Rinse the peppers. Insert the cheese through the incision and wrap the peppers in aluminum foil.

Wrap the onions in foil and place in the smoke side of the pit close to the fire box so they cook thoroughly. Place the peppers in the smoke side of the pit as far away from the fire box as possible.

When the skirt steak is done, place the meat on a cutting board and let it rest for about 10 minutes. Then cut the steak into ⅛- to ¼-inch slices and place on serving plate.

Retrieve the onions and remove the foil and the skin. Place in a bowl and season with salt, pepper, and lime juice. Place the onions on the serving plate next to the skirt steak.

Retrieve the peppers, remove them from the foil, and place them on the serving plate next to the skirt steak.

Slice avocados and add to the serving plate. Make tacos with corn tortillas, top with salsa, and garnish with the grilled onions, sliced avocados, and peppers.

Gloria Perales and Isabella Zano

NANO'S TACO RUN

Tell us your story.

My sons started Nano's more than twenty years ago. We have people coming back every day and year after year. I think people come back because it's comfortable, you're just like family, and they love our food. And we have many people who come here from all over and this is their last stop or this is their first stop. So everyone needs their Nano's fix.

What is your most popular taco and why? What makes it a standout or unique?

The most popular taco I would say is the carne asada. The good thing is you can pretty much mix up your taco like you want it, so however you want your taco, we're going to make it. The carne asada is really, really good.

Our homemade flour tortillas are what people come back for, but as far as our breakfast tacos go, that's the biggest seller. We sell them until we close at 5:00 p.m., and we serve breakfast all day. Our barbacoa is another big seller. We run out quick on the weekends, so everyone knows that you have to get here early.

We get a lot of people from Austin, Houston, Dallas, and even New York City. We've had people freeze our tacos and ship them!

Casey Lain
HOUSE OF ROCK

Tell us your story.

I was born in Corpus Christi and grew up on my family's dairy farm in Sandia, Texas. I was introduced to tacos at a very young age—specifically, tacos on homemade flour tortillas. My father's right-hand man on the farm was named Antonio "Tony" Caballero. Tony lived down the road from us and made the best homemade flour tortillas. My older brother and I always knew when he was making tortillas because we could smell them from far away. Every time we caught a scent, we would stop what we were doing and run to Tony's place to help him roll out the dough. In return, he would send us home with a hot stack of fresh flour tortillas.

Later in life, I joined the workforce in downtown Corpus

Christi and started what turned out to be a twenty-plus-year career in the service industry, specializing in concert promotion, food, and beverage . . . not always in that order. As the managing partner, I have been promoting concerts and managing House of Rock since September 2005. A few years ago, I became a board member of the Downtown Management District, which is a BID, or Business Improvement District, charged with the development of the downtown Corpus Christi area. I have been chairman for the past few years.

What's your connection with tacos?

I was raised on tacos. I still eat tacos every week and I am raising my kids on tacos. The taco is a South Texas staple. Tacos are what you bring to office meetings; tacos are crowd pleasers. You can eat tacos for breakfast, lunch, and dinner.

Give me your top five taco spots and why.

1. **Chaco's Tacos**—the best. The food is delicious, and the Gutierrez family is like family to me.

2. **Hacienda Vieja**—great food and the service is outstanding. You can get in and out quickly, and it's close to home.

3. **San Luis Restaurant**—killer hot sauce and some of the best carne guisada in town.

4. **Taqueria Garibaldi**—great food. Mingo and his family always greet you with a smile.

5. **Tacos El Tri Food Truck**—the best street tacos you will find and they are open late night just about every night of the week.

Edgar and Brooke Montes

MOLÉ

Tell us your story.

I grew up in Queretaro, Mexico and worked in my family's restaurant selling tacos and gorditas. I have worked in the food service industry for twenty years—more specifically, Chili's, where I met Brooke, my wife, who had also been in the food service industry for seventeen years.

I missed the cuisine of Mexico that couldn't be found in Corpus Christi. I often cooked at home,

sharing meals with friends and family, and they encouraged us to open our own restaurant. We created Molé, a place that features the authentic flavors of Mexico that many compare to their grandmother's cooking. I work hard to preserve the freshness, preparation, and authenticity of the cuisine. Many of the items on our menu can be found throughout Mexico, but you will also find many new dishes we created using the classic ingredients of Mexico. Corpus Christi is more known for the delicious Tex-Mex cuisine, so it was a bit of a challenge to introduce a different type of Mexican food. It didn't take long for people to catch on, and they realized they can eat with us at Molé and their favorite Tex-Mex spot and not feel like they had the same thing to eat.

What is your most popular taco and why? What makes it a standout or unique?

Tacos al pastor. We slow cook the meat on a rotisserie, and it's the special pastor recipe from my mother that gives it the awesome flavor.

Vianney Rodriguez

SWEET LIFE BLOGGER AND RECIPE DEVELOPER

Tell us your story.

I'm the founder and developer for the award-winning blog *Sweet Life*. Raised by Mexican parents, I was fortunate enough to be enveloped by both Mexican traditions and the hybrid culture of Tejanos (tenderly known as Tex-Mex).

My blog, *Sweet Life*, reflects this identity of being raised in a kitchen filled with laughter, stories, amor, and the wafting aroma of fresh tortillas on a comal. My palate and blog are filled with an eccentric array of traditional Mexican, Tex-Mex, and Texas dishes. I recently coauthored my first book, *Latin Twist: Traditional and Modern Cocktails*. I've been recognized as *Latism* 2012 "Best Latina Food Blogger," and I've been featured on the *Huffington Post*, Yahoo Shine, *Latina Magazine*, *Glamour*, and *Cosmo for Latinas*.

What's your connection with tacos?

For me, tacos are comfort, they are home, they are a mordida (bite) of life. I was raised in a household where my mom made fresh tortillas with every meal, breakfast, lunch, dinner—she made flour or corn tortillas. My mom, being the eldest of five children, often helped my grandma in the kitchen to prepare meals for the family. From a young age, she was put in charge of making tortillas. My mom would wake up around 3:00 a.m., make tortillas for their lunches (tacos) of frijoles guisidos. It was a meal they could eat quickly, on the go, which fueled them for the day. When my parents married and moved to South Texas, my mom cooked what she knew, she cooked what her definition of home was, and when you're in a new place, alone with no family or friends nearby, food becomes a link to home. I didn't have bologna sandwiches or ham and cheese for lunch. I had tacos. Whatever my mami made for dinner the previous night was transformed into school lunches for us kids.

PALOMA COCKTAIL MARINATED CHICKEN FAJITAS

VIANNEY RODRIGUEZ

Serves 6

2 cups fresh grapefruit juice,
   plus a few grapefruit
   slices
2 teaspoons lime zest
4 tablespoons fresh lime
   juice

3 teaspoons salt
1 cup tequila
1 cup club soda or Squirt or
   grapefruit soda
4 pounds boneless, skinless
   chicken breast

In a large bowl combine grapefruit juice, grapefruit slices, lime zest, fresh lime juice, salt, and tequila. Whisk to combine. Add club soda and chicken breasts. Marinate for 2 hours. Preheat grill to medium high heat and grill chicken 6 to 8 minutes on each side. Slice and serve.

Charlie Alegria

MORGAN STREET SEAFOOD

Tell us your story.

I was born into fish. My dad was a seafood long-haul truck driver during the 1940s and 1950s for Gulf King in Aransas Pass, Texas. I am a true Texan, born and raised in Corpus Christi. I graduated from a local high school and Texas College (Stephen F. Austin in Nacogdoches, Texas) with a degree in accounting, but fish are my life. My parents opened up Seven Seas Fish Market in 1960, but my roots go

deeper than that. Since I can remember, I always had seafood in my surroundings. So my love and appreciation goes so deep with this business. Currently, my family owns and operates Morgan Street Seafood—an extension of what my parents began. I fundamentally operate the business as my father did. Even though the operational part has changed somewhat, the basic part of my business has not, which is quality product at a fair price.

What's your connection with tacos?

When I was younger, my mom always made tacos for meals; breakfast, lunch, and dinner. The seafood taco consists of either fried fish or sautéed fish in a hot tortilla with fresh veggies and condiments. My favorite is the fried fish taco with lettuce, tomato, and either fresh salsa or pico de gallo for a little heat and flavor. I also provide fresh product to local vendors who make fish tacos, which is my connection.

What's your go-to taco and why?

Seafood tacos made of fresh drum or sheepshead. Any other taco not seafood related would become asada.

Why do you think people love tacos in your region and in Texas?

It's easily accessible, quick, and not bound by a knife and fork to eat.

Give me your top fish taco spots and why.

Coastal Sol Food Truck—the freshest fish. Gary and his son focus on quality and really good seasoning with a touch of Louisiana.

La Ribera Restaurant—fish tacos that your mom can be proud of. A great mix of Mexican spices and that homemade flavor.

Railroad Seafood Station—the fish and shrimp tacos are both great and topped off with avocados.

Cruz Leon

TAQUERIA EL POTRO

Tell us your story.

I am originally from Jalisco, Mexico. My wife and I started our business in 2003. It is a family business. Our specialty is breakfast. We make all kinds of breakfast tacos, lonche, and a variety of dishes like fideo con pollo, calabazas with chicken, ribs, salsa

ranchera, chicken fajitas, mini-taquitos. The mini-taquitos are made with grilled steak. We give it our own flavor that I learned from when I worked in taquerias in Mexico, and now we're bringing that flavor to Corpus Christi.

What's your connection with tacos?

I never went to a culinary school. I learned first from my mom. Cooking comes so naturally to me; it gives me a lot of pleasure to prepare a great meal. Just like any other job out there that you love, this is a labor of great satisfaction.

What is your most popular taco and why? What makes it a standout or unique?

The mini-tacos are really popular. I don't know if it's the particular flavors of the mini-tacos or if it's because a lot of people who have traveled to Mexico recognize them from the street food. They've tried them in Mexico, and they feel that they have the true flavors of Mexico. I don't know, but they have become really popular.

Rick Garcia

HI-HO RESTAURANT

Tell us your story.

Hi-Ho was started in 1975 by Mr. Frank Dalton and passed on to his son, Tommy Dalton, in 1978 and was successful. In June 2010, Tommy Dalton decided he needed to retire and sold the restaurant to my parents, Lupe and Maria Garcia. We kept all the same employees, and some of them have been here since the restaurant was opened. I run Hi-Ho now and make sure the restaurant runs in top shape. We are proud of our eagle emblem, which represents that we are Americans, good luck, and peace.

What is your most popular taco and why? What makes it a standout or unique?

Most popular taco is potato and egg with bacon. What makes it stand out is the unique way our cooks prepare them all fresh. Potatoes and egg have been a Tex-Mex tradition, and the bacon adds the flavor to the mix.

Manuel and Maria Aguilar

SOUTHSIDE BARBACOA

Tell us your story.

Manuel: We met in Mazatlán, Sinaloa, Mexico, when she came into town from California to bury her aunt. My family lived close to her family and so that is when we met each other. One day she said, if you want, we can go live in the United States, so we moved

from Mazatlán to Corpus Christi in 1981. We moved here to progress and for the American Dream. After fifteen years of working for others, we finally decided to own our own business. I worked as a cook and my wife worked as a server. Someone once said, if she's good with customers and you're a good cook, why work for someone else? That is when we decided to go into business for ourselves. We have been here for eighteen years. We bought the business with only barbacoa and we added the rest of the menu, like carne guisada, picadillo, and Tex-Mex food. We have two children, a daughter named Diana and a son, Manuel Jr.

Maria: I love to deal with customers because it's my life. I enjoy talking, and even he tells me, "you can make a rock talk to you." I enjoy people.

Manuel: I never worked in Mexico. I only went to school. So when I got here, I started working as a dishwasher and one day was moved over to cook. I really liked it, so I made a point to learn

more. We believe people come back to Southside because of the flavorful food and because of how we treat them. Some customers have said they come because they feel like they're with family. The food also makes them feel like their wife or mother just cooked it, and that is why they come back every day.

Maria: I just want to say thank you for letting us share our story. It is a sacrifice, but if you do it with love, it pays off.

What is your most popular taco and why? What makes it a standout or unique?

Barbacoa. We make it pure with no added salt or seasonings. All natural meat and let the customer add what they want, like onion, cilantro, beans, or avocado.

Monsignor Marcos Martinez
OUR LADY OF THE PILLAR

Tell us your story.

I'm originally from Spain and studied theology. A seminary was opened in Madrid where the pope at the time enrolled priests to serve in South America and Central America. I was in a group that was sent to South America, where priests were greatly needed. This was in the 1950s. I went to the seminary in Madrid for three years and Brazil for eight years in a very remote jungle. There had been other priests who had been there before, so there was a small home and church. And we slowly built a mission and a school. When we finished the contract, I went to study in Paris for one year. I then reunited with a priest in Spain from my earlier years who told me about a need in San Antonio. So via San Antonio I

ended up here in Corpus Christi. Corpus is a very quiet, tranquil town. The congregation feels like a family. The atmosphere is very warm. The people are wonderful and very humble. They don't think of me as a father, but as a brother. They ask me to confess in very informal places—at a park bench or at home. I will visit people on Wednesdays in their home, and I'll prepare a small mass and it feels like a family reunion. We talk about how to raise each other up. How to help each other. We reflect on our lives.

Our church members here in Corpus come to me for spiritual guidance. I bless them, give them communion, anoint them with oils, and prepare them for any personal difficulties they may be facing. So many people come here and I will attend to them at any time they need me.

What's your connection with tacos?

It's what we eat. We begin the catechism and at 9:30 a.m., mass begins. We go to breakfast after the mass. Afterward, we have a bit of recreation. For breakfast, we offer about six hundred to seven hundred meals for children and adults. And we serve tacos. For the children, they'll have tacos and menudo and everyone participates.

And I have personally blessed almost all of the taquerias in town. They call me and ask me to bless their businesses. This includes Taqueria Jalisco and so many others. Many of the business owners come here for mass, and they ask me to bless their taco truck or businesses, usually before they open the business. I think this tradition is really very Mexican. They will ask us to bless their businesses, their homes, their cars—I blessed a car today. I'll bless the *Tacos of Texas* truck for you today.

Why do you think people love tacos in your region and in Texas?

Tacos are very common here in Corpus—it's a Mexican tradition. But, for example, in Spain, the quick, convenient food that everyone eats is the sandwich or bocadillo with a cup of coffee. Here

there are tacos everywhere. And when I go out to the taquerias people will prepare me something because they know me. And there is a church member who sings here who brings me tacos and I enjoy them.

Joe Hilliard

40 THINGS TO DO IN CORPUS CHRISTI
TEXAS TACO COUNCIL

Tell us your story.

Raised in Corpus Christi, I was always puzzled by the oft-repeated gripe from friends and neighbors that there is nothing to do in Corpus Christi. I never had that problem. In 2010, I set out to do forty things I had never done before in and around town to disprove the complainers. I chronicled the depth and breadth of Corpus Christi's natural beauty and all of the offbeat, fun things to do in my newspaper column and on my radio show, blog, and my Facebook page. *40 Things to Do in Corpus Christi* took off and I had one of the best years of my life. Every year since, I've done twenty more new things, including trying almost every new restaurant that opens.

Life is what you make it and life in Corpus Christi is one of the best lives you can hope for.

What's your connection with tacos?

Corpus Christi is the Breakfast Taco Capital of The World, and I have a T-shirt that says so. You can't throw a rock in Corpus Christi without hitting a taco joint. Tacos are a way of life down here, you eat one for breakfast almost every day. Day after day and year after year, the taco experience adds up: everyone in Corpus Christi is a taco expert.

You're on the Texas Taco Council. Why are you the Taco Ambassador for your city/region?

With *40 Things to Do in Corpus Christi*, we try every new restaurant that opens up while also hitting all the mainstays. Tacos are no exception. If a taco is produced in Corpus Christi, I've tried it.

What's your go-to taco and why?

I've moved to a minimal breakfast taco as I've gotten a little older. These days, its egg and avocado a la Mexicana. Slather on some homemade salsa and every day is breakfast heaven.

Why do you think people love tacos in your region and in Texas?

Without a doubt, tacos are the perfect representation of Texas culture and demographics. The farther south you go, the more the authentic flavors of our southern neighbors shine through. If tacos aren't the official state food of Texas, they should be.

San Antonio

As the gateway to South Texas, puffy tacos, Tex-Mex, and Texas history—remember the Alamo?—and home to a huge Latino population, San Antonio comes with some pretty tasty tacos! In the Alamo City, people go crazy for Los Spurs, and they are proud of native sons, Julián and Joaquin Castro. The puro pinche (hell, yeah!) vibe and attitude is in the air, there's a growing culinary scene, Big Red and barbacoa are like religion, and, yes, tacos are part of the daily diet in San Anto.

THE SAN ANTONIO ICONIC TACO: PUFFY TACOS

In San Antonio, there is no shortage of tacos or homemade tortillas. Inhale—you can almost taste the effervescent manteca in the air. And in this great city awaits the puffiest of creations: the puffy taco. No, not a crispy taco or a soft taco, but a corn masa taco fried to golden perfection. Just add ground beef, chicken, and, sometimes, just guacamole for the veggie option because, y'know, health. While the puffy taco is not consumed by the masses, it's what sets the San Antonio taco scene apart from that of other cities in Texas. There's a mascot (yes, a puffy taco mascot), there's Ray's Drive Inn, there's Henry's Puffy Tacos, and there was one of the original puffy taco makers—R.I.P. Arturo Lopez. So next time you're in the Alamo City, make sure you try this unique Tex-Mex creation.

TACO JOURNALISM'S TOP CINCO

1. **El Machito**—Chef Johnny Hernandez focuses on carne, carne, carne.
2. **Mixtli**—Chefs Rico Torres and Diego Galicia introducing the regions of Mexico to San Antonio.
3. **Mi Tierra**—creating a cultural experience since 1941.
4. **Ray's Drive Inn**—old-school drive-in. Puffy all the way!
5. **Taqueria Datapoint**—the only taqueria in San Antonio that matters.

SAN ANTONIO TACO AMBASSADORS

San Antonio was a challenge for the Taco Journalists because the tacos are limitless! We had two amazing Taco Ambassadors who helped us along the way: Edmund Tijerina, food writer and critic with the *San Antonio Express-News*, and Eddie Vega, El Tacolico and taco poet. Then, there was an unexpected taco aficionado who took us by surprise and became an honorary Taco Ambassador— at least for a few hours on our first day in San Antonio. Not only did we meet with him, chat about tacos, culture, and San Antonio, but he also introduced us to locals and made introductions for us.

So that morning, we inducted Dr. Ricardo Romo, president of the University of Texas at San Antonio, into the Texas Taco Council.

As you'll read in this chapter, San Antonio is not only a taco mecca, but this city on the rise is also full of creatives, songbirds, community activists, poets, culturistas, chefs, and taqueros. With so many tacos and so much talent, San Antonio needs its own taco book!

SAN ANTONIO'S TACO VIBE

As we explored this great taco town, we got to know its food, its people, and its vibe. While we have our own impressions, it's best cap-   tured by Texas Taco Council member Edmund Tijerina:

In general, San Antonio is a traditionalist taco town, especially when it comes to breakfast tacos. For the most part, we stick to the classics: bacon and egg, bean and cheese, potato and egg, and a few other basic varieties. Even the nontraditional versions keep things simple: brisket taco (a couple of slices of brisket in a flour tortilla) and a pork chop taco (thin, bone-in pork chop in a flour tortilla). That sense of tradition keeps us rooted and gives San Antonio a beautiful sense of place, but it sometimes keeps our culinary scene from advancing. We need to do a better job of touting our tradition and also pushing forward and trying new things. I'll bet there's a San Antonio answer to the Korean taco— it's just a matter of time before somebody here creates it.

Patricia Torres

RAY'S DRIVE INN

Tell us your story.

I'm married and have six children. I'm a California girl who moved to San Antonio in 2009. My Uncle Arthur and my Aunt Gloria Lopez are the owners of Ray's Drive Inn. I started as a server here and I was asked to be the manager temporarily in 2011. I have been managing Ray's since then.

Ray, the original owner, is my Uncle Arthur's brother. Ray was the oldest of the five boys. He used to show movies outside with carhops and that's where he got the "Drive Inn" name. People used to come and it was a local hangout back in the 50s, and to this day, we continue to have carhops. People park outside and leave their lights on and our servers go out and take their orders. They have the option to dine in their car or take it to go or come inside and eat in the restaurant.

Ray's Drive Inn started in 1956. We have regular customers who come back, and I love their stories, the tradition, the customers who used to come with their parents and their grandparents. Now they're passing on that tradition, bringing their children and grandchildren in. It's an awesome story you hear from a lot of our customers.

What is your most popular taco and why? What makes it a standout or unique?

The puffy taco! Well, when Ray started the restaurant, he used to call it a crispy taco and when my Uncle Arthur purchased it, he said that didn't look like a crispy taco, so he renamed it the puffy taco.

It's a unique taco. It's handmade masa and when it's fried it puffs out. We use a certain technique to form the taco, so it doesn't break when it's stuffed with the fillings. We've been doing this since the beginning, nothing has changed, and we haven't outgrown or become commercialized. We just stick to the original recipe and process of making it and that's what makes our tacos special.

Ricardo Romo, PhD

PRESIDENT
UNIVERSITY OF TEXAS AT SAN ANTONIO

Tell us your story.

My life began in a quiet barrio in the West Side of San Antonio in the 1940s. I am a proud Mexican American descendant, with three of my grandparents having emigrated from Mexico to the United States during the Mexican Revolution and arriving in San Antonio's West Side in 1916. My fourth grandparent, my maternal grandmother, was a seventh-generation Texan, having been born on the border in South Texas. Prior to moving to San Antonio, both families worked as migrant agricultural workers, and my parents met when their two families joined to pick the cotton crops of South Texas.

I was raised in a home where Spanish was the only language spoken. My grandparents were very influential in my upbringing and they only spoke Spanish. In fact, when my brother Henry enrolled in Sacred Heart Catholic School, he was required to repeat the first grade because school officials did not believe he had sufficient English language skills. I was turned down from attending that same school for being monolingual in Spanish. For this

reason, my parents enrolled me in a public school, Davy Crockett Elementary, for one year until I could learn to speak English.

When I reached the first grade, my family moved eight blocks north to a neighborhood known as Prospect Hill. My grandmother worked as a midwife, and because business was always good in the Hispanic community, she did well economically. With her life savings, she purchased a home and moved into a new, diverse neighborhood across Durango Street and crossed the ethnic divide of the West Side.

She was joined in Prospect Hill by my Uncle Benny, then by my parents, and soon by Uncle Arnulfo. My aunt also lived behind my grandmother's house. Eventually, a total of thirty-eight Romos lived within two blocks of each other in Prospect Hill.

My parents were entrepreneurs and owned their own mom-and-pop grocery business in a Mexican American barrio in the heart of San Antonio's West Side. Our business served as a neighborhood gathering place for those interested in social and political causes. Because my dad stressed a strong work ethic, everyone had to pitch in and work long hours in the family store. Now I realize that this hard work paid off in many ways. From my dad, I learned the value of trust, integrity, respect, and public service.

When I was in middle school, I was discovered by my track coach for having a natural talent for running long distances. It was his coaching and mentoring that launched me into becoming a national track champion during my high school years. It was also through my running career that college became a possibility for me. I was fortunate to receive a track scholarship to attend the University of Texas at Austin, and this opened a whole new path in life for me.

Little did I realize that attending UT Austin would not only propel me to become an international track champion, but also that I would meet my future wife. Harriett and I met while standing in line for a Chilean exchange program, and I was absolutely mesmerized by her blue eyes. We were married in 1967, just after graduating, and we headed for California the day after our wedding with teaching degrees and no jobs.

We were fortunate to get teaching jobs in inner-city schools in Los Angeles, in one of the poorest areas in the country. Our love for art was sparked in Los Angeles, which at that time, with all of its galleries, art studios, museums, and contemporary artists, was a city gaining in stature for the art scene.

I earned my PhD in history in 1975 from the University of California, Los Angeles. My academic career as a historian has spanned more than forty years and has included teaching at many prestigious universities, such as the University of California (UC) Los Angeles, UC San Diego, UC Berkeley and the University of Texas at Austin. Through this period, I also pursued an administrative career in higher education, having served as vice provost for undergraduate education at UT Austin for seven years and then becoming president of UTSA in 1999.

I am fortunate to have the opportunity to serve as president of a major university located in the town where I was raised as it gives me a unique understanding of what the community needs. During my sixteen years as president of the University of Texas at San Antonio, I have presided over a period of unprecedented growth in the university's footprint, in its student enrollment, and in the quality of its academic and research programs.

What's your connection with tacos?

My connection with tacos is closely tied to my family's grocery business. One of my fondest memories—and my first introduction to tacos—is of my dad being behind the stove cooking chicharrones and Mexican barbacoa. The chicharrones were cooked in a large pot over a wood fire; the barbacoa was cooked in a deep hole in the ground in the backyard of the store. Now, whenever I am met with the aroma from a well-cooked barbacoa, I am immediately taken back to that memory.

What's your go-to taco and why?

I have many go-to tacos and here is why: I frequent my favorite places on a weekly basis, and location greatly influences when and where I decide to indulge in my favorite taco. A good choice for breakfast on any day of the week is Panchito's, where I can enjoy tacos de chorizo con huevo, de lengua, or de barbacoa. On weekends, you will find me at Rosario's, which is an excellent choice because they serve the best fish tacos in America. Three places I frequent for dinner are Soluna—where I can enjoy tacos al pastor, de carnitas, or de barbacoa—Mary Lou's, and La Gloria, which are conveniently located near my home, making it easy to go there for lunch or dinner to enjoy tacos de lengua or chicken tacos.

Why do you think people love tacos in your region and in Texas?

As a historian who studies his tacos, I believe that we have had tacos in this region dating back to the colonial period. Before the Spanish arrival, the native Indians were producing corn tortillas. It was the Spanish who introduced flour from Spain when they came to America. Thus, the great national debate and divide occurred between those who choose corn tortillas and those who choose flour tortillas. I fall in the corn tortilla camp because they have fewer calories and fewer carbohydrates, compared to their flour counterparts. No offense is meant to anyone who enjoys a good tortilla de harina, as even my own daughter and many close friends do.

I also have concluded that tacos took a whole new form in the 1700s when beef was introduced to the taco world. Until then, tacos had been confined to vegetables, chile, and beans. With the introduction of delicately cooked barbacoa, the taco experience was taken to a whole new level.

Chef Johnny Hernandez
LA GLORIA/EL MACHITO

Tell us your story.

I was born and raised in San Antonio. I was raised in the barrio. My dad, Johnny Hernandez Sr., opened the first Mexican restaurant on the West Side. His restaurant was called Johnny's Cafeteria. My dad got the idea of a Mexican-style cafeteria, kind of like Luby's. There was a small molino next to us, a bakery, and a tailor shop. Dad would send me to the molino, or I would go in the morning before school to pick up tortillas for his restaurant. So I grew up helping out. I helped him with prep work after school. My dad did a lot of catering, so he would have enchilada plates and potato salad. We would peel sacks of potatoes everyday after school. I loved it. Looking back, I think it was an interesting childhood. You think of the young people who want to go to culinary school—I grew up around it and I learned to love it. I certainly enjoyed it a lot, more than my brothers and sisters. I scrambled my eggs in the morning, I learned how to make the tortillas, and this was when I was four or five years old. I would hang out behind the scenes with the cooks in the back.

That experience influenced and definitely shaped me. My dad

was determined to find a way to get me to culinary school. It was a far stretch for us, but Dad always thought that a good education was a path to a better life. Back then, the European and French style was the pinnacle of culinary arts. With my parents' efforts, I was able to borrow and save and get to New York. My dad would tell me that he wanted me to learn French cooking and to cook the finer foods that are in international kitchens. His words to me were, "I don't want you to sell 49-cent tacos all your life." So I was determined not to cook Mexican food for many years. My father was the mentor who shaped my work ethic and my character. It was ingrained in me to learn different styles.

But a trip down to Aguas Calientes reconnected me to Mexico and led to a deeper understanding of our local food. I went as a volunteer for a youth ministry fifteen years ago. I had never been in the interior of Mexico as a chef and an adult. I was blown away by the textures and flavors. The food is very simple, yet complex. The moles, salsas, adobos, tacos de bistec, tacos al pastor were so different from what I was accustomed to. I hadn't tasted anything like that ever because Dad's cooking was Tex-Mex, carne asada, northern style, but in interior Mexico, you taste delicious al pastor, great Mexican cheeses, and roasted salsas. I had never seen or tasted a tomatillo.

After my trip to Mexico, I decided I wanted to focus my restaurant on that style of food. I started thinking strategically about styles and regions and about the fundamental basics of the different sauces. I traveled in Mexico and did a lot of research. I wanted to establish a reputation around the interior of Mexico. I saw it as an opportunity as a Hispanic chef to really own this style in the United States, to create an experience that celebrates the authentic cuisine of interior Mexico and captures its rich, diverse culture.

I quickly realized that people weren't familiar with the food, employees weren't relating to the food, and cooks weren't familiar with the process. So I decided to focus on education about Mexico and its foods. And this aligns well with our city. San Antonio, to me, wants to own Mexican food and be proud of it. So let's do it right. Let's do it better than anybody else. I want to build a culture around something very special—a distinct food culture built around authentic Mexican food. That's my mission in life.

What is your most popular taco and why? What makes it a standout or unique?

My cecina taco is the most popular. It is an Old World tradition of curing meat that is still used today in Mexico and at El Machito. The curing of the meat makes this taco stand out among the slew of others you will find in San Antonio.

CECINA TACOS

CHEF JOHNNY HERNANDEZ

First of all, making cecina is an art form. Although it may look deceptively simple, salting and drying meat must be done with precision and lots of care. Cutting the cecina is one of the most important steps and one of the most difficult.

Makes 10 to 12 tacos

1 whole inside round of beef with no fat, 2½ pounds, boneless	Kosher salt Olive oil

With a carving knife, shave slices of the inside round of beef as thinly as possible (no thicker than a corn tortilla). The next step is to cure the meat. This is done with salt and through drying time.

Lay out the slices of beef on sheet trays, being careful not to overlap any of the edges. Lightly sprinkle kosher salt evenly over all the meat and allow to dry at room temperature for a minimum of 2 hours.

You will notice that the salt will begin to extract the moisture from the meat. Wait for the moisture to dry; this might take up to 4 hours, depending on temperature and humidity. (In Mexico, this step is done in the open air with lots of sunlight.)

After the moisture has dried, rub olive oil freely over the slices and stack.

Grill cecina for 2 minutes on each side. Cut into strips. Serve in fresh corn tortillas with pico de gallo and guacamole.

Rosie Castro

COMMUNITY ACTIVIST

Tell us your story.

My name is Maria del Rosario Castro, but people call me Rosie. I am a native of San Antonio. My mother, Victoria Castro, was orphaned in Mexico at about six years of age. She and her sister came to the US with relatives. She never had a chance to complete elementary school, so she wanted me to have the best education possible. She was a maid, cook, and babysitter. I attended Little Flower School for twelve years, then went on to get my BA in Spanish and English from Our Lady of the Lake University. Ten years later, I received a master's degree in environmental management from UTSA. I am a longtime community activist. I was involved in the Chicano civil rights movement, chaired La Raza Unida Party of Bexar County, and ran for city council at age twenty-three on the Barrio Betterment ticket in 1971. I was part of the efforts to bring single-member districts to the legislature in Texas and in the city as well. I retired from Palo Alto College as interim dean of student success. I am the proud mother of Congressman Joaquin Castro, District 20, and HUD Secretary Julián Castro. I have three grandchildren—Carina Castro, Andrea Castro, and Cristian

Castro—and one on the way. Every one of them loves tacos. My daughters-in-law, Erica and Anna, make better tacos then I do!

What's your connection with tacos?

I have eaten tacos all my life. I worked for the City of San Antonio and would have tacos at the Plaza de Armas every morning. My favorite tacos are guacamole puffy tacos, followed by any kind of guacamole tacos and papas con huevo. For the best puffy tacos, I go to Henry's Puffy Tacos.

What's your go-to taco and why?

Guacamole puffy tacos. I cannot eat enough guacamole. Henry's Puffy Tacos makes the best, just the right amount of lettuce and chile. I love the smooth rich green taste and the puffy shell texture. Two are a whole meal for me, even without rice or beans. Guacamole is a great source of good cholesterol.

Why do you think people love tacos in your region and in Texas?

You cannot be a Texan and not like tacos. The whole world is finding out that tacos can be made of almost any great food. Not only are they compact and earth friendly (no plates required), but they are also nutritious. We Mexicans invented tacos as a gift to the world. Our food is conquering the universe.

Edmund Tijerina

SAN ANTONIO EXPRESS-NEWS
TEXAS TACO COUNCIL

Tell us your story.

In my current role, I'm food writer and restaurant critic with the

San Antonio Express-News. I'm a Houston native who took fifteen years and six cities to make my way west along Interstate 10.

After high school, I received my bachelor's in philosophy from Harvard before deciding that I wanted to go into newspapers. I began my career at the *Bay City Daily Tribune* and then went to the *Corpus Christi Caller-Times* before going to New York for a master's in journalism at Columbia.

After grad school, I worked a one-year internship at the *Chicago Tribune* and then went to the *Milwaukee Journal*. Then after six years at the newspaper in Milwaukee, I took a break from journalism to pursue a dream of being a chef. I quit my job and opened my own restaurant. That wonderful experiment lasted a year, and I left Milwaukee to return to my family's hometown and begin working at the *Express-News*.

I covered education for two years, wrote a local column from 2002 to 2008 called "Around the Town" and "Un Poquito de Todo," a column about Latino culture, history, and current events for *Conexión*, a bilingual publication. I also wrote a blog about taquerias on mysanantonio.com called *You Taco-ing to Me?*

Since 2009, I have worked as restaurant critic and food writer for the newspaper's Sunday food section, *Taste*. Our section has won best in the country in its circulation class three years in a row, and I was runner-up in 2011 for "Best Newspaper Restaurant Critic" in the country.

My wife, Lupita Castrejón, and I live near downtown in a historic district with our son, Andrés.

What's your connection with tacos?

I proudly grew up on the home cooking of South Texas and Northern Mexico, and tacos are an essential part of that cuisine. I learned how to make flour tortillas from scratch from my mother.

Once you know how to make tortillas, everything can transform into a taco—from bacon and eggs to peanut butter and jelly to duck confit, and, yes, I have made all those things into excellent tacos.

When I had my restaurant, I initially resisted making tacos because I wanted to serve a more refined look at Mexican cuisine. But customers insisted on tacos and I relented. Mine, however, were on corn tortillas because I wanted to show off the cuisine of interior Mexico.

Now, the decision to eat tacos on corn or flour tortillas is just one of mood and taste. They're both delicious.

You're on the Texas Taco Council. Why are you the Taco Ambassador for your city/region?

I'm honored to have been chosen as a member of the Taco Council. My knowledge of tacos goes beyond finding great ones in San Antonio, but also includes the history and culture of this city and its people. In San Antonio, tacos aren't just a dining option; they're an essential part of our identity.

What's your go-to taco and why?

Taco al pastor. The combination of the brightly seasoned pork, fresh-diced pineapple, crisp onion, pungent cilantro, and a great salsa on a fresh corn tortilla takes me back to some of my best visits to Mexico. It's also a great way to see how well a Mexican restaurant performs.

Why do you think people love tacos in your region and in Texas?

The classic San Antonio tacos start with a slightly flaky flour tortilla, which has almost a biscuit-like texture. Whether they're breakfast tacos made with scrambled eggs or a savory taco stuffed with only a hunk of Polish sausage, sliced brisket, or a pork chop, our tacos provide comforting combinations.

The San Antonio style has spread throughout Texas, and other cities and regions now claim it as theirs. We're happy to share.

Give us the taco landscape for your city/region. Give us your list of favorites and why they're the best.

In San Antonio, we have three main taco styles: breakfast, puffy, and interior Mexican.

Our breakfast tacos are made with flour tortillas and filled either with scrambled eggs and something else or some type of meat or perhaps potatoes.

Puffy tacos begin with raw corn masa that's tossed in a deep fryer and allowed to puff up. That creates the fragile texture of the corn shell that demands quick eating before the mixture turns soggy.

Then there are the classic interior Mexican tacos, with oil-moistened tortillas wrapped around a chopped filling and topped with diced raw onion, minced cilantro, and a fresh salsa.

We in San Antonio tend to take our tacos for granted and don't realize how our heritage of breakfast tacos is part of what makes this city unique. Then when other cities, such as Austin, are savvy enough to market their breakfast tacos and get credit for it, we get outraged for a few minutes, and then we order another taco.

1. **Taco al pastor at Guajillo's**—as close to the best of Mexico as I have eaten in San Antonio.

2. **Tacos potosinos at La Gloria**—I love the contrast of temperatures and the mild spice of the chile de ancho salsa.

3. **Barbacoa tacos at El Milagrito**—beautifully fresh barbacoa that melds wonderfully with either corn or flour tortillas.

4. **Puffy tacos at Ray's Drive Inn**—when you want to understand the fuss about puffy tacos, one taste of the version at Ray's will explain all.

5. **Puffy tacos at Los Barrios**—their puffy tacos have beaten Bobby Flay and have been served at the White House because they're so good. They're crisp, tender, and not greasy and they demand to be eaten quickly because their peak is evanescent. Fortunately, that's easy to do.

6. **Bacon and egg tacos at Mendez**—freshly made South Texas-style home cooking at its finest.

7. **Carne guisada at Amaya's Cocina**—culinary school grads add depth of flavors to a classic dish.

8. **Pork chop taco at Garcia's Mexican Restaurant**—a thin, bone-in pork chop inside a flour tortilla. God, it's perfect!

Stephanie Guerra

PURO PINCHE

Tell us your story.

I was born and raised in San Antonio. I love my city so much that I started a blog called *Puro Pinche* to showcase all the amazing music, arts, and culture that San Anto has to offer. It started as a hobby and now has more than forty thousand followers online and there's more than one hundred events going on every week. It's hard to keep up nowadays!

I not only talk about the events but I also live the life of a truly happy San Antonian . . . one who loves the multicultural, old-fashioned roots of my hometown but also looks forward to new changes and opportunities. I belong to many organizations like Geekdom, San Anto Cultural Arts, and TechBloc that are all helping to advance San Antonio.

I have a large Mexican American family and a pre-teen son. We love to get together and enjoy meals and margaritas, but we also love exploring the city together. Some of my favorite spots to hang out are the Historic Pearl, Southtown, downtown, and most fruit cup stands.

What's your connection with tacos?

Well, I've been eating tacos since I was a baby. I remember being a baby in my car seat at Lisa's Mexican Restaurant almost every Sunday after church. When I got older, I controlled Lisa's jukebox and ordered bean and cheese tacos all on my own. I practically grew up with a taco in hand, whether homemade by my grandma or from the nearest taqueria. My grandma always made her own tortillas at home, and my uncles hunted the meat she cooked for the tacos. I never quite got the hang of making the tortillas on my own, but I'm pretty good at making tamales.

Give me your top five taco spots and why.

1. **El Milagrito**—their chilaquiles taco, so savory.
2. **La Bandera Molino**—for their all-meat barbacoa taco on corn, not greasy.
3. **El Rafa's Cafe**—any taco. They're huge!
4. **Tacos El Regio**—the best late-night street tacos.
5. **Eddie's Taco House**—because they have a drive-through!

Rico Torres

MIXTLI

Tell us your story.

I was born in El Paso in 1979. Spending my early years in the warm shadow of the Franklin Mountains, I developed a strong appreciation for the flavors of Northern Mexico as remembered and interpreted in the border city. Half my family were Chicanos recently divorced from their Lebanese lineage and the other half were Mexican immigrants longing for their rancho back in Zacatecas. My grandmother knew that food (and occasionally alcohol) was an important tool to keep the family bonds strong. Birthday dinners, holidays, and obligatory religious celebrations were planned and executed with a ritualistic fervor. Preparations could mean days of toasting chiles, grinding masa, and making moles in the same way my Abuelita Lola had grown up with. To an outsider, it may have seemed like a thankless job, but to the family members who ate at those meals, it was a testament to the power of love through food. It was in that time that, as the oldest of a horde of cousins, I was unknowingly bestowed my own torch to carry into the next generation of patriarchs.

As an adult, I'm inspired by the histories of my families, colored by their desires, dreams, compromises to traditions (sometimes tyrannical in nature), and even their folklore. Like the time my grandmother poured hot water on an owl that would perch on her fence for weeks, taunting the family, and it turned into a woman.

Nowadays, I spend my time honoring and rediscovering the foods of my Mexican heritage at Mixtli, where I am a co-owner. This restaurant, created by Diego Galicia and myself, strives to preserve the historically rich foods of Mexico from its pre-Hispanic roots to its contemporary evolution and integrated worldly influences. We seek to protect these values of cooking and promote them through education and example. Currently, the restaurant, still in its modest beginnings, sits in a renovated train car and only seats twelve guests a night. Mixtli, which means "cloud"

in Nahuatl, focuses on one Mexican state at a time for a span of forty-five days. We create menus that exemplify the history, geographies, influences, and traditions of each of the thirty-two states. Mixing ancient cooking techniques, such as nixtamalization—cooking dried maize in an alkaline solution—and fermentations, and modern tools, we create dishes that can be described as progressive yet fundamentally true. This ancient cooking method makes the corn more digestible, easier to grind, and it adds flavor and nutritional value.

Why do people love tacos so much?

I think people love tacos because they satisfy on so many levels.

First, a good tortilla—a taco can live or die based on the quality of the tortilla. Secondly, the filling—which can be anything from beans to braises to simply rajas of chile—can be, and should be, delicious on its own. Unlike the burger or pizza, which lose their essence the more they stray from their original concept, a taco can be as diverse as you want. Lastly, when a taco is complete with an amazing salsa then you have reached the holy trinity of taste. And an experience like that is what makes a good taco an absolute favorite.

BEEF SUADERO TACOS WITH
PASILLA CHILE SALSA

MIXTLI

Suadero is sometimes referred to as "rose meat." This is a light pink cut of meat that looks like a muscle and can be confused with hanger steak, but it is actually the navel beef plate, consisting of the trapezius muscle of the beef.

Makes 18 tacos

BEEF SUADERO

2 to 3 pounds beef suadero

2 teaspoons olive oil

⅓ cup dry chile spice mix
(guajillo, chipotle, pasilla,
árbol, and ancho peppers,
lightly toasted and
ground to a fine powder)

2 heads large garlic cloves
cut in half

½ large white onion,
roughly chopped

8 whole cloves

15 whole black peppercorns

½ cup roughly chopped
cilantro

3 cups whole milk

½ cup water

Plantain leaves

Salt

Coat meat with oil and rub with salt and spices. Move to a medium-sized dutch oven and add the remaining ingredients. Cover with plantain leaf and lid. Cook in preheated oven at 275 degrees for 6 hours, or until meat is very tender. Allow to cool and scrape off any excess fat attached to meat; shred finely. Strain braising liquid and return sauce and meat to dutch oven. Keep warm until ready to use.

SALSA DE CHILE PASILLA

8 cleaned chile negro pods, lightly toasted, then rehydrated in warm water

½ large red onion

3 large tomatoes, blanched and skin removed

1 teaspoon sugar

3 garlic cloves

1 teaspoon white wine vinegar

Salt

For the salsa de chile pasilla negro: combine all ingredients in blender and purée until completely smooth, approximately 5 minutes. Thin out salsa using rehydrating liquid until desired consistency is reached. Strain through fine-mesh sieve if necessary and season with salt.

Heat a large skillet on high heat. Add 2 tablespoons of vegetable oil to hot pan and add salsa to "fry." Stir and cook for approximately 5 minutes to fully combine flavors. Adjust seasoning and cool. Place in a squeeze bottle.

LIME-PICKLED ONIONS

2 large onions
¼ cup fresh lime juice
Pinch sugar

Thinly slice onions into rings; rinse under cold water for 30 seconds. Place in a small bowl and add lime juice and sugar. Allow to sit at least 2 hours.

TORTILLAS

18 ounces prepared yellow corn masa,
    rolled into 1½-ounce balls
Lime wedges

Press masa using a tortilla press and cook tortillas, flipping every 20 seconds until tortilla puffs up. Keep warm in a kitchen towel until ready to use.

Lay warm tortilla on a plate and spoon the suadero meat in the center. Top with pickled onions and chile powder. Squeeze salsa into nice dollops around meat and garnish with lime wedge.

Imelda Sanchez

HENRY'S PUFFY TACOS

Tell us your story.

My father's story begins when he was fourteen. Henry Lopez started his restaurant endeavors when he worked with his eldest brother Ray at his restaurant in the 1950s. It was at a young age that Henry dreamed of opening his own restaurant. While working alongside his brother, they experimented with many deep-fried food items. They became best known for their fried crispy corn dogs and fried chicken. Along came deep-frying corn (masa) dough and they found that they puffed up. They stuffed them and called them crispy tacos.

About eight years later, Henry and his brother Louie opened their first restaurant called El Taco Food to Go. They sold the puffed fried corn dough, also calling it crispy tacos, along with other family dishes. El Taco Food to Go was one of the first pickup windows for fast, easy takeout in the inner city. Thereafter, the drive-through was used among many fast food burger joints in the late 60s.

After a few years in business, Henry bought out his brother but eventually closed his restaurant due to street closures. Henry moved to

California. It was there that he saved money, revamped his original El Taco Food to Go concept, and planned his future of returning to San Antonio to live out his dream of opening a restaurant and specializing in the puffed fried corn masa tacos he renamed "puffy tacos."

In 1978, he opened Henry's Puffy Tacos Mexican Restaurant. This restaurant became very popular in the neighborhood and throughout the city. Henry's children joined the family business, also at a very young age, and together continued to cultivate a puffy taco phenomenon. "Henry" the puffy taco mascot was created by Jaime Lopez, Henry's youngest son, and appears at many

San Antonio events. The mascot is a permanent character of the San Antonio Missions minor league baseball team and is ranked among the best mascots by many publications, truly a sight to see. Through word of mouth, Henry's Puffy Tacos has gained nationwide attention. We have been honored and humbled to be featured in *Texas Monthly, Southern Living, Wall Street Journal, New York Times* magazine, *Sports Illustrated,* and featured by Rachael Ray and Martha Stewart.

What is your most popular taco and why? What makes it a standout or unique?

A puffy taco is something no one had ever heard of. It wasn't until our very own Henry's Puffy Tacos became popular that we started hearing about a few others who claimed to be making the same corn shell many have called crispy tacos, crisped tacos, or puff tacos. There are many imitations and variations out there now. I guess we can say, "often imitated, never replicated."

Throughout the years, we have received many phone calls from other restaurant owners from the southern Valley to up north, asking how we make our puffy tacos. Of course, we do not share our recipe or the process. It is an art form made with love and takes precious time! We currently sell more than one thousand puffy tacos a day and have sold more than 20 million Henry's puffy tacos to date. We offer eight different fillings and numerous toppings. They include the spicy beef fajita that gained national recognition by a compilation of food critic reports as one of the top best tacos in the United States. We take great pride in maintaining a high-quality product, providing a fun, family environment with our friendly staff, and sharing our family dishes for all to enjoy.

Ellen Riojas Clark, PhD

PROFESSOR EMERITA, DEPARTMENT OF BICULTURAL BILINGUAL STUDIES UNIVERSITY OF TEXAS AT SAN ANTONIO

Tell us your story.

I was born in San Antonio and this is where I will die. This is my town, my city. Went to elementary middle and high school here. I attended San Antonio College my first two years, got my BA from Trinity University, my MA from the University of Texas at San Antonio, and my PhD from the University of Texas at Austin.

As a professor in the Department of Bicultural Bilingual Studies at the University of Texas at San Antonio since the 70s, I now serve as professor emerita. My position as research coordinator for the innovative Academy for Teacher Excellence has been most stimulating for we have influenced the field of bicultural bilingual education. My work in visual ethnography is now the highlight of what I do. Three National Endowment for the Humanities grants that focused on Mexican American and Latino literature and culture for teachers started me on this trek. As content director for the Scholastic Entertainment PBS animated series *Maya & Miguel*, I made sure Latino biculturalism was addressed in depth. Now as producer of a prizewinning documentary *The Artist Speaks: Exploring Who I Am* with three more documentaries in the works is what I do in my retirement.

I have been fortunate to have contributed to the cultural and civic life of San Antonio and have been recognized with many awards including being crowned as Queen Huevo by the San Anto Cultural Center. I love being on the Mi Tierra Restaurant mural

wall with people always asking me what did I do to deserve such an honor. As one of the Dos Abuelas who wrote book reviews and travel articles for the *San Antonio Express-News*, I have reached a wider arena. I have retired as La Mera Mera Tamalera for the Guadalupe Cultural Art Center where I taught the cultural art of tamale making for more than eight years to groups as large as four hundred. I am the mother of two engineer daughters, the abuela of four granddaughters, the oldest an engineer, and with another soon on the same path.

What's your connection with tacos?

As funny as it might sound, we never had tortillas growing up as there was not any place to buy them in our neighborhood. Though Jalisco Restaurant did exist, it was south of where we lived. When I was about thirteen, we started going to church on the west side of town where there was a molino—Sanitary Tortillas—by our church.

My siblings and I thought we had died and gone to heaven when my dad would stop and buy fresh corn tortillas. He always brought a salt shaker and he would salt a tortilla, roll it up, and hand us each one. Unbelievable.

On a serious note, I believe there's an important connection between culture, community, and food. It's learning about your cultural identity, which is related to your ethnic identity. Most important is to know who you are, and who you are is related to what you eat and what you know about food and about memories about food.

What's your go-to taco and why?
Leftover steak or roast beef pieces heated in their own juices or pieces of homemade fried chicken in a corn tortilla. My dad would make roast beef for lunch one Sunday and the next, fried chicken. My friends loved it when he would heat up the corn tortillas in the same frying pan and make tacos for our late Sunday supper. My teenage memories of my dad, of the smells, the tastes, and the simplicity of those tacos—all those are part of me as I do the same on Sundays.

Give me your top five taco spots and why.
1. **Mi Tierra**—the egg and crispy bacon slice taco. The egg is always soft scrambled and the thickly sliced bacon is super crispy—just the way I like it.
2. **Los Barrios**—their fried corn tortilla taco with queso and jalapeno slices is magical.
3. **Taquería Aguascalientes (near UTSA)**—good solid tacos with fresh ingredients.
4. **Mario's Taco Truck**—their carne asada tacos.
5. **Old Danny's**—all their tacos.

DOMINGO SANTO BRUNCH:
LENGUA AND SCRAMBLED EGGS
IN HOJA SANTA TACOS

ELLEN RIOJAS CLARK

The leaves of the hoja santa, an aromatic herb commonly called "root beer plant," are used as wrappers or as seasoning for meat, fish, and tamales.

Makes 16 tacos

1 whole lengua, 2 pounds	2 garlic cloves
4 large hoja santa leaves	8 corn tortillas
8 peppercorns	salt to taste

Wash the beef tongue. Wrap in hoja santa leaves with peppercorns and fresh garlic cloves. Cover well with foil and cook at low setting in a slow cooker overnight for 8 hours. Peel the tongue and discard covering. Shred, salt lightly, and keep covered until ready to serve.

SALSA VERDE CON HOJA SANTA

2 serrano chiles

6 tomatillos, fresh

¼ onion

1 small hoja santa leaf

1 avocado

salt

In a food processor, blend the serrano chiles, tomatillos, onion, and hoja santa. Add avocado and blend then add salt to taste. Put salsa in a small bowl.

SCRAMBLED EGGS

8 eggs

1 tablespoon olive oil

2 hoja santa leaves, shredded

8 flour tortillas

Beat the eggs and soft cook them in a little olive oil on low to medium heat. Add the finely shredded hoja santa to the eggs and mix until eggs are done. (Note: a little of this herb goes a long way.)

Add the lengua and the salsa to corn tortillas. Separately, add scrambled eggs and hoja santa to flour tortillas. Don't forget the mezcal and tequila to complete the Domingo Santo brunch!

Xavier Cortez

MI TIERRA

Tell us your story.

My story starts with my father, Pedro Cortez, coming from Mexico as a teenager. He was very excited and especially when he saw the Mercado. He had an entrepreneur's spirit, he loved the music, and he saw how the troubadours were here in San Antonio and how the food was like Mexico. So he named his first little restaurant Mi Tierra, which means "my country," to mean something for all his paisanos (paisano means you come from the same country).

Later, I realized how important the word "tierra" was to the Mayas, the Incas, the Aztecs: tierra was like mother earth. So Mi Tierra had so many meanings, and that is why I selected Emiliano Zapata as the restaurant icon because of his principles. So those who work la tierra, the earth, it belongs to them. The farmers would work the earth, but the aristocrats took it from them, so he fought for those farmers and all the right things. These are the things my father represented, so tierra, mi tierra, mother earth . . . I thought, wow, this is beautiful.

In the old days this area of the Mercado was booming with a lot of Mexicans. And then urban renewal comes in and the neighborhood starts to disappear and I realized how important the Mercado area was for our people. It was so important to preserve all of the traditions. Mi Tierra became an iconic area where many Latinos come to nourish their spirit. Not just with the taco or nacho but also with music and dance and everything that they are.

At Mi Tierra, we have a great mural. In the beginning, I talked to my artist friend, El Indio from Mexico. He showed me a lot of sketches of Indios, Aztecs, Mayans, pyramids, and I said it's getting close to my heart, but I feel it's more about my father, the founder of Mi Tierra, and his heart. So the mural started with my father, my mother, my sister on one side with the four brothers right below them because we were below our parents. And we highlighted my father and mother and it became about the American Dream and his journey.

The mural is done with so much love and passion for who we are, our heritage. I continue to place more and more people and leaders who have accomplished something in San Antonio and in this country. I also put some heroes of Mexico like Francisco Madero and Zapata. I'm very proud of this American story and this mural that hopefully one day will be at the Smithsonian. This mural is about the American Dream.

It is a cultural experience coming to Mi Tierra and San Antonio. The city has so many deep roots and the people themselves are unique. I believe that's what Mi Tierra showcases: our people, the hospitality, the heart—the corazón of our people is incredible. People tell me every day they've never met people like us and it makes me so proud of our culture and being in this country.

Why do you think people love tacos so much?
Well, being born eating tacos, I didn't know what a sandwich was. I would trade my tacos for sandwiches with the gringos so I could eat the bologna sandwiches they had.

The taco is perfection when you spread the little refried bean and you put your chorizo con huevo or your papa con chorizo or your frijoles con chorizo. Of course, we got the bacon and egg and ham and egg, which is a little bit gringo-ish. But then we add the green sauce and it's all Mexican American.

TACOS DE PUERCO EN SALSA VERDE

MI TIERRA

Makes 15 to 20 tacos

3 to 4 pounds pork shoulder	1 cup poblanos
1 cup chicken broth	3 to 5 serranos
1 cup diced white onions	½ bunch cilantro, chopped
5 cloves garlic, diced	Salt
1 pound tomatillos	Sugar

Cut the pork shoulder into large pieces, approximately 5 inches. Season with salt and cook in a slow cooker with 1 cup of chicken broth, the onions, and the garlic for 4 to 5 hours.

Meanwhile, on a large baking sheet, place tomatillos, poblanos, and serranos and bake at 450 degrees until all are charred.

Destem and deseed the poblanos under cold water. Place tomatillos, poblanos, and serranos in a blender and blend well.

Add the blended mixture to the pork and let simmer for 30 minutes. Add the chopped cilantro and turn off the heat. Adjust the seasoning with sugar to reduce any bitterness and add salt to enhance flavor.

Patricia Sánchez

ASSOCIATE PROFESSOR, BICULTURAL-BILINGUAL STUDIES
UNIVERSITY OF TEXAS AT SAN ANTONIO

Tell us your story.

I'm a professor at UTSA and a mom of two daughters who love Abuelita's homemade chicken tacos. I am originally from El Paso but have lived in San Antonio now for eleven years. I knew Mando when he drove a jeep everywhere in Austin and could do a stand-still back flip. Lately, I have been experimenting with chicken, cilantro, tomato, and turmeric for a fusion of Mexican and South Asian tacos—you heard it here first.

What's your connection with tacos?

This is like asking, "What's your connection to breathing?" I've always eaten some kind of taco in my home or at restaurants. Growing up on the border in El Paso, I saw that burritos were more popular, but burritos are essentially tacos with flour tortillas, stuffed with just about anything: beans and cheese, carne, chicken, chile verde, papas con mayonesa, any leftovers in your fridge—even pasta! Just throw it into a flour tortilla. But I've never eaten the US hard shell tacos with ground beef—too Americanized.

What's your go-to taco and why?

Bean and cheese breakfast tacos on flour tortillas—but preferably with white cheese. And, of course, no canned beans.

Give me your top five taco spots and why.

1. La Parrilla—quick breakfast tacos, good prices, near my house, locally owned. They converted an old Arby's into their restaurant.
2. Amaya's Cocina—great picadillo tacos! Family-owned place with a cool East Side vibe.
3. Taco Haven—chorizo and egg and all their breakfast tacos. A good place to have meetings and breakfast.
4. El Piquín—the quintessential Mexico City street taco: mini and spicy. Open super late.
5. Taquería Aguascalientes—best gorditas in town, hands down.

Todd Coerver

TACO CABANA

Tell us your story.

I'm the chief operating officer for Taco Cabana. I came to the company as its chief brand officer in late 2009 and then was elevated to chief operating officer in fall 2012. Taco Cabana was started in 1978 by Felix Stehling in San Antonio in the shadows of Trinity University. It began as a popular late-night stop for the after-bar crowd to fill up at the end of a long night. But its authentic flavors and affordable prices quickly brought the concept success across its twenty-four hours of operation. What made Taco Cabana special was its unique blend of great handmade Mexican food (fresh-made tortillas, salsas made from scratch daily, fajitas grilled over an open flame), real tequila margaritas and selection of beers, as well as its relaxing patios, its twenty-four-hour service, and the convenience of a drive-through . . . all served up at fast-food prices. Today, those foundational points of difference continue to drive the success of the brand at its nearly 170 locations across Texas, Oklahoma, and New Mexico.

What is your most popular taco and why? What makes it a standout or unique?

Surprising to many, our most popular taco is the simplest item on our menu—the bean and cheese taco. Made up of our house-made refried beans, served up on a fresh tortilla, and topped with shredded cheese—it is Texas comfort food in the purest sense of the word. It is the one product on our menu that people order for breakfast, lunch, snack, dinner, and late night. It is *the* Mexican food item for all occasions.

Why do you think people love tacos so much?

In Texas, tacos are comfort food. The taco is pervasive across the state as a staple for any time of the day or night. I think they are so beloved because you can put any combination of flavors inside a tortilla to create a dynamic yet simple eating experience. And the tortilla makes it portable finger food—no knife or fork required. In essence, the taco *is* Texas—relaxed, genuine, and unpretentious, with a uniquely Mexican influence. I think Texans like that the taco is theirs and that people outside of Texas (in the US) don't necessarily "get it." So I think there is a certain Texas pride associated with the taco. It's like our own little secret . . . but the secret is starting to get out there.

Vanessa Del Fierro

LAS CORONELAS ALL-FEMALE MARIACHI

Tell us your story.

I'm a singer, violinist, and director of Las Coronelas All-Female Mariachi. I absolutely enjoy anything that is associated with performance arts. Currently, I have an album titled *Pistolas Y Leyendas: The Mexican-American Experience*. The album touches on topics such as immigration, Mexican legends, stories about love encounters, our Mexican culture including food, and more. I am a proud Mexican American, born of Mexican parents from Matamoros and Río Bravo, Tamaulipas. My Mexican culture is instilled in my soul, and I project that through my music.

I grew up on the south side of San Antonio, an area filled with vast amounts of food, culture, passion, and music. I have one sister, Monica, and two brothers, David and Eric. We all grew up loving la comida Mexicana. It was the only food served in our household, with the exception of the occasional hamburger. Being that my dad was from Matamoros, he loved tortillas de harina. I grew up thinking tortillas de harina were served at every restaurant because we had them all the time, at every meal, but I was soon corrected by my American friends at a Bill Miller's restaurant encounter. But guess what? Bill Miller's serves breakfast tacos now!

I love that our parents instilled our culture in us at such a young age. I feel that a part of my soul would have been missing if they had done things differently. Culture is important; it's the essence of who we are as human beings, what we represent, and our foundation for what we can become.

What's your connection with tacos?

Tacos are a tradition in my family. It is a part of our culture. In our family, it is important to have great food because it is what unites us. We have great conversations, and food has always been an important centerpiece. Tacos are also easy to pack on the go. Our mother always made it a part of our breakfast and lunch to take to school, plus it was cost effective for our large family. At dinner time, we make anything into a taco. I can't ever have a steak or pork chop with silverware like a normal human being; I always turn it into a taco with a tortilla de harina, refried beans, lemon, and jalapeños.

Why do you think people love tacos in your region and in Texas?

Every region, city, or country has its own stamp that identifies them—in culture, food, or music. Tacos for us Texans are

important because we can include them in every meal and in so many different formats. Whether it be an elegant gathering or a fun family dinner, you can adapt your tacos to fit any occasion. You can make them as fancy or as simple as you'd like.

Give me your top five taco spots and why.

1. Chago's Taco Truck—a small, family-owned taco truck that's open late. The food is delicious. It's the best place for mini-taquitos.

2. Cristan's Tacos—for breakfast tacos. And they serve the best barbacoa tacos with refried beans in town. The tortilla de harina is perfect. It was close to my mom's house so we would go there every morning.

3. Don Pedro's—for dinner tacos. Also family-owned, Don Pedro's is an iconic place in Southside SA, where I grew up. They have authentic Mexican cuisine, but also delicious Tex-Mex. I love their beef fajita tacos and carne guisada with cheese and jalapeños.

4. **Mi Tierra**—I love the musical ambience, and they *never* close. After a night out with friends or family, we go there, listen to music, and have some tacos. On Thanksgiving one year when my sis and I didn't want turkey, we opted for papa con huevo tacos with coffee at Mi Tierra instead.

5. **Taco Cabana**—for drive-through tacos. I usually order the two taco combo, chips and queso, and a sweet tea. After performances, I pick up tacos and watch Netflix.

Eddie Vega

EL TACOLICO
TEXAS TACO COUNCIL

Tell us your story.

It all started at a little house on 11th Street in McAllen, from where I went to two elementary schools, one junior high, and three high schools. No, I wasn't kicked out of any of them—it was just grown-ups thinking of my best interests and moving me around. After high school, I moved to San Antonio where I've spent most of the last twenty years.

I say "most" because I also spent a year as a missionary in

southern Mexico, working in rural development. That's where I first learned to cook and was made aware that some beans are black and rice can stay white. Refried pinto beans were not the main reason I left Veracruz, but they were definitely a contributing factor.

Presently, I am a high school teacher, father of two children, and a working poet/spoken word artist. I read and perform at various venues around town, gaining fame with poems about Tejano culture and food. My taco poems (yes, plural) endear me to audiences who understand the value and joy of a good breakfast taco.

What's your connection with tacos?

I woke up to the sound and smell of flour tortillas being made by my mother all throughout my childhood. My father ate tortillas with every meal, usually corn. Every barbecue in the Valley involved tortillas, with each person making their own tacos.

Today, along with my writing partner, Teno Villarreal, I review different taco spots around town for our blog, *We Taco Bout It*.

You're on the Texas Taco Council. Why are you the Taco Ambassador for your city/region?

I'm on the Council because I dream about tacos, write about tacos, give tacos as gifts and compensation, and perform taco-themed poetry.

Why do you think people love tacos in your region and in Texas?

Tex-Mex was born in San Antonio and breakfast tacos reign above all others. Every person has a favorite go-to on their morning commute, and families get together on weekends at houses and restaurants to share barbacoa (and Big Red).

Give us your top ten list and why they're the best.

By no means is this a ranking order; just ten favorites.

1. **La Bandera Molino**—great tortillas, great fillings, perfect authenticity. There's nothing fake about this place.
2. **Los Angeles Tortilleria y Panaderia**—my go-to for best breakfast tacos. An excellent place to take the family for weekend breakfast. Great barbacoa de res and barbacoa de borrego.
3. **Taqueria Datapoint**—excellent at all hours. Breakfast and late night. Mini-tacos de asada at 1:00 a.m. are magical.
4. **Garcia's Mexican Restaurant**—try the brisket taco. You won't regret it.
5. **Tacos El Regio**—yes, it's in front of a male strip club, but don't let that detract or distract. A great late-night destination; they don't open until 10:00 p.m.
6. **Ray's Drive Inn**—in the heart of the West Side. They invented and have the patent for the puffy taco. Others have tried, but they are pale imitations of this specialty.
7. **Taco Haven**—the flour tortillas you'll dream about. An excellent gathering spot for every level of San Anto society.
8. **Tommy's**—the one on San Pedro disproves the myth that there are no good tacos on the North Side. They have a barbacoa and Big Red special.
9. **El Taco Tote**—best of the chains. Selection is excellent for late-night munching. Also, they have an excellent selection of salsas and dressings for your tacos.
10. **Your abuelita**—she still makes tortillas from scratch and can manage to feed a large family with any meat available, plus all the eggs she can spare. Most importantly, affordable. Requires cariño as payment and who doesn't have cariño to spare?

FRIDAY FOOTBALL TACOS

EDDIE VEGA

These tacos are to be eaten on the Friday after Thanksgiving as you watch all the college football you can stand.

Makes 2 tacos

1 tablespoon vegetable oil

2 tomatoes, diced

1 cup diced onion

1 serrano pepper

Leftover turkey

Cayenne powder

Garlic powder

Salt

Pepper

Add oil to pan over medium high heat. Add tomatoes, onion, and pepper. Sauté until onions are clear. Add turkey and seasonings. Reduce heat and cook about 10 minutes. Place filling into corn or flour tortillas. (Your preference; mine is whichever I have in the fridge at the time.)

Carmen Tafolla

STATE POET LAUREATE OF TEXAS

Tell us your story.

I am a native San Antonian who comes from a family that has been eating tacos here since before there were flags! I write poetry, prose, fiction and nonfiction, children's works and academic works. But one of the topics I'm known most for is the meaning of food and the cultural and survival messages transmitted through food traditions. Among the twenty-something books I've authored are *The Holy Tortilla and a Pot of Beans, Tamales, Comadres, and the Meaning of Civilization,* and *What Can You Do with a Paleta?*

While I have a PhD and have taught at many colleges and universities throughout the Southwest, the knowledge I most prize is kitchen knowledge, the things my mother and grandmothers taught me. And my family members keep me humble. After I was named State Poet Laureate of Texas in 2015 in the Texas Senate chambers, with a bunch of well-dressed legislators and some pretty cool state artists and musicians, my primita Rosie said to me, with a sigh, "Well, that's nice. Almost as impressive as the time you won the Golden Palote for best tortilla!"

What's your connection with tacos?

My mom made homemade flour tortillas for my dad at every meal, and her special, super-garlicky salsa for huevos rancheros for breakfast. I loved the way her flour tortillas puffed up so toasty and light, and the way the salsa sitting in her molcajete had a fresh-from-the-garden flavor that floated into the air and enticed your nose . . . so my morning tacos all through high school were tacos rancheros—just the tortilla with the ranchero sauce. (Because I didn't like eggs, so I always had my huevos rancheros without the huevos!)

What's your go-to taco and why?

Bean and cheese, with a sprinkle of fresh salsa. If you can get it in a handmade, thick corn tortilla, that's out of this world! If not, a well-toasted flour tortilla that puffs up, estilo Tejas, is right up alongside it. This one gives me the strength and the protein to warm that tummy and keep it going, especially on days that seem to never end. Besides, somehow it always tastes like comfort food, something your grandma would have given you. Even when there was nothing en la cocina at the end of the month, there was always bean and cheese tacos.

Give me your top taco spots and why.

1. **Peter El Norteno**—great tortillas.
2. **Panchito's**—sabor in the ingredients!
3. **Henry's Puffy Tacos**—great puffy tacos.
4. **Mi Tierra**—because Zapata's eyes wouldn't let anyone do injustice to tacos!

Melissa Guerra

MELISSA GUERRA LATIN KITCHEN MARKET

Tell us your story.

I never thought of tacos as a category until I went outside of Texas for college. I was a little horrified by "taco night" in our cafeteria: fried beef crumbs flavored with rancid spice mixes, shoved into a half-moon-shaped corn chip that broke when you got it near your face. "What is that?" I asked. "It's a taco." said one of my Yankee student friends. *What?*

At home, we had freshly made tortillas at every meal, usually both flour and corn. We used them to scoop up guisado, rice, beans, and even soup and mashed potatoes. Who needed a fork? A tortilla was the blank canvas on which every dish was presented. Sometimes I wonder which was the side dish, the tortilla or the hot meal? The main dishes changed, but the tortillas were always there.

Making a taco is actually a more formalized process of the way we served our meals at home. Someone else had filled and folded your tortilla, as opposed to you doing it yourself at the table. Fancy stuff.

Eventually, I decided to go on my own taco crusade, and I opened a taco restaurant. It was a lot of fun, but I had to close it. In its heyday, we served a lot of satisfied customers. I guess it was my attempt to right all the taco wrongs I had seen in my lifetime, starting back in my college years. (I wonder if they ever got it right in my old cafeteria. I have a feeling they probably switched to soy crumbles instead of beef. Sigh.)

So now I write taco recipes and blog about Latin American food. I get to try out new recipes and techniques, and I can make awesome tortillas. The secret? Practice, practice, practice. (Having OCD tendencies doesn't hurt either.) I even wrote a taco app, which features some pretty easy, delicious recipes.

These days, we eat loads of tacos in my household, but I have to say we enjoy them the way we did when I was a kid. We roll our own.

What's your connection with tacos?

Our favorite drive-though place was El Pato on University Drive, right across from Pan American University in Edinburg. El Pato was this little clapped-together shack, painted white with red trim, and long yellow or white fluorescent light bulbs trimming the eaves. At night, the taco stand buzzed from the hum of the lights, the clamoring of the customers, and the frenzy of junebugs that flew blindly into both. Everyone had his or her favorite Pato. I always ordered the beef guisado with beans. The ladies in the back rolled out fresh flour tortillas and ladled in the hot fillings while you waited. I doubt any of our orders made it home to be served on a plate. We always ate them in the car on the way home from football games.

What is your go-to taco and why?

Honestly, my favorite taco is chicharrones (pork rinds) en salsa. Chicharrones are bacon's naughty cousin, the one the family doesn't talk about. Always ready for a party, chicharrones hang out at the local gas station or convenience store, ready to go. "Anytime, anywhere"—that's their motto. And when we are caught with a bag . . . well, you should take a picture of that guilty face. You know you love 'em. So why keep pork love a secret? Gimme some skin and eat 'em out loud.

TACOS DE CHICHARRÓN
WITH SPICY CABBAGE

MELISSA GUERRA

Serves 2 generously

1 cup finely shredded
   cabbage
1 small can sliced jalapeños
1 pound fresh tomatoes
1 clove garlic
4 teaspoons vegetable oil
Salt

Pepper
1 ounce chicharrones
   (pork rinds)
8 corn tortillas, heated
¼ cup crumbled queso
   fresco

Place the shredded cabbage in a small glass bowl. Pour liquid from the can of jalapeños over the cabbage, toss well, and allow to marinate for about 10 minutes, while you prepare the tacos.

Fill a 2-quart saucepan with water and bring to a boil. Add the whole tomatoes and allow to simmer for 1 minute. Remove the tomatoes and discard the water. Peel the tomatoes, cut in half, and remove the seeds. Add the tomato pieces to a blender, along with the clove of garlic. Make a puree.

Add the vegetable oil to a 9-inch skillet and heat for about 1 minute over a medium flame. Add the tomato puree and simmer for about 3 to 5 minutes until the sauce is reduced.

Divide the chicharrones between all of the tortillas. Top with the warm sauce, sliced jalapeños, marinated shredded cabbage, and crumbled queso fresco.

Houston

I love Houston. It's a great city. It has great art, music, and food scenes, and it is one of the most multicultural cities in the United States. With that comes a diverse selection of places to eat. And the people of Houston love it and they own it. They wear their Houston pride on their arms and shirts, they hashtag it, and they support each other and love to have fun! The biggest city in Texas with more Latinos than any other city in the state . . . you're going to have a lot of taco options!

THE HOUSTON ICONIC TACO:
TACOS ON WHEELS!

Regional Mexican, street, and taqueria style—it doesn't matter as long as it comes from a truck. And there's no shortage of roaming taco trucks parked downtown, in a neighborhood, and by the gas station. Houston's taco scene owes it big-time to taco trucks that serve up the best al pastor, bistec, carne asada, tripitas, and, yes, even some fajitas. There's nothing better than eating standing up in front of your favorite taco truck, jamming to your tacos at Boombox Taco, trying the red chile creations at TacoKeto, or chasing down LaMacro truck on your bike. In diverse and immigrant-friendly Houston, taco trucks are the kings of the road.

TACO JOURNALISM'S TOP CINCO

1. **TacoKeto trailer**—The koketadas are one of a kind and blazing red hot!
2. **Estilo Taco Tierra Caliente**—taqueria-style barbacoa and bistec, authentic all the way.
3. **Villa Arcos**—the breakfast taco spot on the East End.
4. **Boombox Taco trailer**—nothing compares to Alejandro's style in music and tacos.
5. **Gerardo's Drive-In**—cooking up to 140 cabezas de vaca every weekend.

HOUSTON TACO AMBASSADORS

Yes, we had an in with our lead photographer Marco Torres, a.k.a. Marco from Houston. Marco is H-town and knows what's up with the tacos. But we had to leave room for más gente to enter the Texas Taco Council. Jay Roscoe, a.k.a. Guns and Tacos, has been scouring Houston looking for tacos for ten years now, and he was a perfect fit. Iveth Reyes not only captures the tacos but she also brings her crafty DIY style, her Latina culture, and her family as she introduces us to her mom's cochinita pibil tacos. #QueRico!

THAT HOUSTON TACO VIBE

So what's Houston like from a local's perspective? Our own Marco gives it to us in his own words:

Houston is one of the most diverse cities in the country, and its residents are supremely committed to succeed by any means necessary. It is a hustle town, and the idea of receiving something of quality at a bargain price is optimal for many of its citizens. Which is why I think that Houston is so enamored with the taco. On any given day, Houstonians have access to a vast array of delicious tacos, from traditional carne asada, trompo, and barbacoa to exotic, experimental, and fusion offerings. We stand in line for that perfect breakfast taco on our way to work, grab a quick lunch at the local taco truck, and then sit down with the family at the neighborhood taqueria in the evenings. Eating tacos in Houston is more than just a meal, it's a lifestyle.

THE *TACOS OF TEXAS* TATTOO

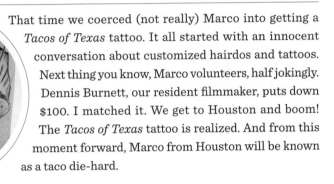

That time we coerced (not really) Marco into getting a *Tacos of Texas* tattoo. It all started with an innocent conversation about customized hairdos and tattoos. Next thing you know, Marco volunteers, half jokingly. Dennis Burnett, our resident filmmaker, puts down $100. I matched it. We get to Houston and boom! The *Tacos of Texas* tattoo is realized. And from this moment forward, Marco from Houston will be known as a taco die-hard.

Saul Obregon Banda

LAMACRO

Tell us your story.

I was born in Monterrey, Mexico, in 1971. When I was nine, my dad decided to migrate to the United States with the whole family of ten to give us a better life, a hope of the American Dream, and an education. I can honestly say that out of all my brothers and one sister, I was the only one who did not want to leave my native city and country, due to my dreams of becoming a professional soccer player.

As time went on, I adapted to the US and started working hard. At the age of fourteen, I was doing everything from helping my parents at night, cleaning offices as a janitor's helper, washing cars, mowing lawns, welding (as I got older), bartending, etc. Soon after graduating from high school, I became a metal sculptor and fabricator, then I went on to finish college and worked in the oil and gas industry as a mechanical designer and engineer for fourteen years. After my layoff in December of 2011, I decided to open what we now know as Taqueria LaMacro.

The name had to be unique, and I swore that if I ever opened a business, I would pay tribute to my native city. Thus the name "LaMacro" was born. It was a no-brainer to my oldest brother Ishmael and me as I blurted it out by accident and we agreed that this would be the ultimate name of my restaurant, due to the fame of La Macroplaza in Monterrey. The plaza has political demonstrations, concerts, houses, the governor's palace, and shopping venues, and it's the place where many tourists, families, and friends meet up. Whenever I go back to Monterrey, I tell my local family and friends, "hey, nos vemos en La Macro." This has become my slogan now for my place of business back in Houston. Now I can hear my customers saying to each other over their phone conversations, "hey, nos vemos en LaMacro." This is very touching to me as I have brought a piece of my birth city to life here in the States.

LaMacro was built by myself and general contractors in the heart of Northside, or, as it is now known, North Central Village. While it was fun and many memories were made, it has also taken a toll on me between the hustle and struggle of staying afloat. My first two years were amazing, thanks to my good friend Marco Torres and other local food critics. After my second year, sales went down, and I had to close my original brick and mortar storefront due to local construction of a light rail and traffic diversion. Immediately after closing my doors, my cell phone was ringing nonstop, social media outlets were blasting what had happened, and the local newspaper even wrote a story quoting me saying that we would reopen. Thus, two weeks after we closed, I went over to the flea market and bought a tiny six-foot food cart that had a trompo base on it, paid cash, and we were back in business—this time east of downtown or, as they call it, "EaDo." We now operate out of a huge food truck and have been in that neighborhood ever since.

What is your most popular taco and why? What makes it a standout or unique?

Our most popular tacos are al pastor or, as we call them in Monterrey, "trompo taquiza." It consists of five mini-corn tortillas filled with pork meat that has been slowly roasted on a vertical spit. Then we add cilantro, onion, and pineapple if desired.

What makes them stand out is the unique pork marinade flavor and the fact that you can actually see our trompo on the food truck. I have also been known as a renaissance entrepreneur for bringing this style to Houston.

Sylvia Casares, "Enchilada Queen"

SYLVIA'S ENCHILADA KITCHEN

Tell us your story.

I'm originally from Brownsville and serve the food of my mother in my three restaurants. I graduated from the University of Texas at Austin, I'm a former food scientist, and I opened my first restaurant twenty years ago.

I love to share my Texas border cuisine with my customers—so much so that I built a private cooking school in my Eldridge location, where I teach cooking classes most Saturdays. My most popular class is Tamale 101. Growing up in the Rio Grande Valley, my grandmother would gather everyone together early on Christmas Day for a multifamily, multigenerational tamale-making party, and we duplicate this event after each class.

Some of my recent recognitions came from *USA Today*, where my restaurant was named one of the "Ten Great Mexican Restaurants across the USA." We were also listed in *Texas Monthly* magazine's "Top 50 MexTex Restaurants in Texas," and Rachael Ray wrote that our food "is out of this world!" I was anointed the "Enchilada Queen" by *H-Texas* magazine and was named the cuisine's official spokesperson. I competed on the Food Network's *Beat Bobby Flay Show,* and my book *The Enchilada Queen's Cookbook* will be published in 2016.

I'm the proud mother of three wonderful children: Jason, Celeste, and Nicholas. They exceeded my wildest hopes for education, attending Rice and Harvard, Georgetown University, and Rice University, respectively. They all happily reside not far from Royal Oaks.

What's your connection with tacos?

I grew up eating them at home and then made them for my children. Now I serve a few varieties in my restaurant.

What's your go-to taco and why?

Tacos al carbon because the beef is wood grilled and very tender. The flour tortilla is a recipe from South Texas and is really fresh.

My second go-to is the cabrito taco. It's made from the milk-fed young cabritos (under ten pounds), and we cook them over mesquite wood so they have the flavor of South Texas.

Why do you think people love tacos in your region and in Texas?

Tacos are finger food and are usually budget-friendly. They are typically "fast food" made fresh, so they accommodate our busy lifestyles. I think this applies everywhere you go.

Give me your top five taco spots and why.

Other than my own tacos at Sylvia's Enchilada Kitchen and at home, I enjoy Taqueria Laredo, Mexico Deli, Merida breakfast tacos, the breakfast tacos at Café Amiga in Brownsville, and the shrimp tacos at The Vermillion in Brownsville.

SYLVIA CASARES

Using a baby goat is very important for the flavor and tenderness of this recipe. The milk-fed-only cabritos are a little harder to find, but will make a difference in the final product.

Serves about 7 to 8

SPICE BLEND

¼ cup salt

¼ cup + ½ teaspoon garlic powder

3 tablespoons + 1 teaspoon onion powder

5 teaspoons cayenne

5 teaspoons smoked paprika

2½ teaspoons black pepper

Measure each ingredient accurately. Combine in a small container with a lid. Cover and shake to blend well. Use for seasoning cabrito.

CABRITO PREPARATION

1 10-pound cabrito (baby goat that has only been fed mother's milk)

½ cup corn oil
½ cup spice blend

Brush the oil all over the cabrito, then rub the meat with the spice blend. Cover and allow cabrito to rest and season for about one hour or until your wood or coals are red hot.

Place the cabrito on the hot grill and cook for about five minutes on each side so the skin is slightly golden. If possible, raise the grill to about 18 inches above the fire and grill another 30 minutes. Remove meat from the grill and set it aside until it is cool enough to handle. Cut the grilled cabrito into 8 pieces.

Wrap the pieces in heavy duty aluminum foil and place on a large baking sheet. Bake at 325 degrees for about 2 to 2½ hours.

Serve with corn tortillas, charro beans, guacamole slices, fresh chopped onions, and cilantro.

Chris Shepherd

UNDERBELLY

Tell us your story.

I'm from the Midwest and my family was always down for cooking. My mom and dad were open to letting me cook. When I was eight, we used to go through cookbooks, go to the store, buy everything, and turn around and make it for dinner. And we ate whatever, hot dogs and pizza—a menu out of an eight-year-old's mind. So it kind of progressed from there.

I was probably twenty-one or twenty-two when I realized I wasn't meant to push paper or sit behind a desk. I fell in love with spending time in the kitchen, so I thought, man, this might be fun to do for a living. I decided to make the jump and go to culinary school. But I was also in junior college when I was told it might be good to take a couple of semesters off to figure it out. I thought, "I think I just got kicked out of college."

What I did had to be different, it had to be fun, it had to be something I wanted to do. So I went to culinary school.

With my restaurant, I wanted to show the way we eat. And basically, the decision on the style of the restaurant was to show where we lived, show what we do, showcase the farmers, ranchers, and fishermen, and show the culture of our city. This is my passion and what I love. I love to cook, I love to learn from all cultures, and I decided to do it all at Underbelly. I've been fortunate to receive awards and accolades, but for me it's about learning and expanding, stepping outside your own box, and showcasing our food.

What's your connection with tacos?

Food is food. When it's delicious, it's good and you gotta eat it in Houston. I usually stop by Saturday afternoon after service at Estilo Tierra Caliente. I usually get an al pastor, barbacoa, and a quesadilla to put me over the edge. Food in Houston is based on the cultural diversity of the city, whether it's Vietnamese, Middle Eastern, or tacos. It's all here. With tacos, I like to have three or four, so size matters as well as ingredients and the salsa. I like my tacos small; you should be able to eat your taco in three bites.

What's your top taco place in Houston?

For the most authentic and delicious tacos, I go to Estilo Taco Tierra Caliente and El Hidalguense.

Jessica Villagomez and Alejandro Martinez

BOOMBOX TACO

Tell us your story.

The concept of the gigantic boombox came to Alex about a year ago. He said that he wanted to do something to include his love of music and food into one project, which came out to be Boombox

Taco. When he first mentioned he was going to build it from scratch, no one believed him. I seriously doubted he would be able to turn an ex-plumber's truck into a fully functioning food truck. He left everyone in awe after the truck was completed, including our neighbors who saw him work at it for more than six months. He built everything from the inside to the outside, with a little bit of help from some artist friends. He continues to make improvements on it.

The truck got all its permits on a Friday and the next day, Alex had already confirmed a show that was expecting about two thousand people. Unfortunately, or fortunately, it rained the day of the show and way fewer people showed up. But with the rain and all, Alex and I still decided to do our first sell. Neither of us had worked on a food truck before, but we each had a bit of an idea on how to run a business because we had each worked at family businesses before. Alex helped his father at a butcher store and I helped my mother at a hair salon. There was still a lot of learning to do, but that night we managed to do our first sell.

Of course, we had our kinks. Alex forgot to fill the generator tank and we ran out of power and onions and cilantro. But we were fortunate to have friends who helped us that night. After that nervous but successful night, we realized it was the beginning of something we both love. We have a strong passion for delivering good quality and tasty food to our customers, a lot of whom have become very good friends.

What is your most popular taco and why? What makes it a standout or unique?

It is a tough competition between the steak taco and chorizo taco. What people compliment us a lot about the steak taco is the quality of the meat. The meat is never chewy or greasy. We always strive to cook the steak to a point where it is juicy and full of flavor with a good texture. The chorizo taco is a great contender. People like the chorizo's home-cooked taste. They know it is hard to find a chorizo like the one made by Boombox Taco. Again, it is the quality of the meat cut and the way it is seasoned. The barbacoa is also making a strong mark on our customers. They tell us they love the juiciness of the meat and smoky flavor that the maguey leaf gives it.

Chef David Rodriguez

Tell us your story.

I was born in Mexico City and moved to Houston when I was thirteen years old. I got my first kitchen job when I was fifteen and I've been cooking ever since.

What's your connection with tacos?

In Mexico City, tacos were an essential part of everyone's meals. Since we were pretty poor, stuffing a tortilla with what-ever was the way to make food last. Also, since most of the people walk everywhere or ride public transportation, street vendors are where most people get their food.

What's your go-to taco and why?

I prefer an al pastor taco above them all—something about the complexity of making the meat and how much goes into it.

TRIPITAS (INTESTINE) TACO

CHEF DAVID RODRIGUEZ

Make sure you have a bad ass salsa and some good tortillas.

Makes 10 tacos

5 pounds pork intestine

1 to 2 gallons water

3 cups fresh-squeezed
orange juice

½ cup fresh-squeezed
lime juice.

3 bay leaves

½ cup canola oil

Salt

Pepper

1 onion, medium diced

½ bunch cilantro, roughly
chopped

10 corn tortillas

Make sure the intestine is thoroughly rinsed. This is *very* important as you can only imagine what it holds and you don't want that flavor in your tacos. This should take you at least 30 minutes.

After you rinse the intestine, make sure you remove the excess fat. Take your time and try to keep the intestine's cylinder shape. Fill a medium stockpot with water. Add the intestine. Bring to a boil and lower the heat. Add the orange juice, lime juice, and bay leaves and simmer for about 2 hours. Remove the intestine from the heat and let cool.

Cut or slice the intestine into 1-inch sections. Bring a black cast-iron skillet to high heat, then add the canola oil. Once the oil starts to smoke, add the intestine and fry until golden brown.

Remove from heat, add to tortillas, and top with onions, cilantro, and salsa of your choice. (Cold intestine develops fat, so serve immediately.)

Jay Roscoe

GUNS AND TACOS
TEXAS TACO COUNCIL

Tell us your story.

I'm a welder in Houston, with a big appreciation for Mexican cuisine and culture. While serving in the US Navy, I was stationed in San Diego, so I rented an apartment in Tijuana just a short trolley ride away. It didn't take long before I discovered all the taco stands, which I enjoyed almost daily. I lived there for about nine months and enjoyed every day of it.

Years later in Houston, I came across Patricia Sharpe's *Texas Monthly* article, "The Greatest Tacos Ever Sold." My friend Jake and I decided to hit up all these Houston spots on the list on our lunch breaks. Before long, we were hooked on Houston's taco trucks. Google Maps was a new technology at the time, so I decided to put together a public map of all of the taco trucks in the city. I started writing about tacos on a blog called *Guns and Tacos*, and I posted the map there, encouraging others to send me addresses of their favorite taco trucks to add to the map. The blog became popular on a local level, and I soon had the opportunity to share my favorite spots in other publications such as the *Houston Chronicle, Free Press Houston, My Table Magazine, Texas Monthly, Sugar and Rice* magazine, even *Playboy*. I organized "Taco Truck Crawls," where a convoy of cars and buses traveled around the city to hit up some favorite spots. I also organized taco scouting trips, where a small group would split up and find new taco trucks to add to the map.

You're on the Texas Taco Council. Why are you the Taco Ambassador for your city/region?
I'm not sure who nominated me as Taco Ambassador for Houston, but if I were to guess the reason why, it's probably because I'm the only person who writes pretty much exclusively about Mexican food and drinks. There are a handful of incredibly talented food critics in Houston who write about tacos from time to time, but not exclusively.

In Austin, there are enough taco bloggers to start their own militia. In Houston, it's just me.

What's your go-to taco and why?
I love a great basic fajita taco on corn tortillas with the works. However, if there is a beautiful trompo nearby, I will choose tacos al pastor every time.

Why do you think people love tacos in your region and in Texas?
If you spend a bit of time in Houston, you'll find that we've got one

of the most diverse populations in the nation. You can find food from just about any ethnicity you can think of—if you're okay with driving a few dozen miles.

In short, we've got a lot of variety here due to trucks and restaurants owned by families from many different regions of Mexico. I've spent several years eating Mexican "street food," and I am still constantly discovering new dishes I've never heard of.

I think Houston's lack of zoning laws also makes Houston more of a "mixing pot" than other Texas cities. Our neighborhoods and cultures aren't quite as segregated as they are in other areas, and, as a result, I think most Houstonians are generally a little more tolerant and hospitable.

Give us the taco landscape for your city/region. Give us your top ten list and why they're the best.

Some of my favorite areas include Airline, Long Point, Edgebrook, Telephone, and Hempstead Highway. If you see tire shops, you're getting close. I've always tried to avoid writing top ten lists—I just don't think they're fair. I prefer to send people to a certain area or street, and let them figure it out on their own. After all, the adventure is the fun part—and you might find a better taco truck than the one I sent you to.

Robb Walsh

AUTHOR

Tell us your story.

I came to Austin in 1970 when I was seventeen years old. I was blown away by the barbecue joints and Tex-Mex food. It was like nothing I had ever seen anywhere in the country. It was only a few years before that Fritos bean dip was introduced and my father was addicted to it. I learned how to make guacamole and bean dip and made it for my family and they loved it.

In my later years in Austin, I lived close to El Patio. I was fascinated by the buttered saltines and hot sauce tradition. So when I was researching the food, some of the old-timers said that they ate the buttered saltine with hot sauce before they ate chips and salsa. But it is a taco world. I remember El Matamoros down on East Avenue off I-35 and they were the home of the crispy taco. Austin varied the taco a bit from the puffy taco. So the crispy taco tradition was a big draw in the early Austin Tex–Mex in the 70s. Matt's El Rancho and La Tapatia were super busy, and then interior Mexican came along with places like Fonda San Miguel and Tex-Mex became less popular. Now everyone wanted authentic interior Mexican. And there went the crispy taco tradition. Which was a real Tex-Mex standard for so many years.

When I launched the popular *Taco Truck Gourmet* blog for the *Houston Press* in 2006, it was the first regular coverage of taco trucks in the state. I served as restaurant critic at the *Houston Press* from 2000 until 2010 and at *Houstonia* magazine from 2012 to 2014. I have also served as the editor in chief of *Chile Pepper* magazine and food columnist for *Natural History* magazine, and I'm a frequent contributor to *Gourmet, Saveur,* and *Fine Cooking*.

My 2002 book *Legends of Texas Barbecue Cookbook: Recipes and Recollections from the Pit Bosses* was nominated for the James Beard Award in the Americana category. My first book, *The Tex-Mex Cookbook: A History in Recipes and Photos*, was nominated for the IACP Cookbook Award in the American category. My book *Sex, Death & Oysters* was voted one of the best food books of 2009 by Amazon.com. I also wrote *The Tex-Mex Grill and Backyard Barbacoa Cookbook* and *Texas Eats*.

What's your connection with tacos?

As a restaurant critic and food writer for the *Houston Press*, I became an advocate for taco trucks. In my *Taco Truck Gourmet* blog, I wrote about a new truck each week.

What's your go-to taco and why?

Barbacoa taco at Gerardo's on Patton in Houston. One of the last whole-cabeza barbacoa tacos in Texas.

Give me your top five taco spots and why.

I don't believe in rankings or ratings, but I will recommend five tacos. (To avoid conflict of interest, I will omit the excellent shrimp puffy tacos at El Real Tex-Mex in Houston because I am an owner.)

Crispy tacos at **Amaya's Taco Village** in Austin.

Puffy tacos at **Henry's Puffy Tacos** in San Antonio.

Mollejas tacos at **Tacambaro,** the taco trailer behind Canino's in Houston.

Barbacoa tacos at **Gerardo's** in Houston.

Fajita taco at the **Taconazo** trailer in Houston.

SHARK-BLT TACOS

**DAVID GARRIDO AND ROBB WALSH
(FROM *NUEVO TEX-MEX* BY DAVID GARRIDO
AND ROBB WALSH, CHRONICLE BOOKS)**

Note: since this recipe came out in the Nuevo Tex-Mex *cookbook more than twenty years ago, I have started to substitute "sriracha remoulade" (an ad hoc blend of 1 tablespoon mayo, ½ tablespoon sriracha sauce, and ½ tablespoon creole mustard) for the haba-nero mayo called for here. You can also substitute swordfish, mahi mahi, or another firm fish for the shark.*

Makes 8 tacos

1 pound ½-inch thick shark
steaks, very fresh
1 onion, peeled and cut
into rings
2 tablespoons olive oil
2 teaspoons chile powder
8 freshly fried taco shells
4 strips crisp-cooked bacon,
crumbled

1 head soft lettuce, such as
Boston lettuce, washed
and julienned
1 tomato, seeded and diced
homemade sriracha
remoulade (see note
above)

Preheat the broiler. Marinate the shark steaks and onions in the olive oil and chile powder. Place the onions and the shark under the broiler and turn after 2 minutes. Cook the shark and onions for 3 more minutes or until just done. (Overdone shark is very tough, so be careful.) Cut the cooked shark into long strips, removing any skin or bones. Put the shark meat and onions in the taco shells, top with crumbled bacon, lettuce, tomato, and plenty of homemade sriracha remoulade.

Leo Chavez
TACOKETO

Tell us your story.

My wife Rosie and I, owners of TacoKeto, and our children, Blanca, Leo, and Rocio, are taco lovers. For years, the family tradition was to go out to eat on Sundays, and tacos were a family favorite. However, the family was never 100 percent satisfied with the tacos. Mom's recipe always seemed to please the stomach. Our family's motto has always been to put the needs of others before ours, and so we figured, let's share with others the Mexican food that makes us so happy! After a couple of family meetings and coordinating of schedules, our food truck made its grand opening in February 1997. Dad and daughter Blanca, only thirteen at the time, opened the food truck with no experience and not knowing what to expect. We sold $40-worth of tacos to the very first customer. Nineteen years later, that very first customer still remains loyal. The Chavez family is blessed to have gained taco lovers from numerous cultures. The TacoKeto family's goal is to provide delicious food and friendly service to all our customers. Mom's recipe has come a long way since 1997.

What is your most popular taco and why? What makes it a standout or unique?

Our most famous taco is the koketada. The name comes from the business name, Taco*Keto*. It's basically our small quesadilla with a twist. While most quesadillas are served on a flour tortilla, our koketada is served on a corn tortilla brushed with Mom's secret red sauce recipe, stuffed with Mexican quesadilla cheese and meat of choice, and topped with grilled onions, grilled peppers, cilantro, limes, and a side of grilled potatoes.

Iveth Reyes

TEXAS TACO COUNCIL

Tell us your story.

I was born in Morelia, Michoacán, Mexico, and raised in Houston. My Mexican identity and culture have always been a big part of me and my interests—which, of course, include food. I strive to incorporate the Mexican culture into anything that I create. I believe it is extremely important to highlight the beauty of cultures.

I was raised by an artist mother; she is an inspiration, someone who creates on a daily basis, whether it be in the kitchen or outside of it—my mother does it all. I'm married to a touring musician, and even from afar, he always encourages me to create and follow my dreams.

What's your connection with tacos?

My connection to tacos comes from my family. In our home, there was never a tortilla shortage, meaning that everything in the fridge had the potential of becoming a taco.

You're on the Texas Taco Council. Why are you the Taco Ambassador for your city/region?

I believe I was lucky enough to be chosen to be a Taco Ambassador for Houston because I have a connection to tacos as far back as I can remember. I grew up eating some of the best tacos, and I won't take anything less than the best.

What's your go-to taco and why?

Like SPM (South Park Mexican) once said: "2 tacos with the beans and nopales." My go-to taco would have to be a taco with refried

beans and sautéed cacti, topped with homemade salsa, simply because these are ingredients that are sure to be in my fridge at all times and always take me back to my childhood.

Give us your top ten list and why they're the best.

In no particular order:

Tacos chelo from Cuchara—crunchy tacos filled with potatoes and topped with green salsa. You won't find these anywhere but Mexico, Mom's kitchen, or Cuchara. Cuchara has a kitchen full of moms who definitely know what they're doing. An authentic experience.

Any breakfast taco from Laredo Taqueria—tortillas handmade as you order. Is there anything better?

Tacos al pastor from Tacos Tierra Caliente—these are sure to hit the spot any time of day.

Tacos de suadero from Taqueria Mi Jalisco—at any time you drive by this taco truck, they are sure to have a line. Once you try these tacos, you'll understand why: they are the closest thing to Mexican street tacos outside of Mexico streets.

Tacos de barbacoa from Tortilleria La Reyna—you have to order the barbacoa and tortillas separately and build your own taco at home. Legit barbacoa on top of tortillas made Mexican tortilleria style.

Gringas, piratas, and tacos de trompo from Tacos del Julio—delicious drunk or sober food. Always paired with charro beans and delicious green salsa.

Pretty much any taco from Taconmadre in South Houston—the tacos are amazing and the salsas are so good.

Tacos from La Moreliana—in the hood and legit. The guys who work here are butchers at the meat market and always get the best stuff for the tacos.

Any tacos from Tacos La Bala—these are legitimate Mexican street tacos. They have the best salsas!

Tacos de chapulines (grasshoppers) on blue corn tortillas from Hugo's on Westheimer—yep, grasshoppers. Don't think about it; just eat it. You'll thank me later. A little high end, but definitely worth it.

Olga Farias

Tell us your story.

I am originally from a small town in Michoacán, Mexico, where I was raised by my father and mother, in a self-proclaimed gastronomical capital. I grew up around delicious food, both eating it and cooking it. I am the third of ten children, and I am the oldest of the women, so, as tradition has it in Mexican families, I was always my mother's helper.

I am a self-taught apparel designer, seamstress, pastry chef, and artisan with an eye for detail. As far back as I can remember, I was always making dresses and cakes, among other things, for people. I immigrated to Houston soon after marrying my husband, who I have now been married to for twenty-eight years. Here in Houston, I raised my three children and have created many connections that have allowed me to continue creating for others.

What's your connection with tacos?

Tacos have always been a part of my life. As Mexicans, we make tacos out of anything. They are so normal in my life—it's actually rare if I go longer than three days without a taco.

COCHINITA PIBIL TACOS

OLGA FARIAS

Serves 10

Habanero salsa (see recipe
  below)
6-pound boneless pork
  shoulder (not lean), cut
  into 3-inch chunks
2½ teaspoons salt
½ cup fresh bitter orange
  juice
1 teaspoon black
  peppercorns
1 teaspoon cumin seeds

½ teaspoon whole allspice
3 tablespoons annatto
  (achiote) seeds
6 garlic cloves
1 teaspoon crumbled dried
  oregano
1 large red onion, halved
  lengthwise, then cut
  crosswise into thin slices
3 fresh banana leaves
10 corn tortillas

HABANERO SALSA

2 cups of red wine vinegar
2 cups finely chopped onion
1½ cups fresh bitter orange
  juice (or substitute
  lime juice)

2 teaspoons dried oregano,
  crumbled
1 teaspoon salt, or to taste
1 to 2 tablespoons chopped,
  seeded fresh habanero
  chile (1 to 2 chiles)

Bring red wine vinegar to a boil, then turn off the heat. Add all other ingredients, stir, and let sit for at least 30 minutes. Set salsa aside.

Put pork in a large bowl and rub with 1 teaspoon salt and 2 tablespoons juice.

Toast peppercorns, cumin seeds, and allspice together, then cool slightly. Transfer to grinder along with annatto seeds and grind to a powder. Transfer to a small bowl.

Mince garlic and, using side of a large heavy knife, mash to a paste with remaining 1½ teaspoons salt. Add to ground spices along with oregano and remaining 6 tablespoons juice and stir to make a paste.

Toss pork with paste to coat well. Add onion and toss to combine.

Holding both ends of a banana leaf, drag leaf over a burner on moderately high heat slowly until it changes color slightly and becomes shinier, then turn over and toast other side. Toast remaining banana leaves in same manner.

Line roasting pan with leaves, shinier sides down, by arranging 1 leaf lengthwise and 2 leaves crosswise, letting excess hang over sides. Trim overhang to about 8 inches on all sides. Transfer pork mixture to banana leaves, then fold overhang of leaves over pork to enclose completely. Cover pan tightly with foil and chill for at least 6 hours.

Put oven rack in middle position, then place pan with pork in oven and heat to 400 degrees (to take the chill off the pork gently). Once oven has reached 400 degrees, bake until pork is very tender, 2¼ to 2¾ hours.

Discard foil and open banana leaves, then serve pork with habanero salsa and tortillas.

Jonathan Jones

EL BIG BAD

Tell us your story.

I grew up in the small industrial Gulf Coast town of
La Porte, Texas. My best friends and second family
were the Zapata family of Monterrey, Mexico. I was
seven years old when we met. And I was hungry . . .
literally. The Zapata family shaped my culinary passions
from the very beginning. Before I was in third grade, I had had
entomatadas, pozole, menudo, fideo, very hot salsas, and, of course,
tacos. *Real* tacos. In the twenty-nine years I have cooked professionally, I have traveled the globe of foods. But the hold that Mexican food has on my soul wins out every time. I have for many years
embraced al alma la cocina Mexicana.

I was fortunate to have a great friend in Steve Sharma. He is the
owner of El Big Bad, and he gave me a great opportunity to show

off the bold, colorful, and spicy flavors of *my* Mexico. Our foods are soulful and interpretive, delicious, and *fun*.

What is your most popular taco and why? What makes it a standout or unique?

Our most popular taco would be our chicken tinga taco. It is a wonderful mixture of textures and flavors. Its composition is a homemade corn tortilla stuffed with shredded chicken that has been stewed with onions, chipotle, and tomatoes and then topped with a smoked crema Mexicana, crunchy radish, a mild green blistered shishito chile, and finally crowned with crunchy fried chicken skin chicharrón! I love it because it isn't just a chicken taco! It is a fun and exciting play on what is normally ubiquitous.

Why do you think people love tacos so much?

Tacos are edible personality. Tacos are homemade fast food. Tacos are good any day, all day, every day. Tacos are fun and serious. Tacos are a multitude of flavors, colors, and textures all dancing together. Tacos look like they are smiling at you!

GERARDO'S DRIVE-IN

Tell us your story.

I am originally from Copandaro, Michoacán. It is a peaceful place where there are no wars, no enemies, and no fighting. I migrated to the United States and lived in Laredo for twenty-five years before moving to Houston. I've been in business for about thirty-eight years beginning on May 14, 1975. Gerardo's is named after my son.

A friend offered me the opportunity to open a business. Before

owning my own business, I worked in meat-packaging companies, hotels, and restaurants, and I knew there had to be a day when I was going to be the owner of a business. When the opportunity was given, I took it, and I am grateful more and more each day.

What is your most popular taco and why? What makes it a standout or unique?

We offer all types of tacos, but our most popular is the barbacoa taco, our barbacoa de cabeza. It is popular because of the Mexican flavor, and we make our barbacoa the way it should be made. Other places make it with borrego and cabrito, but it should really be made with cabeza de res. We make about 110–120 cabezas on a weekly basis. Well, back in the day, we only made it during the weekend, but now it is served every day.

Rafael Ramirez Cariño

CARIÑO TACO TRUCK

Tell us your story.

I grew up in mom's kitchen, in her restaurant in Puebla, Mexico. My mom, Hortencia Cariño, had a small restaurant, where she cooked many traditional Mexican dishes. I was surrounded by cooks and that's how my mother made a living and I believe that's what I do best, too. I've learned from the best.

Just like my mom's style, I would describe my cooking style as comforting, natural, and creative. I want people to feel like home when they taste my food, give them a sense of comfort. Cooking is my passion, so I enjoy getting creative and using a mixture of seasonings to get a delicious result.

I've worked all my life for others and I wanted to start something of my own. I felt I had reached a point where I was ready to become independent, start my own business. The taco truck is a tribute to my mother, which is why it's named after her "Cariño" (her last name). She had so much passion for food and really enjoyed giving to others. I wanted to do the same, give something of my own to my customers.

What is your most popular taco and why? What makes it a standout or unique?

My favorite taco would be the good old fajita taco on a corn tortilla. It cannot get any better than your traditional-style taco with juicy tender fajitas dressed in cilantro y cebolla with tons of salsa!

We use high-quality outside skirt steak and marinate it with our own special ingredients. We use fresh organic produce, homemade flour tortillas, and top-quality meat. By infusing our cultural heritage with our fresh ingredients, we want people to experience and enjoy our family recipes.

Dina Duran Gutierrez

VILLA ARCOS

Tell us your story.

I grew up in the East Houston area. I have five children—three girls and two boys—and thirteen grandchildren. My husband, Morris Gutierrez, is from San Antonio. We've always lived in the area, and everyone here knows us and knows about the taqueria. We've been here almost thirty-nine years.

My mother started Villa Arcos in 1976. She owned the property. Her name is Velia Rodriquez Duran and she's from San Antonio as well, but she grew up here in Houston. They use all her recipes and she taught all of us about the business. I was very proud to work there and very proud of my mom for what she did and what she left us, a legacy.

She taught us to work hard and don't be lazy. She was a hard worker and only knew the basics of running a business: to serve great food, be clean, and provide good service, and the people will come. And she was right!

They serve different meat tacos, but the supers are the most popular. They'll sell bacon supers all day long. They serve mainly Tex-Mex breakfast tacos like barbacoa, bacon and egg, hamburger meat and potatoes, and fajitas. Those are real popular. They just like to do Tex-Mex.

What is your most popular taco and why? What makes it a standout or unique?

The most popular one right now is the bacon super. It has bacon, egg, potato, bean, and cheese. The reason why it's so delicious

is because they make their own tortillas. They make them from scratch, about eighty to one hundred tortillas a day. So they start with a fresh homemade flour tortilla and, of course, the bacon. It takes about thirty to forty-five minutes to cook the bacon because they use the ends and pieces. Not the strips—those cook real fast and are really thin. Their bacon is chunkier and meatier. They scramble six to seven cases of eggs every day. They have a lot of fresh eggs. They save all of their clean grease and fry the potatoes and their refried beans with the same bacon grease and that's why it tastes so delicious. They also scramble the eggs with the bacon. Once everything is done, they spread the beans on the tortilla then add the eggs, potatoes, bacon, and top it off with cheese and hot sauce. Then you're ready for a super bacon!

Maria Samano

ESTILO TIERRA CALIENTE

Tell us your story.

I'm from Guerrero. I've been in business for fifteen years in Houston. I've been working in the food industry for a long time. I was a chef in a Mexican restaurant in Mexico. Then I came to the US and I started my own business and, thanks to God, I have a lot of happy customers. My customers really like the food and they love me. Tierra Caliente is an area in Guerrero and I bring that style to the food. Today I serve barbacoa, fajita, pastor, and lengua. I have customers from everywhere. And most people tell me that they come here because I serve the flavors of Tierra Caliente, Guerrero, Mexico. They like that I bring authentic flavors, and they like the service.

What is your most popular taco and why? What makes it a standout or unique?

Well, people love all the tacos I prepare. There's not just one: fajita tacos, al pastor tacos, tongue, chicharrón, chicken, barbacoa tacos, *all* of them. Here, they love them all!

You always have to prepare the tacos with two tortillas. And we get here at five in the morning to prepare all the ingredients that day—fresh and flavorful. All the meats are prepared on the same day, and all the vegetables and seasonings are prepared on the same day.

Many of my customers tell me that I prepare the food with flavors of Mexico. People follow the flavors, but they also really love the salsa that comes with the tacos. And you can't forget about the service: when people feel like they are at home, like they are with family, they really enjoy the food. They feel comfortable with me and in my restaurant.

Roberto Diaz and Trancito Diaz

LA GUADALUPANA BAKERY & CAFÉ

Tell us your story.

We come from a family of bakers. My dad, Trancito Diaz, worked for different French bakeries in Houston and he learned how to make bread, cakes, and pastries. In 1995, my dad was the head baker at Carrabba's, but then he was laid off. That was when we decided to open up our own bakery. We started as a bakery servicing local restaurants then we started offering Mexican bread and coffee. Our customers started to ask for breakfast foods so we started making tacos, huevos rancheros, and migas. At first, we only had a chalkboard menu, but when our customers started to ask for lunch, we made our big menus and offered table service. We transitioned from bakery to restaurant after that and that's what we're known for now.

It wasn't easy, though. It took a lot of hard work, dedication, and sacrifice. In the first two years, we were working seven days a week, and I was only making $180 a week. We did everything here, we ate here with our families, and we all worked. Whatever we made was to pay the bills. Now we have to work just as hard to stay at the level we're at now. Our magic combo from the beginning has been to provide great food and service. When someone comes into our the bakery, we always greet them and tell them "we'll take care of you better than they take care of you at home."

What is your most popular taco and why? What makes it a standout or unique?

Breakfast tacos especial. They come with onions, potatoes, peppers, chorizo, egg, and cheese. We get a lot of the morning traffic and even for lunch. We serve breakfast all day long and people love to eat them through the afternoon.

Our mole is popular, too. We have mole enchiladas and we make a special mole taco that's not on the menu. I think what makes it good is that we get our paste from Puebla, Mexico, from our uncle. We add our own seasoning, chicken stock, and more chocolate to give it that special flavor.

Dallas-Fort Worth

Big hair, J. R. Ewing, and ranchers, move over. There's a new Dallas scene and it loves tacos! Sure, when you think of Dallas, you wouldn't necessarily think of tacos, but all that has changed in recent years. There's been a taco boom in different neighborhoods, and chefs are taking their creativity with tacos to new levels. Old Tex-Mex haunts are reinventing themselves, and new styles from Monterrey to Mexico City are popping up everywhere.

And no one knows more about the Dallas taco scene than our Taco Ambassador team, writer José Ralat and photographer Robert Strickland. These guys have been in that taco terrain for years and know the good, the bad, and the ugly. You'll learn more about some of their local favorites in this chapter.

Dallas, you definitely surprised us—in a good way. You introduced us to a tortilleria-turned-taco shop, we hung out with longhorns in the downtown area and ate your gas station tacos, you sizzled us with some amazing al pastor with crispy cheese, we met with the gunslinger taquero, we almost drank out of a paleta-inspired keg cart, we had some classic crispy tacos, we entered a taco speakeasy and experimented with hibiscus tortillas and huitlacoche quesadillas. Dallas definitely gets the "most improved taco scene" award in this book.

THE DALLAS ICONIC TACO: GOURMET, CHEF-INSPIRED TACOS

Dallas history is full of Tex-Mex families and recent arrivals—Tacos Regionales—people bringing their own styles from different regions in Mexico. But where Dallas tacos are headed is the New Americano way. Gourmet or chef-inspired tacos are making an impression on Dallas, from Revolver Taco Lounge and Urban

Taco reintroducing tacos and Mexican food from the finer side of life to Velvet Taco putting an international vibe into each taco creation. It's only fitting that the taqueros y taqueras at these places are making it their own, Dallas style (cue velvet rope).

TACO JOURNALISM'S TOP CINCO

1. **Revolver Taco Lounge**—gunslinger and designer taquero crafting up high-end and authentic tacos. Try the pulpo or the jalapeño relleno tacos.
2. **Urban Taco**—Mexico City with a Dallas twist. Al pastor a la tuma with a crunchy and crispy manchego layer.
3. **Trompo**—like al pastor but different. This taco hustler makes a trompo onsite or in your backyard.
4. **El Come Taco**—authentically Mexican. The arrachera with nopales taco will make you say ajuaa!
5. **La Nueva Fresh & Hot**—tortilleria turning up hot guisados on demand.

TROMPO: A TACO SPEAKEASY

It was dusk in the Oak Cliff neighborhood, and we could have easily hit up two to three taco shops within walking distance. But instead, we entered Trompo for an intimate gathering of taco-makers and aficionados hosted by Luis Olvera, proprietor and El Rey del Trompo. As with most speakeasies, you enter through the rear or, in this case, the driveway. In the back was an old casita with chairs and tables in the open-air garage (pronounced

"garajeh"). The trompo grill (a vertical broiler or rotisserie) was prepped with layers of pork shoulder seasoned with chiles and paprika, giving it a bright red hue. Nearby were two flat griddles, salsas, and yellow corn tortillas. As Luis y familia of helpers slowly cooked the meat, everyone waited patiently, salivating-ly, as the pork shoulder rotated on the trompo. It was mesmerizing. Thin slices of pork were cut off the trompo, creating a spin-top shape (hence the name "trompo," which is what these are called in Mexico), and placed on corn tortillas. To give them that extra crisp and sizzle, the tacos were laid down flat, with the carne on the bottom side, for a minute or two; then they were ready to be salsa-fied with reds and greens and layered with cebollas asadas, cilantro, and fresh limes. By that time, the beers were flowing and everyone was asking for one more taco!

Luis Olvera

TROMPO

Tell us your story.

Cooking for me began when I was a preteen, during my yearly summer vacation to Monterrey, working in my Tío Toño's puesto, Kalifa Burger. At the time, it was a refurbished log cabin, specializing in northern Mexican comfort foods. I did a lot of jobs, from cleaning tables to washing dishes, cutting potatoes into French fries, and, of course, the specialty, the Holy Grail, flipping up to thirty burgers at a time over an iron mesquite charcoal-burning grill!

Back in Dallas, as more and more family members migrated to our great state of Texas, family gatherings became a weekly routine at my parents' house (my current home). Butchering and cooking livestock and watching my father build outdoor ovens (ataúd or caja china) and underground pits (horno en pozo) to cook in. My godfather Mario could take a recently slaughtered goat or pig and turn it into carnitas, chivo en salsa, montalayo, you name it. If it could be cooked outside, you better believe my family was going to make it their own.

In 2008, one of my uncles custom built a food trailer. His specialty? Tacos de trompo. Every first Sunday in Canton, Texas, Juan Carlos would sell thousands of tacos to a very happy crowd. Although I grew up eating these tacos de trompo every time I crossed the border, I'd never given them a second thought. I noticed there were less than a handful of true trompo vendors in Dallas. That year my interest in the world of tacos began. Fast forward a

few years, and with a couple of recipes modified by yours truly, my vision became a reality. Along with a cousin, Omar, Dos Primos Tacos, the speakeasy whispered throughout Oak Cliff, began. First with only family, then shortly after, we'd welcome people from all walks of life into my backyard, the same backyard that served as the gathering place for my family for many years.

I will never forget January 2013 though. I hosted a party at my parents' house. Having played with this most treasured secret family recipe for what seemed like a lifetime, I relished the looks on my family and friends' faces as they bit into *my* savory tacos. "I don't know what you did to that recipe, but I can't stop eating them!" It boosted my confidence to believe in myself and my product. Of course, there have been hour-long wait times, family arguments as to whose fault it was that an order was wrong, more advice than I could have ever dreamed of hearing, and so many smiles, hugs, and compliments.

I can only hope to continue to share my "Mexican street tacos," as they are best described by the locals in my town, for many more moons with my loved ones (whom I have to thank for the endless recipes and tips throughout the years), and to pay it forward one taco at a time.

What is your most popular taco and why? What makes it a standout or unique?

El taco de trompo, a savory twist on its iconic predecessor, el taco al pastor. It looks more vibrant with its fiery red contrast on a yellow corn tortilla, and the inviting aroma and taste of paprika over pork helps the palate embrace the "just one more taco" feeling!

Why do you think people love tacos so much?

Because tacos are life! In all seriousness, I like a good protein, I like my share of veggies, I enjoy a little tang in my food, not to

mention a kick of spice, but in one glorious bite, I can have it all
... wrapped in the greatest invention of all time, the tortilla! Does
that sum it up?

Gloria Vazquez-Summers
LA NUEVA FRESH & HOT

Tell us your story.

My parents started the tortilla business in Mexico back in 1967.
As a kid, I used to help my parents in the store even when I did
not like it. As I was getting older, I started to like being part of my
parents' success, and as an adult getting divorced and with two
kids, I decided to start my own tortilla place in Mexico in 1999. I
struggled for a year and then I did good. But after a few years, I felt
I wanted to do better and to offer my kids better opportunities in
life. So I decided to come to the United States and try the American Dream. My sister and I opened La Nueva Fresh & Hot in 2006,
selling tortillas and guisados. It wasn't enough for two families,
so my sister sold me her part. I thought it could be a great idea to
sell tacos with the best tortillas in Dallas, so I called my mom for
recipes because I wanted my food to taste like home.

Back in Mexico, my mom used to cook a very good, big breakfast. Always with fresh tortillas, some meat, delicious salsas, and
family. It was like a family reunion, and it was the thing I missed
the most when I came here—good homemade Mexican food and
family. I wanted my kids to experience that! So now that my business is more successful, I want all the families to share good food
and fresh tortillas at their tables.

What is your most popular taco and why? What makes it a standout or unique?

Guisado verde taco (green pork stew). I think this taco is very popular because it is different from any other taco. It is very spicy, not only with the hot flavor but also because of the spices we use to cook the stew, and it is always fresh!

This taco is unique because of its flavor and also because of the fresh tortillas we use to make it. Its flavor is very Mexican, and if you are not used to eating spicy food, we recommend having a big glass of water handy when you eat this taco.

Why do you think people love tacos so much?

I think people like tacos because they are so delicious and different. You can have a taco with anything you want—chicken, fish, pork, beef, shrimp, or vegetables. Also, you can invent your own tacos. All you need is a good, tasty, fresh tortilla and you can get them at La Nueva Fresh & Hot!

Also, tacos are becoming part of Texas culture because Texas has a lot of Mexicans living here and its taco culture is expanding to the rest of the country. There are different types of cuisines that are adopting the taco culture and creating their own version of tacos, which I personally think is very cool.

GUISADO VERDE TACOS

LA NUEVA FRESH & HOT

Makes 10 tacos

SALSA

1 pound jalapeño peppers

1½ pounds peeled green
   tomato

6 black cloves

Pinch cumin

Pinch black pepper

½ teaspoon oregano

4 fresh garlic cloves

Salt

Place a pot with water on the stove and add the jalapeño peppers. Cook for 15 minutes, then add the peeled and cleaned green tomatoes and cook for another 10 minutes. Place the peppers and green tomatoes in a blender along with the rest of the ingredients and a cup of water. Blend until everything is thoroughly mixed. (If you want more spice in your stew, add 5 serrano peppers.) Set aside until guisado is ready.

GUISADO

4 pounds diced pork meat

2 teaspoons cooking oil

1 medium onion, finely diced

Salsa (see recipe above)

15 corn tortillas

Place the meat in a pot with the oil. Cook on medium heat, stirring the pot every 2 to 3 minutes. Cook until all the meat juice is almost gone. Add half of the diced onion and cook until transparent. When the meat juice is all gone and the meat is cooked to perfection, add the salsa and keep it on the fire until the meat sauce (guisado) comes to a boil. Remove from heat.

Warm the tortillas on a skillet and fill with the guisado. You can add fresh onions, cilantro, and a slice of avocado to make them even more delicious.

Regino Rojas

REVOLVER TACO LOUNGE

Tell us your story.

I design and sell guns. I own a gun shop with my father and Revolver Taco Lounge with my mother. I'm a collector and I design guns and, yes, tacos.

My family started in the gun business in the 1500s. I come from a family of blacksmiths from the Mexican Revolution. I'm from Michoacán and my family settled there. It's a crazy story. Back then, my grandfather was on the run for being a blacksmith for the rebels, so he settled in Michoacán.

Now our family lives in Texas. It's a nice place to raise a family. My dad and I opened the gun shop and soon after opened Revolver Taco. One day I noticed my mom was in the corner, knitting, looking sad and bored, and I knew she needed her own place. She's worked in the kitchen all her life, and there was no way I could take the kitchen away from that woman. Our shop became a place for my mom to cook for a few people and once the media came, it just exploded. Now our whole family is part of the taco bar.

What's your connection to tacos?

Me gusta el tango! I love to cook. I love to entertain. That's what I had growing up. Back home, people used to come knock on my mom's door to see what she was cooking up. So my mom would sit them down, and they would eat tacos or whatever she was cooking. I grew up with that catering style, but just in the home. So when we opened up Revolver, it just came natural.

Now on the taco, well, you know it was created in the homes of families. It is meant to feed friends and family. It doesn't matter the style of taco. It's about sharing a meal with your best friends and family. After that, whatever you do with the taco is extra. The important thing is sharing, cooking it with love. If you do it as a business and keep that essence of Mexican food, cook from the heart, people will love it.

José Ralat

TACO TRAIL
TEXAS TACO COUNCIL

Tell us your story.

I was born in Arecibo, Puerto Rico. When I was a toddler, my family moved to the mainland, where we moved around almost every year. Eventually I landed in New York City, where my family had roots. For me, it was a homecoming. It was there that I met my wife, a native Texan and Mexican American and a significant influence on what I see as my life's work.

We lived in Sunset Park, a Brooklyn neighborhood that offered my wife and me plenty of Puerto Rican and Mexican elements. What's more, Sunset Park has a sizeable southern Mexican immigrant population. The neighborhood was the best of both worlds. I had my first real taste of Texas and Mexico and began transitioning from editor of a neuropsychiatry journal to food writer—specifically, a writer on Mexican food and tacos.

After our son was born in 2008, we hightailed it to Texas, where I dedicated my life to food writing and writing focused on tacos. Now I am the food editor of Dallas-based *Cowboys & Indians*, a nationally circulated Western lifestyle magazine. Working at *C&I* has allowed me the opportunity to write about foods like Indian fry bread tacos and South Texas barbacoa, and it's only deepened my love, understanding, and passion for tacos.

Acclimating to Texas wasn't easy, but, I got to say, I love the Lone Star State, its culture and its food—especially the tacos.

What's your connection with tacos?

As I mentioned, my wife is a native Texan and Chicana. While living in Sunset Park, she insisted I try some of her taco de lengua at Matamoros Restaurant. She grew up eating lengua, so for her it was no big deal. For me, it was a really big deal. The lengua was earthy but mellow and so soft. It was world-silencing. Before that, though, while we were dating, she made me chorizo and egg breakfast tacos on fresh flour tortillas made at the Chinese-run Tex-Mex joint in the neighborhood. One bite, and everything stopped. I was hooked, needed to eat more, needed to know more about tacos— their history, cultural significance, permutations. This elderly woman sold $2 barbacoa de chivo tacos out of a street-side stall in Sunset Park. Her gamey food fueled my errands, filled them with so much happiness.

After my family moved to Texas, I got a call from Mark Donald, the editor of the *Dallas Observer* back then. He asked me if I liked tacos. "Of course, I like tacos," I answered. So he told me to pitch an online taco column. And that's how *Taco Trail* began in 2010. Each week for a year, I visited and reviewed a taco joint for the newspaper's food blog, *City of Ate*. A year later, *Taco Trail* went independent with a website. And I got serious. I've done loads of research and traveling. I've written about the history of the taco holder; dug deep into the regional styles of tacos cooked on the trompo, the vertical spit al pastor is cooked on; written about a kosher taco truck in El Paso; visited more than five hundred taco places nationwide (most in Texas, of course); amassed a library; and become more curious. But, more importantly, through reading, eating, writing, traveling, and talking to taqueros across the US and Mexico, I've learned that there are significant erroneous preconceptions. There are so many myths. They are culturally harmful. They also harm the enjoyment of tacos, which is ultimately what it's about.

The websites—Imbibe, Munchies, and First We Feast, as well as *D Magazine*, the *Dallas Morning News*, CNN, and other media outlets—have featured my taco work. It also led to my invitation to contribute to the 2015 *Texas Monthly* taco issue. For the issue, I visited ten cities—many with my friend and photographer Robert Strickland. I also wrote supplementary material and cowrote the introduction. It was an honor and a dream come true to share tacos with Texans. Hopefully, it spurs someone to expand his or her horizons and find a new favorite taco.

You're on the Texas Taco Council. Why are you the Taco Ambassador for your city/region?
Since starting the *Taco Trail* and working as a freelance writer specializing in tacos and visiting as many taco spots as I have, I've gotten to know and befriend many taqueros and restaurant owners—not to mention champion their deserved place in the regional

taco scene. It's allowed me to cofound and/or curate events and festivals such as the North Texas Taco Festival and the big one, ¡Taco Libre!, a music and taco festival that featured Grammy award-winning Ozomatli as the headliner.

I love Dallas-Fort Worth's tacos. I've been fortunate to become acquainted with the diversity of tacos available here. I'll steer you to the great tacos, not the merely popular ones, and I am dedicated to spreading the good word.

What's your go-to taco and why?

The tacos al pastor at Urban Taco and El Come Taco. I'm also a big fan of the fish taco and the Jose's taco, a classic refried bean nosh, at El Come. They hit all the marks of traditionalism with touches of modernity and plenty of deliciousness. They're just tasty.

But, really, my go-to tacos are the ones I make at home: break-fast tacos with bacon and tater tots, fajita tacos, and a slice of salted avocado in a tortilla. Tacos estilo casero are always the best.

Why do you think people love tacos in your region and in Texas?

Tacos and Texas are inseparable. Tortillas were available in our great state before it was part of the US. It's in the DNA, and, along with barbecue, one of our national cuisines.

Give us the taco landscape for your city/region. Give us your top ten list and why they're the best.

Dallas-Fort Worth has perhaps the most diverse and dynamic taco scene in Texas. Sinaloan, Sonoran, DF, Tex-Mex, Oaxacan and Monterrey-style tacos can be enjoyed within minutes of each other. Zacatecan, Jaliscienses, Tijuana, Michoacano and Durango-style tacos are also readily available. Guisados—from picadillo that you want to slurp and smoky rajas con queso to pillowy chile rellenos and mellow costillas en salsa roja—are easy to find and delicious. For adventurous locals looking to explore traditional Mexican delicacies, there are even chapulines (roasted grasshoppers). It's awesome and incredible.

In no particular order:

Los Torres Taqueria—a homey taqueria specializing in Sinaloan-style tacos with an emphasis on goat braises. The norteño-style flour tortillas, handmade with beef tallow at nearby La Norteña Tortilleria, are fantastic. The taco to get here is the taco ahogado (drowned taco), goat and Monterey Jack cheese in a handmade corn tortilla that has goat consommé poured over it and is finished with a squiggle of jalapeño mayo. For many, it's a preconception-challenging selection, as it requires a fork and knife. But eating it is like slipping into a warm bath.

Urban Taco—a pioneer of what is now considered Modern Mexican. Urban Taco balances ultratraditional components like tortillas made from nixtamalized masa and al pastor cooked on and sliced from a trompo with contemporary elements like the design and the best agave spirits collection in the region. So many rarities and delicious options.

El Come Taco—this taqueria is part modern and part classic, like Urban Taco. The restaurant design is dominated by neon-colored Día de los Muertos calaveras, but there are tacos al pastor, Mexico City-style cabeza, an excellent fish taco, and a refried bean-avocado-queso fresco taco. All of which are my must-orders at El Come. Occasionally, chapulines are on the menu.

El Tizoncito—a member of the Mexico City-style trinity, tacos al pastor on a trompo that includes Urban Taco and El Come

Taco. Walking into the original El Tiz location in Oak Cliff is like being transported to a Mexico City taqueria.

Oak Cliff Trompo—the best example of Monterrey-style tacos de trompo, the northern cousin of tacos al pastor.

La Nueva Fresh & Hot—a family-owned tortilleria that specializes in guisados—consider them Mexican breakfast tacos—such as rajas con queso and the fiery guisado verde.

El Corazon—my favorite DFW Tex-Mex restaurant. El Corazon is the latest from the first family of Tex-Mex, the Cuellars, who founded the El Chico chain. Their tacos norteños are handmade corn tortillas filled with refried beans, fajitas, cheese, avocado, and pure comfort.

Taco Stop—another taqueria that appears modern but is actually very traditional. This walk-up joint serves excellent breakfast and lunch tacos. The potato and egg taco is among the finest I've had in the state, especially with a few drops of the peanut habanero salsa. It has claws.

Mi Lindo Oaxaca—the only Oaxacan restaurant in Dallas. The owners and staff take traditionalism seriously. The mole is literally made from scratch, as in they shell each cacao bean by hand to make the chocolate that goes into the mole.

Revolver Taco Lounge—what I consider the best taqueria in the state. Revolver Taco Lounge offers deeply traditional Mexican food with a focus on the cuisine of the owner's native Michoacán. There's relleno, huitlacoche, and a lot of seafood. Carnitas, of course. And then there are the tortillas: made to order, they're so hot when they reach your table, you need to give them a minute. Otherwise, you'll burn your fingers. There's plenty of fun, too. Pulpo carnitas, for example.

Luis Villalva

EL COME TACO

Tell us your story.

I'm from a family surrounded by taqueros in Mexico City. I was introduced to the business of tacos at the age of ten. My family owned two taco places in Mexico, so basically tacos are in my blood. The taqueria is a place full of nostalgia, and I keep it simple and authentic. I use all original recipes for my street tacos.

What is your most popular taco and why? What makes it a standout or unique?

Our taco de la casa is the arrachera taco. It's one of the specialties. We use 100 percent grass-fed arrachera (skirt steak) with our house seasoning (salt, pepper, and garlic), topped with sautéed onions, diced potatoes, and slices of cactus. I think it's popular

because of the nopales. As soon as customers try one, they ask for more on the same visit or the next time they come back.

Daniel Vaughn

BARBECUE EDITOR, *TEXAS MONTHLY*

Tell us your story.

I am the barbecue editor at *Texas Monthly* and the author of *The Prophets of Smoked Meat*. I have logged tens of thousands of miles on the highways and back roads of Texas and eaten at more than one thousand barbecue joints across the country. Thankfully, exploration is a hobby.

What's your connection with tacos?

Since moving to Texas from Ohio in 2001, I've been fully immersed in the food culture of the Lone Star State. Tex-Mex, tacos, barbecue, and juicy steaks make up most of my diet. The number of tacos I have consumed hasn't been as well documented as the barbecue, but there have been plenty. I love them all, especially breakfast tacos on flour tortillas, and I'm always confounded when I travel back to Ohio to find they still haven't discovered the breakfast taco.

What's your go-to taco and why?

While running carpool for a first grader and then to daycare, I need something portable for breakfast. I don't want a prepacked breakfast bar. I want meat, eggs, cheese, and salsa wrapped in a warm flour tortilla.

Why do you think people love tacos in your region and in Texas?

Because once you've discovered the beauty of meat and vegetables wrapped in a tortilla, you realize how inferior two slices of bread are. You also have to factor in the possibility for variety. Three or five different tacos for lunch is more than acceptable, which means you don't have to commit to one flavor.

Give me your top five taco spots and why.

1. **La Nueva Fresh & Hot in Dallas**—it's a tortilla factory as well as a taco shop, so the corn tortillas are always perfect. I like the guisado verde, which has great depth of flavor and a rich spiciness.

2. **Rusty Taco in Dallas**—flour tortillas grilled fresh to order. That helps make a great breakfast. Whether it's the bacon-egg-cheese-avocado or the homemade chorizo, a squeeze of habanero salsa reminds you that you're awake.

3. **Valentina's Tex Mex BBQ in Austin**—this South Austin trailer puts out incredible smoked brisket, ribs, and pulled pork, but it's even better in one of their fresh flour tortillas. A regular old chopped-brisket sandwich has nothing on this brisket taco topped with guacamole and spicy salsa.

4. **Vera's Backyard Bar-B-Que in Brownsville**—the only place left in Texas that cooks whole beef heads in the ground over wood. It's the best barbacoa in the state, and it's even better

in a tortilla from the nearby Capistran Tortilla Factory with a few chili pequins and avocado salsa.

5. **Urban Taco in uptown Dallas**—the al pastor pork, ruddy with chiles and spices and singed on a trompo in the kitchen. A cool slice of sweet pineapple is placed atop the taco. Get it "a la tuma" for an unusual cheesy crust on the outside of your taco, and a surprising slice of raw jalapeño.

Markus Pineyro
URBAN TACO

Tell us your story.

I moved to Dallas from Mexico City when I was eighteen and I immediately realized how much I missed a good taco. I struggled

with that for a few years until one day I decided that I wanted to be responsible for bringing that good taco to Dallas. So, at the age of twenty-three, I embarked on my dream.

I opened our first location in 2007. In the beginning, the biggest challenge was that people didn't understand what a "taqueria" was because our demographic had not been exposed to it. Our mission was to familiarize our clientele with our taqueria concept. In the next few years, we saw a boom in taco concepts around our city and at a national level. Being one of the first taquerias in town helped us pave the way to be able to open multiple locations in Texas. I truly think I have the best job I could've asked for. Eight years later, I eat tacos every day and I love it.

What is your most popular taco and why? What makes it a standout or unique?

Tacos al pastor. We focus on Mexico City street food and naturally that is the most popular in the city, so it reflects the same way on our menu. We slow cook it on our trompo with a delicious char.

Why do you think people love tacos so much?

Tacos are the new burger, what can I say? I think tacos are so popular because there is a taco for everyone due to the amount of creative things you can do with a taco.

TACOS AL PASTOR A LA TUMA

URBAN TACO

Indigenous to Mexico, chiles japoneses are one of the most popular dried chiles used in Mexican cuisine. This chile is similar in heat to the árbol, so use with caution in your recipes.

Makes 50 tacos

PASTOR MARINADE

10 ounces guajillo pepper

5 medium cloves garlic, peeled

2 medium-sized white onions

3 pounds medium-sized oranges

1½ pounds medium-sized limes

½ medium-sized pineapple

1 two-pound bar of achiote spice, paste

10 ounces white vinegar

1 ounce cumin

2 ounces japonés pepper

2 tablespoons salt

Add water to a deep pot and boil the guajillo pepper, the garlic, and the onions for about 30 minutes. Strain the guajillo, garlic, and onions from the pot and put aside.

Peel the oranges, limes, and pineapple and cut each into 4 pieces. (Save one piece of the pineapple to grill, slice, and use for the garnish.)

Blend all the ingredients together, adding the paste, vinegar, salt, cumin, and japonés pepper as well. Blend till smooth.

AL PASTOR A LA TUMA

10 pounds pork butt

Manchego cheese

Corn tortillas

Onion, chopped

Cilantro, chopped

Avocado, sliced

Salsa

Slice the pork in medium slices and place in a plastic or metal container. Add the pastor marinade and cover completely with the marinade. Cover the container and let the meat marinate for 8 hours.

Cut thin slices of the marinated pork, approximately 1½ ounces per serving/taco. In a medium skillet or flat top, fry pork in oil over high heat. Cook until a little char can be seen. Approximately 8-12 minutes.

Serve on a tortilla. To make an a la tuma taco, sauté 1 ounce of manchego cheese on a flat top for about 1 minute and then place a corn tortilla on the cheese and let it cook and crisp into the tortilla. Garnish the taco with onion, cilantro, salsa, avocado, and a slice of roasted pineapple.

Chef Anastacia Quiñones

Tell us your story.

I'm originally from East Dallas. I went to the Culinary Institute of America in Hyde Park and then I moved to San Francisco to pursue a culinary career in French food. Never in my wildest dreams did I imagine I'd be making a living cooking Mexican food. It's been fun introducing people to real Mexican food.

What's your connection with tacos?

Tacos have always been a comfort dish. Some people have mac and cheese or pot roast. I always have tacos!

What's your go-to taco and why?

Fajita, cebolla (raw), cilantro, and lots of lime with a chile torreado to bite. Keep it simple and classic.

Why do you think people love tacos in your region and in Texas?

It's so Texas to eat tacos. They're easy on the go or they can be dressed up in a restaurant. People of all walks of life can relate to them.

RED SNAPPER TACOS

CHEF ANASTACIA QUIÑONES

I crave these tacos. I am allergic to swimming fish, so if I am going to eat fish, it had better be worth it. These are!

Makes 3 tacos

- 1 cup flour
- 1 teaspoon ground cayenne
- 1 teaspoon garlic salt
- 6 ounces red snapper

Mix flour, cayenne, and garlic salt. Toss fish in the flour mixture, then fry coated fish in fryer for 3 to 4 minutes until cooked.

JICAMA SLAW

½ cup shredded red
   cabbage

¼ cup chopped cilantro

¼ cup julienned jicama

¼ cup sliced red onion
   marinated in lime juice
   for 1 hour

Combine all ingredients and set aside.

AVOCADO SERRANO PUREE

2 avocados, peeled
   and seeded

1 serrano, capped
   and seeded

Juice of 2 limes

Salt

Puree ingredients until smooth.

Place fried fish in a tortilla with jicama slaw and avocado serrano puree.

Gilbert Cuellar Jr.

EL CORAZON VINTAGE TEX-MEX

Tell us your story.

My father Gilbert Cuellar was one of the five Cuellar brothers who started El Chico. I was introduced to Mexican food (Tex-Mex) at a very early age. My dad was forty-three when I was born, and I was the only boy after five girls.

Although my dad was very busy with his growing company, he would take me to the El Chico restaurants on Saturday for guys' day out. We'd have either menudo or tacos that were fried with ground beef inside. I remember that great flavor of the tacos and also burning my mouth because they were so hot inside!

I worked with El Chico for several years and then went on

to open my first restaurant, Casa Rosa in Dallas. We introduced Dallas to beef fajitas in 1981 in addition to our other upscale Tex-Mex offerings. Nevertheless, our customers asked for "those old-fashioned tacos" they remembered from years ago. So alongside our carne asada and pollo con rajas were the humble but delicious old-fashioned tacos. People loved those tacos and they were great sellers for us.

During the following years, I moved back to El Chico for a while then on to Nashville to open a Texas-style restaurant called Texana Grill featuring fajitas, steaks, and ribs. We served only soft tacos there and we used smoked chicken and shredded beef. The tacos were really good and reflected my love of the Texas Hill Country.

Most recently, my cousin John Cuellar and I opened El Corazon Vintage Tex-Mex in Oak Cliff. El Corazon is an opportunity to reflect on my life in Tex-Mex and show folks the foods John and I really love. We aren't trying to follow new trends, just serving great, fresh homemade vintage Tex-Mex. We were awarded "Best Tex-Mex" in Dallas this year by the editors of *D Magazine*, proving there is a desire for what we do.

We've been open at El Corazon for more than two years now and a few months ago, customers started asking for "those old-fashioned tacos." Funny how some things just never change! So, we started making the tacos people love and we serve them every Wednesday. It's great seeing the expressions on people's faces as they try the tacos. It's like they've been transported to earlier times.

So I know that, no matter what year it is or how complicated the menu, customers will always love the standards of Tex-Mex and "those old-fashioned tacos."

What is your most popular taco and why? What makes it a standout or unique?

Our most popular tacos at El Corazon are our tacos norteños. The tacos start with our handmade corn or flour tortilla; we spread a thin layer of our refried beans on the inside and then add Jack cheese and beef or chicken fajita meat. Then we cook it on the plancha (griddle) with a little butter until it's crispy and golden brown. We serve them with sliced avocado and the customer's choice of sides.

I never thought something so simple could taste so good! I always made these at home with leftover grilled steak or chicken and we just called them "Dad's tacos." When my daughters were living at home, we'd grill steaks or chicken outside and they'd always remind me to cook extra so we would have leftovers for Dad's tacos.

I believe customers love the tacos norteños first because they taste great and second because they are just the right size to hold. And they combine that crispy outside with the soft and creamy inside. I'd like one right now!

EL CORAZON VINTAGE TACOS
(OLD-FASHIONED TACOS)

EL CORAZON VINTAGE TEX-MEX

Makes 2 tacos

Canola oil for frying
2 fresh yellow or white corn
   tortillas

Seasoned ground beef,
   shredded chicken,
   or calabacitas and
   mushrooms

Heat ½ inch oil to 350 degrees in a skillet. Using tongs, carefully place a tortilla, one at a time, in the oil for about two seconds until the tortilla is soft. Remove from the oil and place on a cookie sheet to drain and cool.

Once the tortillas are cool to the touch, take your prepared filling and place in the middle of the tortilla using a tablespoon. Leave about an inch on the sides for closing. You will need about three ounces of filling per tortilla.

Fold the tortilla over to form a half-moon. Place the tortilla on a cutting board and lift up the part where the edges of the tortilla meet. Place two toothpicks in the tortilla using an over-under sewing method (one toothpick between the fold and the middle). This holds the filling in place during frying.

After you have made all your tacos, make sure the oil is 350 degrees and about ½-inch deep in the pan.

Add the tacos one by one to the oil and fry until crispy on one side. Turn over and cook until crisp and golden brown. Remove from the oil and cool slightly. Hold the taco with a dish towel and carefully remove the toothpicks. Serve hot.

I like to garnish the tacos with lightly dressed lettuce and tomatoes. You can open the tortilla a little to add the garnish.

The filling inside will be hot for a while so make sure to warn the kids. Happy tacos!

Robert Strickland

PHOTOGRAPHER
TEXAS TACO COUNCIL

Tell us your story.

Food photographer. Father and husband. Native Texan. After ten years as a graphic designer, I made the leap into professional photography by focusing on the food industry—from the people to the plate. With a camera in hand, I've documented everything from fine dining to barbecue on the back roads of Texas. Recently, tacos have become a focus of my work, thanks to assignments for the *Texas Monthly* taco issue—and I couldn't be happier about it! Focusing on tacos has really helped heighten my appreciation for

the dedication that good taquerias require and has furthered my understanding of the taco's importance across cultures.

My photos have been featured via websites such as Eater, Munchies, and First We Feast. They've also appeared in print via *Life & Thyme* magazine, *Billboard* magazine, and *Cowboys & Indians* magazine.

What's your connection with tacos?

Being a native Texan, I've always grown up with tacos in my life. Sure, I'm half-Korean and half-Anglo, but that doesn't mean I didn't crave good tacos. That said, my most recent connection is through my friendship with José "Taco Trail" Ralat. He's been an amazing mentor when it comes to learning about the sheer variety and nuance of tacos from region to region, both in Mexico and Texas. I learn so much being around him.

You're on the Texas Taco Council. Why are you the Taco Ambassador for your city/region?

My friendship with José has grown from purely similar interests in food to a really well-oiled working relationship. Often, he comes to me when he's looking for someone to photograph tacos, and in turn, I've developed a real love and respect for what goes into the taco—especially in a dynamic taco scene like Dallas–Fort Worth.

What's your go-to taco and why?

Not sure if I have a single go-to taco—so much of that has to do with the taqueria and the region that their food represents. I will say that right now I'm loving the tacos de trompo of Monterrey. That bright red stack of pork is a beautiful thing.

Why do you think people love tacos in your region and in Texas?

Like I said before, Dallas–Fort Worth has a ton of variety when it comes to tacos, and I think that's a huge selling point. Mexico City, Sinaloa, Michoacán, Oaxaca, Huasteca, and more are all represented here and represented in really delicious ways. We're not in your face like other places, but people who overlook this area's tacos are missing out.

Give us the taco landscape for your city/region. Give us your top ten list and why they're the best.

In a word, Dallas is dynamic. So many different styles, and you can find really good examples of each of those styles. I hate top ten lists, so I'll give you a top nine (in no particular order):

Revolver Taco Lounge—top to bottom, maybe the best taqueria I've ever been in. The prices can be jarring, but you get what you pay for: stunningly good food. And those made-to-order, hand-pressed corn tortillas are worth fighting over.

Urban Taco—the pastor a la tuma—stunning and worth every penny.

El Come Taco—the tacos al pastor and the Jose's taco . . . so good.

Los Torres Taqueria—Sinaloan birria, barbacoa roja, and taco ahogada. No more words needed.

La Nueva Fresh & Hot—the bean and cheese taco is simple and so freaking good.

Taco Heads—I'm often disappointed in brisket tacos, but these are damn satisfying.

El Tizoncito—get the choriqueso appetizer. Thank me later.

El Corazon de Tejas—the tacos norteños are comfort food turned up to eleven.

Morales Restaurant—the taco rojos estilo Huasteca are not to be trifled with.

Veronica Torres

DALLAS CONVENTION & VISITORS BUREAU

Tell us your story.

I'm a Latina originally from Austin. I'm a graduate of Johnson and Wales University with a degree in hotel and restaurant management. I'm currently the director of business development at the Dallas Convention & Visitors Bureau and serve as the president of the Hispanic 100 board of directors.

I'm very passionate and consider myself an advocate for health and wellness programming along with young professional leadership and entrepreneurship. I received my yoga teaching certification from the APY Institute in Dallas. My husband and I built a Fit Couple brand while advocating for Latinos and African Americans in the world of healthy lifestyle and exercise. My love for culture is rich and organic; my family roots originate from Mexico and tacos were a staple at home.

What's your connection with tacos?

Basically born with a taco in hand before a bottle. My family origin is from Mexico. Growing up in a small community in Austin, we were poor and culturally rich. My lunch bag for school was leftover dinner in a taco wrapped in foil or sometimes just a napkin. My mom made breakfast tacos for the morning bus ride—sometimes it would be leftovers from dinner the night before. No eggs, maybe beans and carne picada. My grandmother always made fresh flour tortillas—my grandpa was very particular about fresh tortillas. A must—beans *always* included.

Give me your top five taco spots and why.

1. La Ventana—breakfast taco. The quality of their tacos is the best. Easy access to pick up and run without compromising the taste.

2. Mesero Miguel—slow-cooked brisket "mama's style" and the tomatillo sauce. Mico, the owner, is serious about his taco and tequila! Home-cooked, fresh, and bangin' flavor.

3. Velvet Taco—buffalo chicken. Just enough spice. This place reminds me of Austin.

4. La Popular Tamale House—the best morning taco: chorizo and egg. Old fashioned, no gimmicks, just like my mom's!

5. El Come Taco—best street carnitas. Old-school flavor.

John Franke

VELVET TACO

Tell us your story.

I grew up in Maryland, went to school at Johnson and Wales University for culinary/food service management, and moved down to Dallas in 1995. I moved from Dallas to Chicago in 1998 and back to Dallas in 2000. From 1995 to 2003, I worked in several restaurants in a chef or sous chef role. In 2003, I moved to Burkina Faso, West Africa, to do missionary work with street children. I returned in

2007 to continue my career as a chef. I have four children and live in the DFW area. Having lived in Africa and in many parts of the US and visited multiple countries, I have been exposed to so many cultures and foods. Velvet Taco has given me the opportunity to express those cultures and flavors into fun and innovative tacos. Velvet Taco opened in 2012 and has grown from one to four locations in the past three years. It is an eclectic taco joint with internationally inspired creations that are served in house-made corn tortillas, locally sourced flour tortillas, or lettuce wraps. Each taco has a story behind it, all of the meats are marinated and/or brined in house, every recipe is made from scratch, and the flavor combinations are unique and memorable.

What is your most popular taco and why? What makes it a standout or unique?

Our most popular taco is our spicy crisp tikka chicken taco. It is two crispy fried chicken tenders tossed in our house-made spicy

tikka masala sauce and served over cilantro lime basmati rice. It is finished off with a touch of raita sauce and a thai basil leaf. It is popular because of its uniqueness, its heat level, and its appeal to people with an adventurous and international palate. There is nowhere in DFW that serves anything like it in a taco form and people come from far and near to get their tikka fix.

Why do you think people love tacos so much?

Tacos are simple, small, handheld, flavorful, and invite an atmosphere of family and sharing. People these days love to get quick food that is unique, inexpensive, and packed with a punch of flavor. Tacos do that, and more and more people are becoming taco converts. Velvet Taco is taking it to another level in terms of combinations, but still staying simple, small, handheld, and flavorful.

Maria Teresa G. Pedroche

LATINA, ARTIST, AND TAQUERA

Tell us your story.

I'm an award-winning artist, curator, educator, community engagement expert, and taquera. My artwork has been shown in the United States, Mexico, and Spain. I'm originally from Brownsville and have more than twenty-five years' art museum experience that includes fifteen years at the Dallas Museum of Art.

I believe the arts are the soul of the community, helping to reflect and promote the city's history and the community's cultural diversity: past, present, and evolving. Quality creative arts and cultural opportunities create a sense of community pride and a sense of place.

What's your connection with tacos?

I was born eating tacos! As far back as I can remember, my grandmother Ester and mother Maria were always reinventing taco recipes passed down from many generations. I grew up in South Texas (Brownsville), where fresh ingredients were everything, from our backyard garden to Padre Island. Chickens were never pets because they were eventually grilled or made into chicken soup.

My father Julian had a passion for cooking fish and making tacos for breakfast, lunch, and dinner. He taught me how to make tortillas! I was more concerned with making artsy tortillas than cooking. Every Sunday after mass, we would drive from Brownsville to Padre Island. He would go fishing with my brothers, Arturo and Jorge, while my mother Maria and sisters Nelda, Lisa, and Elva would play and paint. We returned home and my father cooked a feast. I have stories to last a lifetime.

SOUTH TEXAS SHRIMP TACOS

MARIA TERESA G. PEDROCHE

Makes 16 small tacos

GARLIC CILANTRO LIME SAUCE

¼ cup water

½ cup chopped green
onions

½ cup cilantro

2 to 3 cloves garlic

½ teaspoon sea salt

Juice of 2 limes

½ teaspoon paprika

Pulse all the sauce ingredients in a food processor. Taste and adjust as needed. Set aside.

TOMATILLO SALSA

Makes 4 cups

1 pound fresh tomatillos

1 large Spanish onion, about
12 ounces, cut into large
chunks, about 3 cups

3 garlic cloves

½ cup packed, chopped
cilantro

½ serrano chile or jalapeño

Juice of ½ lime

½ teaspoon cumin

Fine sea salt

Pull the husks from the tomatillos and wash them under cool water until they no longer feel sticky. Cut tomatillos and put them into a food processor. Add the onion and garlic and process. Add the cilantro, serrano or jalapeño, lime juice, and cumin and process until the pepper is finely chopped.

Place mixture into a small saucepan. Season lightly with salt and bring to a boil over medium heat. Cook, stirring occasionally, until most of the liquid is boiled off, about 15 minutes. Cool before using. The sauce can be refrigerated for a few days.

SHRIMP TACOS

2 pounds shrimp, peeled and deveined, tails removed

1 teaspoon chili powder

1 teaspoon cumin

1 teaspoon sea salt

¼ teaspoon cayenne pepper

pepper to taste

2 to 3 cups shredded green cabbage

8 corn tortillas

1 to 2 avocados

Queso fresco

Additional cilantro for topping

Lime wedges

6 radishes

Heat a drizzle of olive oil in a large skillet over medium-high heat. Pat the shrimp dry with paper towels and sprinkle with the spices. Add the shrimp to the hot pan and sauté for 5 to 8 minutes, flipping occasionally, until the shrimp are cooked through.

Toss some of the sauce (not all) with the cabbage until it is coated to your liking. Use leftover sauce on top of the tacos.

To serve tacos, heat corn tortillas, add a slice of avocado on the tortillas, a few pieces of shrimp, top with shredded coleslaw, and finish with queso fresco, cilantro, radishes, tomatoes diced, lime wedges, and remaining lime sauce.

Add Tomatillo Salsa on your tacos and you're ready to eat!

Catherine Cuellar

ENTREPRENEURS FOR NORTH TEXAS

Tell us your story.

I'm the director of Entrepreneurs for North Texas at the Communities Foundation of Texas. I was recognized by the *Dallas Business Journal* as one of the "40 Under 40" in 2013, and was a White House Fellows regional finalist in 2011.

What's your connection with tacos?

My grandfather Frank X. Cuellar Sr. was one of the five brothers who cofounded the El Chico Tex-Mex restaurant chain, which grew to be the largest Hispanic-owned business in Dallas in the twentieth century. My parents own El Corazon de Tejas, a former El Chico that has been in operation since 1955, making it the oldest family-owned Tex-Mex restaurant in Dallas County.

What's your go-to taco and why?

A soft cheese taco smothered in chili con queso, just bequeso (pardon the pun; I have a cheesy sense of humor and taste).

Why do you think people love tacos in your region and in Texas?

Tacos are the quintessential American food. The ingredients in a crispy beef taco and a cheeseburger are the same: ground beef, lettuce, tomato and cheese, but the kick of salsa and crunch of a tortilla shell give tacos the advantage.

Give me your top taco spots and why.

I only have three: El Corazon, my parents' place, then the two closest to my home in downtown Dallas; La Ventana for breakfast tacos; and Fuel City, which is always open.

John Benda

FUEL CITY

Tell us your story.

I am a Dallas native, born and raised. I started in the convenience store business back in 1980—I had a small grocery store in downtown Dallas. Over time, I purchased more stores in the Dallas metroplex and eventually began building my own. I believe the genesis of the taqueria/c-store combination was my store on Harry Hines and Northwest Highway called Friendly's.

Originally I had a chef preparing and serving tacos out of a cart in the patio area at Friendly's. We were wildly successful, and soon the street tacos became so popular that we outgrew the cart. We designed a kitchen inside the store with a walk-up window. Using the same recipe, I opened a taco kitchen inside my new store on Riverfront Boulevard. I called it Fuel City. Sprawling over eight acres in the mix of downtown Dallas, Fuel City was the largest c-store I had ever built—or seen for that matter.

When designing Fuel City, I tried to create it as if it were a ranch in downtown Dallas. I wanted to show all the people what the city used to look like way back when I was a kid. I grew up on a family ranch my father had, and those are still some of the best memories for me. I wanted to share those experiences with the city. I dedicated three acres behind my store for Texas native wildlife. To this day, we still have longhorns roaming out back, donkeys playing with their colts, and gigantic cactus plants all in a three-acre paradise behind Fuel City in the heart of downtown Dallas. Our famous Fuel City tacos are best enjoyed dining in the rustic area called "The Patio," with a view of the ranch out back where the donkeys and Texas longhorns roam.

What is your most popular taco and why? What makes it a standout or unique?

All of our tacos are delicious, but which is the most famous? I would say the picadillo. It's an authentic Mexican-style picadillo served on either flour or corn tortilla, cooked with care and the perfect balance of fresh ground beef, potatoes, cilantro, onions, and a secret green sauce.

The element that makes all our tacos so special is the availability of twenty-four-hour service. You can get the same, superior quality product at 3:00 p.m. or 3:00 a.m. for just $1.75.

Why do you think people love tacos so much?

People love tacos because people are smart and tacos are awesome. We have a couple of Fuel City T-shirts that we sell, and here are a few examples of the sayings on back:

Fuel City Tacos: Where Dreams Come True

Fuel City Tacos: Say No to Drugs and Yes to Tacos

Fuel City Tacos: I Love the Smell of Fresh Tacos in the Morning

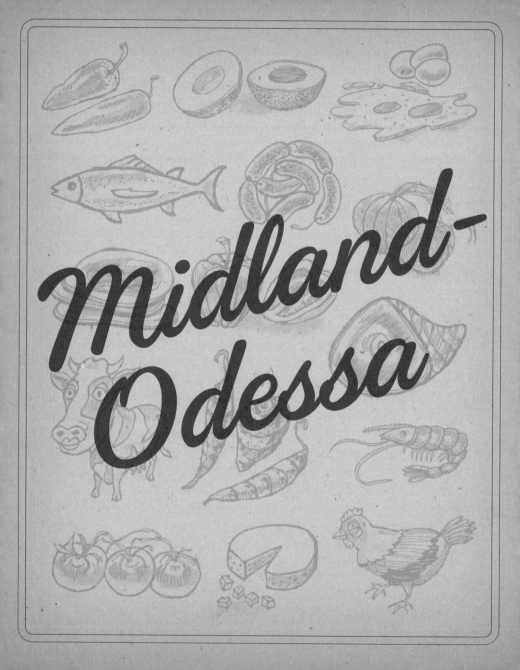

Midland-Odessa

Midland-Odessa: Friday Night Lights, the Tall City, former President George W.'s childhood home, the place where Hispanics speak with a Texas drawl, and plenty of taco spots to go between these two West Texas cities. Midland-Odessa is located in West Texas on the Permian Basin. Originally founded as the midway point between Fort Worth and El Paso on the Texas & Pacific Railroad in 1881,

it's the cradle of the Petrobelt, the land of white pickup trucks, oil derricks, good people, and tacos as far as the eye can see—and that eye can see pretty darn far out there!

We started our trip by visiting the only mayor-slash-Mexican-restaurant-owner in our travels, we invited ourselves to a family discada, and we secretly ordered chile verde tacos at a seventy-year-old tortilla and tamale factory at the tiniest of the taco buildings in West Texas. Our guides and local Taco Ambassadors, Carlos Hernandez and Dennis Harris, took us to the tastiest tacos in the Petroplex.

P.S. What's up with all the drive-throughs? There is a drive-through for everything: liquor, tacos, pizza, medicine, you name it!

THE MIDLAND-ODESSA ICONIC TACO: THE CRISPY TACO AT ROSA'S CAFÉ AND TORTILLA FACTORY

No one can deny Rosa's place in the Midland-Odessa taco and popular culture. Taco Tuesdays is a thing, and it is alive and well at Rosa's Café! They've perfected their crispy tacos with the right amount of crunch and enough (not too much) seasoning to the ground beef that makes you want to double down pretty much every Tuesday. It's one of those quick-serve places making tacos for the masses and serving them well.

TACO JOURNALISM'S TOP CINCO

1. **Elva's Taco Casa**—do not judge this book by its cover. The taco de carne deshebrada is cooked and pulled gently by Elva herself.
2. **Twister Tacos**—tripitas done right!
3. **Rosa's Café and Tortilla Factory**—iconic crispy tacos, wood-fired beef, Taco Tuesdays!
4. **Manuel's Tortilla & Tamale Factory**—the fresh tortillas and the pork with chile verde and asadero cheese have the right kick.
5. **El Taco Tako**—A West Texas institution. Fajitas on your tacos, nachos, and yes, even burritos.

MANUEL'S TORTILLA & TAMALE FACTORY

This place was special. One-hundred-year-old machines, fresh masa brewing, a huge warehouse full of tortillas. They have been supplying restaurants for miles and miles for years and years. The next generation, a.k.a. "The Son," has lots of great things brewing, including making some of the most amazing tacos in this state. Stewed meats in dark sauces piled on fluffy, fresh, and warm tortillas. The kind of comfort food that makes you feel like you are wrapped up in a down comforter—*that* kind of comfort. And then you bite into this gorgeous taco creation and . . . well, that bite was one of the best things we ate this entire trip.

Elva Porras

ELVA'S TACO CASA

Tell us your story.

The name of my restaurant is Elva's Taco Casa. I started working by making tortillas—corn and flour—for about thirteen years. I'm from Candelaria, Texas. I've been in Odessa for thirty-five years. I have always cooked since I was a little girl. I come from a family of ten sisters and three brothers. That's how they made families back then!

What's your connection with tacos?

My mom taught us—everything I learned, I learned from my mother. My mom made everything from scratch (breads, cakes), and it was a lot of work every day. And we didn't make just a few tortillas—we made a lot in order to supply breakfast, lunch, and dinner. That's something I really enjoy—making the tortillas by hand. I make them really quickly! I have the fastest hands in my family.

What's your go-to taco and why?

We make tacos with carne deshebrada, shredded beef. Our shredded beef is low in fat. We don't use any extra grease or manteca. We leave the natural oils in the beef. And we shred it, we don't fry it. We prepare it by steaming it for two hours. We remove the extra grease and shred it by hand. It is a very popular dish. We don't add anything other than salt. So it's very natural and minimally processed. Because it's so fresh and low in fat, I think people really like the natural flavor.

Why do you think people love tacos in your region and in Texas?

I've been doing this for thirty years. People like that we prepare the ingredients by hand, fresh every day. The corn flour tortillas are prepared by hand as well. We keep things simple. All the ingredients stay very minimal—vapor and amor!

Mayor Jerry Morales

GERARDO'S CASITA

Tell us your story.

Tex-Mex restaurants have been my life. I was born and raised in Midland, Texas. Growing up in an oil and gas town, you would think that, sometime in your life, you actually would have been employed in some capacity in the industry that drives your community. Not me. My parents were successful entrepreneurs; their real passion was owning an insurance business and a popular Mexican restaurant named Gerardo's Casita. In 1977, when our family opened up Gerardo's Casita, I learned how to bus tables, polish silverware, wash dishes, roll burritos, and fry sopapillas. My brother, sister, and I provided support by filling in where we were needed.

In 1996, my wife and I cashed in my stock from my previous employment and purchased my parents' building and restaurant. We were starting a new life and a new dream . . . living the American Dream. We had a lot of fun and tears redesigning the building, creating our menu, buying used equipment, painting, and hammering away.

Nineteen years later, we are still living our dream. It now includes our twenty-five-year-old son running our two stores and our catering company. Our twenty-one-year-old son has recently graduated from Le Cordon Bleu Culinary School.

My passion includes serving not only our guests but also our community. I was elected to the city council in 2008, and then mayor of Midland in 2014. I love serving people, and I love it more when people are happy!

What's your connection with tacos?

My mom and my aunts were incredible cooks. My dad was a hard food critic. My mom was always getting creative in the kitchen and our family loved eating her experiments. Owning your own restaurant, you're always trying to find that signature taco or burrito that will put you on the map. Tacos have been my life.

What's your go-to taco?

I love our tacos Durangos! The tender meats, spices, cilantro, and avocado all combined give it a flavor that is unique. I can eat it two ways and have two different experiences. On a soft white corn tortilla, it gives a little sweet taste. When I eat it grilled, I feel like I'm in Mexico.

Why do you think people love tacos in your region and in Texas?

If you're not eating barbecue, you're eating tacos! Tacos

are in fast-food restaurants, breakfast shops, and mobile food vendors. They are easy to make and consume and make a great meal or appetizer. In this region, we are not confused like Austin. In Austin, they roll their tacos? A taco is not rolled.

Carlos Hernandez
ROSA'S CAFÉ AND TORTILLA FACTORY
TEXAS TACO COUNCIL

Tell us your story.
I was born and raised in Odessa and was one of five children. My mom was an incredible cook and instilled in me a great love for authentic Mexican food. While I was still a student at Odessa High

School, I began sweeping floors after school at a corn products plant that supplied tortilla chips and chalupa and taco shells for the Taco Villa restaurant chain, which was founded in 1968 by legendary restaurateur Bobby D. Cox. Once I was old enough to drive, I was making product deliveries to the chain's locations and eventually was promoted to general manager of the plant at age nineteen. From there, I have worked my way up in the industry to become the

vice president of operations for Rosa's Café, a fast, casual restaurant concept that has grown from nine locations in 1995 to forty-two restaurants in 2016 throughout Texas. My wife, Norma, and I still live in Odessa where we love to experiment with special Mexican dishes that are based on our families' recipes.

What's your connection with tacos?

Mexican food, and particularly tacos, are in my blood. They were a way of life for me and my brothers and sisters. My mom cooked with great passion—and she still does today! Her tacos were incredible, and she would make so many different kinds—picadillo, carne asada, chile verde, chile colorado, and so many other types—using both fresh corn and flour tortillas. Nothing is better than homemade tacos using fresh ingredients and authentic seasonings.

What is your most popular taco and why? What makes it a standout or unique?

Our crispy beef taco is by far our most popular at Rosa's Café. It is the foundation upon which we built our highly popular taco plate promotion every Tuesday at Rosa's. It is made with fresh-cooked picadillo, which our customers love! And we pile on the vegetables and cheddar cheese. It is truly delicious.

Why do you think people love tacos in your region and in Texas?

It's plain and simple . . . tacos are comfort food in West Texas. They are the go-to food that is perfect for any time of day—breakfast, lunch, supper, and late night. It is hard to beat a fresh, flavorful taco, period.

Give me your top taco spots and why.

1. **Manuel's Tortilla & Tamale Factory (Odessa)**—the best chorizo tacos anywhere.
2. **Rosa's Café (throughout Texas)**—I may be playing favorites, but I think we have a delicious picadillo taco that competes with anyone.
3. **Clearsprings Café (Midland)**—they serve a very tasty fish taco.
4. **Fajitas & More (Odessa)**—the best barbacoa taco made with handmade tortillas.

Valeriano and Oralia Flores

FAMILIA FLORES

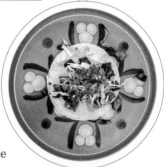

Tell us your story.

We've been in Odessa since 1973. I was raised in Sheffield, Texas. My wife and I met when I was in the service and we were married in 1968. I mostly worked in construction. We have four children and they're all grown up.

I guess we started with this food thing when we had a quinceañera for my daughter and we cooked all the food; we had goat, brisket, asado, carne con chile verde, and all our family helped out. My aunt cooked the beans and we had so many beans left over that we had to put them in the freezer. My wife cooked the menudo, and I liked it so much that she taught me how and now I do the menudo. After that, we started cooking food at festivals in West Texas. We cooked tacos, flautas, and carnitas, and we still get asked to come out and cook at festivals. That's something I'm proud of.

What's your connection to tacos?

We always cooked all kinds of Mexican food. Then one day, a friend of mine in Odessa invited me to a discada. After that, I started doing it at home with mostly meats, pork butt, sirloin steak, German sausage, and Mexican chorizo. You cook all of that together and you make a good taco. My wife and I like to show our kids how

to properly make Mexican food, with the right amount of cuts and flavors. I want my kids, my boys, to learn. I give them pointers, coaching them so they can learn to make their own discadas.

Give me your top taco spots and why.

My wife Oralia's beef tacos—my favorite because they are homemade. She gets them just enough crispy and her hot sauce is to die for. We top them off with finely chopped lettuce, tomatoes, and cheese. We always add the meat, then the hot sauce and top with lettuce and tomatoes to avoid burning our lips when we bite into it.

Rosa's Café—just an all-time favorite. They're quick and easy to go pick up, and they have the ground beef with potatoes that we like. They're pretty inexpensive for a plate of three with rice and beans.

La Hacienda Vieja—the taquitos are with small tortillas and are about as close as you can get to the street tacos they sell in Mexico. They also serve them with a salsa de tomatillo that makes them one of my favorites.

Raymond Martinez III

REYNA'S DELI

Tell us your story.

I currently own and operate Reyna's Deli here in Midland. I opened this establishment December 4th of 2013, to continue to share this particular style of cooking. This business had been opened before me by none other than Reyna Martinez, my mother, back in 2001. The roots of our cooking style stem from Puebla, Mexico. Her cooking—ranging from her tacos and enchiladas to the fried banana dessert that we offer—has been recognized by *Texas Monthly* on different occasions. We've also had the pleasure of serving Barbara Bush and family.

Our success here in the Permian Basin has been my mother's recognition for her cooking for more than fifteen years, a legacy that we continue.

What is your most popular taco and why? What makes it a standout or unique?

The taco al pastor is one of our most popular here at Reyna's. I believe the reason is because the flavor that is associated with that taco is amazing. We use a red pepper, basil, garlic, and apple vinegar-based sauce. It's a sauce with great punch that doesn't overpower the taste buds. Usually when pastor is being prepped, slices of pork and onions are layered and topped with a peeled pineapple in a vertical broiler (a trompo) for optimal marinating.

Dennis Harris
TEXAS TACO COUNCIL

Tell us your story.

Born and raised in Pecos, Texas. Upon completion of high school, I enlisted in the army as a combat medic and was lucky enough to live and travel all over the United States. After the military, I attended Texas Woman's University located in Denton, received a master's in music education on the classical guitar and a master's in teaching with a minor in mathematics.

A math teacher in Dallas and in Odessa and a guitar instructor at the University of Texas of the Permian Basin and Odessa College, I am also the founder and owner of Permian Basin Guitar located in Odessa, teaching guitar full time and playing shows for various functions.

My love for Mexican food has led me to constantly seek out the best local eateries wherever I go. One of my major rules is "no chain restaurants!" Chains use their name to help lure customers in. Look for a local place that has plenty of cars in the parking lot. If the locals are supporting the location, then you know it's good.

You're on the Texas Taco Council. Why are you the Taco Ambassador for your city/region?

I chose to be the Ambassador because it makes me feel like I'm giving back to my community. I love going to hole-in-the-wall-style places that are only known by the locals. These small business owners are my neighbors, my customers, my community, and my friends, and I want to support them.

What's your go-to taco and why?

My go-to taco was al pastor until I met with the Taco Council. I tried the alambre and now I'm hooked. I now choose one or the other, depending on what mood I am in.

Why do you think people love tacos in your region and in Texas?

Tacos are amazing and should be added to the food pyramid!

Give us the taco landscape for your city/region. Give us your top five list and why they're the best.

Choosing a number one would be hard, and that usually depends on what mood I am in. However, here is my list:

Taqueria Guadalajara—when I want to feel my mouth burn from the heat.

El Taco Tako—when I want to sit down and eat.

Dumplins y Amigos—don't let the name fool you; their breakfasts are amazing.

Taqueria El Gallo de Jalisco—most of their plates are combinations (taco and burrito, taco and torta, etc.). My only complaint is that my stomach hurts from eating so much every time I go there.

Twister Tacos—basic plates, so you can go to their self-serve section and pile on all the goodies you want. Just be careful with the salsa—it will sneak up on you.

Bobby Gonzalez
MANUEL'S TORTILLA & TAMALE FACTORY

Tell us your story.

The Gonzalez family was one of the first of five Hispanic families to move and settle in Odessa. I was born into this business that my grandfather, Manuel E. Gonzalez Jr., established in 1946. It started as a tortilla and tamale factory then grew into a restaurant. A lot of famous people have eaten there, including Roy Orbison, Cisco Kid, Waylon Jennings, and ZZ Top, to name a few. Back in the day,

Manuel's Restaurant was *the* place to eat! It was on the only main road that went through town until the interstate was built. Grandfather always said give the customer what they want, at a fair price, and they will keep coming back.

In 1971, my father, Manuel E. Gonzalez III, bought the tortilla and tamale factory from his father and moved it to the current location. Today I help my father manage and run the business. We offer four kinds of tamales, including pork, chicken, cheese and pepper, and beans and cheese. Red and green salsas. Chile con queso, chorizo, taco shells, chips, and burritos. This year we are celebrating seventy years of continuous service in the Permian Basin.

What is your most popular taco and why? What makes it a standout or unique?

Our most popular taco is our chile verde because it's hot but has the right amount of flavor and spices.

Eliseo Bello Gonzalez

EL TACO TAKO

Tell us your story.

I'm from Monterrey, Nuevo León, Mexico, but before I moved here, I lived in San Antonio and worked for a food company called Gatsford. That's where I learned a little more about seasoning, on top of what I knew from my mom and grandmother. In 1980, I had the opportunity to own this business, so I said, I'll do it, and as of November 2015, I will have been here thirty-five years. I believe that service and food go hand in hand, so we put a lot of emphasis on those two things. We have clients who have been coming back for all those years, and I'm proud to say that their children keep coming back to visit.

What is your most popular taco and why? What makes it a standout or unique?

Crispy fajita taco, and people like our burritos, too.

Why do you think people love tacos so much?

First of all, we're Mexican, right? Even on this side of the border. And, of course, a taco should be well prepared and have good flavor. They must go well with condiments and salsa—you can't be missing the salsa.

Patricia Loya
TWISTER TACOS

Tell us your story.

I am from Chihuahua and I've been in Odessa for about fifteen years. We moved here because this is where my husband found work. I started with a trailer, selling burritos, but then I switched to making tacos. I like to cook, and I guess I'm a good cook because our customers seem to like it. We have traditional tacos like tripas, bistec, al pastor, and carne asada.

What is your most popular taco and why? What makes it a standout or unique?

The tripas taco sells a lot and so does the al pastor. Tripas are pork intestines and we clean and cook them here. Then we fry them up to the customer's order, like medium or extra crispy. We have a lot of salsas like chile de árbol, vegetables, crema salsas, avocado, and guacamole.

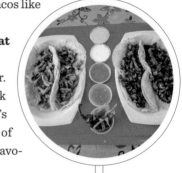

Lenora Mancha

BEN'S LITTLE MEXICO

Tell us your story.

We've been around a very long time. My husband got started with the restaurant after World War II. He used to work at a Piccadilly

and didn't want to do that forever. He said he wanted to open a restaurant in the Mexican side of town. Ben helped everyone; he had a lot of friends and basically the whole town knew Ben. I met Ben at his place and he would always invite me to eat. I told him that I couldn't because I needed to stay skinny. He was a charmer and I ended up marrying him. When we were married, it was the talk of the town since I was much younger than Ben. We had our only daughter Niemo and now we're in charge of making the tacos.

What is your most popular taco and why? What makes it a standout or unique?

It's our crispy beef tacos with pico de gallo, cheese, and tomatoes. People order them by the dozen. I don't know what makes them popular, but we've been making them the same way since Ben started the restaurant.

Abilene

Abilene, "Big Country," is the crossroads where desert meets the plains and the Hill Country. A place where you can catch the rodeo on any given weekend and where you can eat delicious fajita tacos at the Farolito Restaurant, one of the oldest Mexican restaurants in West Texas, circa 1936. One of my favorite and one of the most surprising cities on this trip was Abilene. The city itself is

extremely charming. My girls loved the Dr. Seuss statues downtown and the really awesome and unexpected children's literature library nearby.

THE ABILENE ICONIC TACO: CARNE GUISADA TACO

La Popular's carne guisada has all the locals excited every morning. The tender and perfectly stewed meats wrapped in a warm, freshly made thick flour tortilla may have been one of my favorite tacos on the seven-thousand-mile journey. Grab a dictionary, look up "comfort," and you should see a picture of this taco. They say if you're a true Abilenian, you eat at La Pop!

TACO JOURNALISM'S TOP CINCO

1. **Armando's Mexican Food**—just solid taqueria-style tacos and delicious meats done very right.

2. **Farolito Restaurant**—everything you want in a classic Tex-Mex restaurant and more. The beef and chicken fajitas are done to a crisp.

3. **La Popular**—carne guisada tacos are heavenly and pretty much melt in your mouth.

4. **Taqueria La Ranchera**—the tacos regionales in this family-run place are made with love.

5. **Lola's Mexican Café**—the breakfast tacos are only half the experience.

TACO AMBASSADOR

My good friend, coworker, and now Taco Ambassador Blake Kammerdiener was a major reason that Abilene made the ten-city taco cut. Blake is a native Abilenian and well versed in the art of Taco Journalism. In short, he is one of us. So when he told me tales of a carne guisada so delicious and savory that it would put all others to shame, I just had to taste it myself. He brought us to some really amazing places and introduced us to some passionate and loving people who served us that love in the form of tacos. Thank you, Blake.

LOLA

We met so many wonderful people on our journeys across this great state, but one of the most memorable was Mrs. Maria Dolores Molina, better known as simply "Lola." She is a force to be reckoned with and runs her little slice of taco heaven in Buffalo Gap, just outside Abilene, by her rules. The men wait on the women, no cussing, be nice, help out in the kitchen—these are not just good ideas at Lola's restaurant, these are the rules.

We had heard stories about Lola's tacos and her rules from many an Abilenian, and if you've ever eaten at the awards-winning Perini Ranch Steakhouse outside of town, you've probably driven right past Lola's.

When you walk into her place, it feels like home. Pictures on the walls, mix-and-match tables and chairs, kitchen door open, and people congregated, talking, cleaning, cooking. Some on their way to work and more just arriving. All smiling.

Ordering with Lola is just having a conversation. What are you hungry for? What do you have? We'll take that. You want some drinks? Get them. You need some dishes? Wash some. Can you flip that? Yes.

If you are ever in Abilene and need a home-cooked meal and a more-than-interesting conversation, just visit Mrs. Lola.

HOUSE RULES
(Guidelines for Survival)

1. We do not specialize in service....wait on your self!
2. This is not the Country Club and you do not pay dues here, so don't boss us around with that attitude!
3. You eat what we tell you to eat (unless you're a regular customer)
4. If the tables are sticky, go get a rag & clean them; if there is no coffee....make some!
5. If you have a bad outlook on life, go sit on the porch until you can change it!
6. Don't talk for your children here!
7. Don't even THINK about leaning back in our chairs!
8. MEN WAIT ON WOMEN HERE!!
9. Leave our tips alone !!!
10. Come back and see our clean, little kitchen!

Armando Ortiz

ARMANDO'S MEXICAN FOOD

Tell us your story.

I co-own Armando's Mexican Food with my brother. I have another brother who has a business in California. I helped him out a lot, and I was interested in starting my own business. So we moved here to Abilene from California. We've been here for three years and we try to make our food authentically Mexican. Some of the Mexican dishes we make are the cama-

rones rancheros with salsa and taquitos callejeros (barbacoa, al pastor, carnitas). No one really knew about these taquitos callejeros with onions and cilantro and corn tortillas. They were used to the flour tortillas and ingredients from this side of the border, but now the taquitos callejeros are the most popular.

What's your connection with tacos?

We are a family business. My son comes and helps out. It's a small business, we have a few employees, and we make sure that our customers are happy and satisfied. When we started our business, my wife and I said that, no matter what, we want to make sure that our customers come out and eat and enjoy the meal—if they don't come back, it's for another reason and not because they didn't enjoy the food.

What is your most popular taco and why? What makes it a standout or unique?

The steak taco and the tacos al pastor are very popular. Maybe the name of the pastor taco threw people off at first. Most people would only choose the steak because they were familiar with it, but now they know that the al pastor is good and it's become very popular.

I think people like our tacos because everything is fresh. We make everything when the customer orders it, nothing is frozen, nothing is precooked. I think that's why people like it.

Why do you think people love tacos so much?

I think tacos are a familiar food. We get a lot of construction workers or other workers from Mexico, and they all grew up eating this food, so it's familiar. If they see al pastor or carnitas on the menu, they know what they're ordering, so it's a sure thing.

Blake Kammerdiener

TEXAS TACO COUNCIL

Tell us your story.

I was born and raised in Abilene, where my peanut butter and jelly was the carne guisada burrito (which is a West Texas taco). I started cooking at a very young age, with the first dish I ever cooked on my own being a big pot of pinto beans when I was five years old. This immediately began to evolve into more complex dishes as the love for cooking was passed down to me from my parents. After one Thanksgiving in my early teens, I grew tired of eating turkey sandwiches and began experimenting with making turkey tacos with the leftovers. It was an unusually dry turkey that year so I tried a couple different ways to add moisture back into the delicious meat. This progressed over the next ten or so years to become a chicken taco recipe that is famous in our small circle. If I cook my chicken tacos and not everyone gets invited to partake, I get a lot of sad/angry messages about it for the next week.

In 2011, I began working full time with South by Southwest Film Festival as the production coordinator, and in 2012, I started producing the Taco Meet Up events during SXSW where we showcase some of our favorite tacos from around Austin. Since then I have moved up through the ranks and now function as the Film Festival production manager and an associate programmer. I've continued to work on new tacos, including my own carne guisada recipe.

What's your connection with tacos?

I love everything about tacos and they make up about 70 percent of my diet and have for as long as I can remember.

You're on the Texas Taco Council. Why are you the Taco Ambassador for your city/region?

There are a few special places in Abilene that really needed to be shown to the rest of the world. I felt it was necessary for me to make that happen.

What's your go-to taco and why?

I have to say it's a carne guisada taco. No matter where you are, every carne guisada is different and I need to try them all.

Why do you think people love tacos in your region and in Texas?

It's definitely part of the West Texas heritage (and Texas in general). It's cattle-and-cowboy country and there is nothing better out on the range than a great taco.

Give us the taco landscape for your city/region. Give us your top ten list and why they're the best.

West Texas is actually more defined by what they call burritos. They are not the big-as-your-head burritos in general, but more taco-sized burritos with the ends folded in.

My top 10 tacos/burritos in Abilene are (in no particular order):

Alfredo's—carne asada taco.

Alfredo's—crispy chicken taco.

Armando's—street taco (carne asada).

Hernandez Bakery—carne con chile.

La Popular—carne guisada.

La Popular—chorizo, bean, and cheese.

La Popular—potato, egg, and cheese.

Lola's Mexican Cafe—whatever she wants to make for you.

Taqueria La Ranchera—barbacoa.

Taqueria La Ranchera—carne con chile roja con arroz.

BLAKE'S FAMOUS CHICKEN TACOS

BLAKE KAMMERDIENER

Makes 15 tacos

1½ pounds boneless chicken

Pepper

Salt

1 tablespoon granulated
   garlic

Dash Worcestershire sauce

1 large poblano pepper

Dash olive oil

½ large white onion

2 jalapeño or serrano
   peppers

2 large (or 3 medium)
   Roma tomatoes

¼ cup milk (2 percent
   or whole milk is best)

1 tablespoon cumin

Generously coat the chicken with salt, pepper, and granulated garlic. Add dash of Worcestershire sauce and rub to evenly cover the chicken. Grill (I like to use mesquite bricks and chunks for my fire) until fully cooked, making sure to get the chicken nice and charred. Remove and let rest for 15 minutes.

Lightly salt and pepper the poblano and then rub with olive oil and roast at 350 degrees until skin is bubbly. Remove and skin.

Dice the fresh jalapeños or serranos, onion, and tomatoes and sauté in a little bit of olive oil until sweated and soft. Add a dash of salt and pepper to the vegetables to help the layers of flavor develop. Dice the roasted poblano and grilled chicken and add to the pan. Add in garlic and cumin and shred the chicken as it cooks. Salt and pepper to taste. As you shred the chicken in the pan, add the milk, a little at a time, and cook it into the meat. Repeat this process for about 20 minutes or until the chicken is fully shredded.

Maria Dolores Molina

LOLA'S MEXICAN CAFE

Tell us your story.

I'm from southwest Mexico and I came to the US in 1980 looking for my father. I didn't like growing up without a daddy, and I wanted to meet him so I came up north to Dallas and I found him! We connected and he encouraged me to stay. Soon after that, I moved to Buffalo Gap.

I started working here washing dishes and now I own the place. I enjoy seeing the generations of families come in and eat at the restaurant.

When the people come in, they know what to do. They go get their drinks, get their tea, and their hot sauce and chips. They come to the kitchen and tell me what they want. I make it if I have it. If not, I send them to the store. Once the food is ready, they come get their plates. Everything is self service just like at home.

We have house rules to make sure we keep the place neat. We're a family place and gentlemen have to take care of the women. We have rules like "you eat what we serve you" or "if the tables are sticky, go get a rag and clean it" or "if you have a bad outlook on life, go sit on the porch until you change it." People like the rules; they keep coming back.

What is your most popular taco and why? What makes it a standout or unique?

People like the breakfast tacos that have bacon and potatoes and eggs and cheese.

A lot of people come in and order breakfast tacos, especially the workers. Sometimes they order fifty, it depends on the group.

I also make green enchiladas. Green enchiladas with hamburger meat with onions, garlic, and green chiles, the New Mexico green chiles.

Mindy Howard

THE MILL WINE BAR & EVENT VENUE

Tell us your story.

I am the owner and general manager of the Mill Wine Bar & Event Venue. I'm a small-town Texas girl, lover of Jesus, of good atmosphere, community, and fine wine. I'm an entrepreneur and visionary who loves creating something out of nothing. I'm the mother of twins and a baby boy.

What's your connection with tacos?

I'm a Texan . . . need I say more? Tacos are a way of life in Texas.

What's your go-to taco and why?

Ground beef loaded with all the veggies on a corn tortilla.

Why do you think people love tacos in your region and in Texas?

Something about Mexican food and tacos in particular are just a way of life in Texas. Trying out new and different ways to enjoy a taco is a weekly occurrence at my house for my kids.

Give me your top five taco spots.

1. La Popular
2. Fuzzy's Taco Shop
3. Farolito Restaurant
4. Lola's Mexican Cafe
5. Taco Bueno (sorry, but I have to! It's one of my favorites!)

Tacos

Meat $2
Chicken . . . . $
Combo . . . . $
Bean . . . .

¡QUE VIVAN LOS TACOS!

Texas is a big state with lots of history, culture, and tacos. In our taco journey, we traveled more than seven thousand miles in the Lone Star State, we met familias carrying on their tradition of taco-making, we made new friends who opened the doors to their homes and businesses, we captured their stories and recipes, and we learned a lot along the way, one taco at a time.

The taco is very close to our hearts and bellies. It's home. It keeps us connected to our Texan and Mexican culture. And we're not alone, as you have read. The taco is ingrained in the state's culture. It's part of what makes Texas Texas. Texans are whole-heartedly embracing the taco, whether it's Mexican immigrants bringing their flavors and styles to Texas or ranchers enjoying a good breakfast taco. The tacos are here to stay.

So enjoy them while they're hot. Support your local taquero, break tortillas with your neighbor, find new ways of filling that folded tortilla, venture to the undiscovered taco stand, make them at home, bring them to work, and share a little piece of your culture and heart. Enjoy the national food of Texas y que vivan los tacos!

EL GLOSSARY

SOME ENGLISH, SOME SPANISH,
AND PLENTY OF SPANGLISH

achiote: a red spice made from annatto seeds; often turned into a paste with garlic, vinegar, oil, and salt

aguacate: avocado

ajo fresco: fresh garlic

al pastor: sweet pork with dried chiles and achiote, topped with pineapple chunks; we prefer the ones prepared using a trompo

alambres: beef with bacon, peppers, onions, and Oaxacan cheese

albóndigas de kurbina: red drum (fish) meatballs

antojitos: similar to a snack or appetizer

arepas: a thick, corn-based tortilla or pancake, traditionally eaten in Colombia and Venezuela

arrachera: Mexican flank or skirt steak

asados: barbecue or roast

ataúd: outdoor oven (literally, a coffin)

barbacoa: beef head

birria: goat meat

bistec: thin beefsteak

borrego: lamb, mutton

buche: pork stomach

cabeza de res: cow head

cabrito: young goat

cachete: cheek

cacheteados: "slapped" or spread with refried beans

caja china: outdoor oven

calabacita: squash

calabazas: squash

callejeros: street, as in street tacos

camarones: shrimp

campechana: mixto-style with beef, pork, and chorizo

cariño: with care, with love

carne asada: grilled steak

carniceria: meat market

carnitas: fried pork butt or shoulder

cascabel: dried, red, bell-shaped chile, about an inch in diameter

cazo: pot

cebolla: onion

cebollitas de chambray: scallions

cecina: lightly cured beef (salted), thinly sliced and grilled over mesquite

chapulines: grasshoppers (sometimes refers to crickets)

chicharrones: pork rinds

chilaquiles: corn tortillas cut in quarters and lightly fried, typically made with eggs, chiles, and chile sauce or salsa

chile colorado: dried New Mexico red chile, narrow, 5–8 inches long

chile de árbol: narrow red chile, 2–3 inches long, sold fresh but more often dried

chipotle: smoked, dried jalapeño, also sold in cans packed with adobo sauce

chivo en salsa: goat in sauce

chusma: riffraff

cochinita pibil: slow-roasted pork, cooked in citrus juice

comal: a flat griddle, traditionally made of earthenware (a cast iron skillet is a good substitute)

comino: cumin

de volada: immediately, instant

deshebrada: slow-cooked shredded beef

disco (discada): beef, bacon, sausage, chorizo, jalapeños, onions, and tomatoes cooked in a disk-shaped pan—think Mexican wok

ejido: small farming community

elotes: corn

en pozo: in-ground pit

entomatadas: fried corn tortillas bathed in a tomato sauce, like enchiladas but with tomato sauce

epazote: pungent herb, sometimes referred to as Mexican tea; has a slightly tangy flavor, frequently used in black beans

estilo mexicano: Mexican style

fideo or sopa de fideo: Mexican pasta with tomato sauce, noodle soup

flautas ahogadas: rolled tortillas, stuffed with meat then bathed or "drowned" in tomato and chile sauce

fritangas: fried feasts

gorditas: a small fried patty made with corn masa and stuffed with cheese, meat, beans, and salsa

güera/o: light-skinned or blonde person, often refers to people who are white

guisados: stewed meats with green or red chile

hoja santa: herb with an anise-like aroma, sometimes called root beer plant; its large leaves are used to wrap tamales in parts of Mexico

huaraches: a long, oval-shaped fried masa patty topped with meats, cheese, beans, and salsas (literally, sandals)

jeta: face

lengua: tongue

lonche: sandwich

lonchera: food truck

machaca or machacado: dry shredded beef

mariachis: breakfast tacos, commonly used in Laredo (literally, musicians who play traditional Mexican folk music)

masa: (corn) dough used to make tortillas, huaraches, gorditas; can also refer to wheat flour dough

matanza del marrano: pig slaughter

migas: pieces of fried tortillas or tortilla chips made with eggs, cheese, and pico de gallo

molcajete: a stone tool, mortar and pestle, used to make salsas

mole: Mexican sauce, typically made of chocolate, chiles, and spices

molino: grinder

montalayo: minced goat organs

morcilla: blood sausage

mordida: bite

morita: smoked, red jalapeño, though the smoke is usually not as strong as with chipotles; always sold dry

muy ricas: very good

paleta: popsicle

panza: belly

pequin: very hot chile about the size of a fingernail, grows wild in Texas, rarely seen in stores; can be used fresh or dried

piratas: a taco with fajitas, beans, and cheese

plancha: griddle

pláticas: talks or chats

poblano: mildly hot, fresh, green chile, about 4 inches long, somewhat heart-shaped; when dried, it is called an ancho chile

pollo asado: grilled chicken

puesto: a stand, as in a taco stand

rajas: roasted and peeled poblano peppers

requesón: farmer's cheese, similar to ricotta

sabores: flavors

serranos toreados: lightly roasted serrano peppers

sesos: beef brains

suadero: a lean cut of beef that lies between the lower flank and sirloin cuts, also known as rose meat or roast meat

tacos callejeros: often found at taco stands or trailers; slightly smaller in size and served with a double corn tortilla and various fillings that include alambres, al pastor, barbacoa, bistec, chorizo, lengua or tripas.

tacos dorados: deep fried tacos stuffed with meats, beans, potatoes, and salsas

tamalada: a tamale-making gathering or party

taquero: taco maker, cook

testales or testal: small balls of wheat flour masa (dough), shaped prior to rolling out tortillas

tripas: or tripitas are small intestines of farm animals that have been cleaned, boiled, and grilled or fried

trompo: vertical broiler or rotisserie

ACKNOWLEDGING THE REST OF THE *TACOS OF TEXAS* TEAM

Muchísimas gracias to everyone in the book and those of you who helped us along the way.

Dennis Burnett: Lead Filmmaker and Photographer

I am a freelance photographer based in Austin, Texas, who recently arrived from the beautiful, historic city of Savannah, Georgia. I earned a BFA in photography with honors from the Savannah College of Art and Design. During the past decade in Savannah, I honed my skills as a director, photographer, and filmmaker, first in the work-study program and then as a staff photographer at SCAD. Relying on my eye for detail, sense of humor, and a style rooted in documentary photography, I have built a career working for private and commercial clients. Much of my personal work focuses on stories of observation and authentic emotion in an attempt to capture what it means to be human. I'd like to thank Lindsey Mongrain for her patience and support, my father Mark Burnett who taught me what it means to have a work ethic, and Mando Rayo who introduced me to the dietary importance of tacos.

Marco Torres: Lead Photographer

I am a freelance editorial photographer and music journalist based in Houston, Texas, where I have documented my city's rich music, art, and taco scene since 2004. As a Mexican American, I grew up surrounded by food and family, listening exclusively to corridos and cumbias in my parents' home. I was raised on the north side but later attended Jones Senior High in Houston's South Park district at the height of the DJ Screw era, fueling my love for Houston rap. I credit my high school band director, Mr. Ronald J. Cole, for introducing me to jazz, funk, blues, and soul music. I graduated from the University of Saint Thomas with a degree in international studies and business. As a photography assistant, I have worked under famed San Antonio photographer Rolando Gomez and Los Angeles–based entertainment photographer Estevan Oriol. My work has been featured in multiple Voice Media Group outlets, including the *Houston Press, LA Weekly, Dallas Observer*, and *Miami New Times*. My photos have also been published in *Texas Monthly, New York Times, Billboard* magazine, and *Rolling Stone* magazine. My clients include Red Bull, Nike, Remy Martin, the National MS Society, and CenterPoint Energy.

I would like to thank the Torres-Martinez family, my editors and colleagues at the *Houston Press*, the incredible Texas photography community, and everyone I have ever shared a taco with. In loving memory of my mother, Rosa Maria Torres, and abuelita Daria Salazar, may they forever rest in peace.

Tanya Ramirez: Graphic Designer

(Tacos of Texas Map, TacoLife Lessons, Texas Taco Council members designs)

I'm a native Laredoan living and working in Nashville, Tennessee. As a Texas-made graphic designer, I strive to create innovative, fun, and engaging work (with a little Tex-Mex flair), through the art of visual design. When I'm not designing, I'm out searching for my new favorite taco joint and occasionally drinking tequila.

Pepe Yz: Artist

(Illustrations and portraits)

Pepe Yz is a Chilean-American visual artist who has been working professionally for the past fifty years with a focus on abstract expressionism. He has exhibited in New York, Europe, and Chile. He has two children, two beautiful granddaughters, and now resides in Austin, TX.

Taco Interns

Ciri Haugh: Taco Research and Public Relations
John Peña: Taco Research
Camilla Rodriguez: Graphic Designer, Taco Infographic
Jordan Schwartz: Taco Research

And Especially...

April Alejandro, Gabe Van Amburgh, Becky Arreaga, Liz Arreaga, Paulina Artieda, Cristina Balli, Ted Barnhill, Cindy Casares, Chevy for the #ChevyTacoTruck, Tony Cooke, Vanessa Cortez, Robert Crowe, Leslie Dennard, Trish Dressen, Andrew and Cassandra Dungan, Alejandro Escalante, Dr. Lino Garcia, Patty Gonzales, Iris Graebner, Argentina Granada, Laura Hernandez, Maria Isabel Ibarra, Moraima Ibarra, J. P. Kloninger, Daniela Lopez, Ant Macias, Glen and Tahj Mayes, Adan Medrano, Mercury Mambo, Mario Montaño, Carmen Murcia, Eric and Diana Orta, Jackie & Will Padgett, Dora Rayo, Javier & Stacy Rayo, Astolfo Rodriguez, Manny Ruiz and Angela Sustaita-Ruiz, Titus Ruscitti, Llyas Salahud-Din, Bryana Salcido, Joel Salcido, Luis Carlos Sandoval Jr., Shelley Seale, Carl Settles Jr., Steven Smith and Becky Pastner, Joyce Stahmann & Larry Gobelman, Laura Tansey and Polo Valdes (YAPA Artisan Empanadas), Texas Beef Council, TexasFolklife, Nick and Adrienne Thompson, Terry Thompson-Anderson, Robert & Rosemarie Torres, Rosie Uyarra-Salcido, Javier Valdez, Monica Maldonado Williams & Norwood Williams, Rosemary Wynn.

THANK YOU!

INDEX OF RECIPES

INDEX OF PEOPLE AND PLACES